Date Due

THE THREAT AT HOME

THE THREAT AT HOME

**Confronting the Toxic Legacy
of the U.S. Military**

Seth Shulman

BEACON PRESS   BOSTON

Beacon Press
25 Beacon Street
Boston, Massachusetts 02108-2892

Beacon Press books
are published under the auspices of
the Unitarian Universalist Association of Congregations.

99 98 97 96 95 94 93 92   8 7 6 5 4 3 2 1

Text design by Dan Ochsner

Library of Congress Cataloging-in-Publication Data

Shulman, Seth.
    The threat at home: confronting the toxic legacy of the U.S.
military / Seth Shulman.
        p.   cm.
    Includes bibliographical references (p.   ) and index.
    ISBN 0-8070-0416-2
    1. Arsenals—Waste disposal—Environmental aspects—United
States.
    2. Hazardous wastes—Environmental aspects—United States.
    3. United States—Armed Forces—Environmental
aspects.   I. Title.
    TD899.A76S48   1992
363.72'87'0973—dc20   91-41373
                                                       CIP

*In memory of Nancy Sosland Shulman,
who taught me not to be afraid to fight when
something is important, and to Elise Sosland
Shulman-Reed, that she may be inspired by
the same lesson.*

Contents

Acknowledgments   ix

Preface. The Most Toxic Mile   xi

Part I. **The Threat**   1

One. Minefield in the Heartland   3

Two. Teaching a Camel to Fly   10

Three. "Toxic Time Bomb"   20

Four. A Roadside Attraction   32

Five. The Latest Model   43

Six. Eastern Europe at Home   52

Part II. **Secret Legacies**   61

Seven. Lakehurst, New Jersey: "The Dark Years"   63

Eight. Grand Island, Nebraska: "Overly Anxious"   74

Nine. Sacramento, California: "Moving Target"   83

Ten. Hanford, Washington: "Sacrifice Zone"   93

Eleven. Between the Cracks   104

Part III. **Facing the Future**   113

Twelve. The Pentagon Gets Religion   115

CONTENTS

Thirteen. Dead Guppies Make Waves   126

Fourteen. Nerve-Wracking Prototype   136

Fifteen. A Military Toxic Network   147

Epilogue. Watertown and Local Strategies   157

Appendix A. Strategies for Action   165

Appendix B. Suspected Sites of Contamination by Type   171

Appendix C. Pertinent Laws   189

Glossary   203

Notes   213

Index   247

Acknowledgments

Throughout the several years I worked on this project many people and institutions provided support, moral and financial. First, this book would not have been possible without a generous grant from the John D. and Catherine T. MacArthur Foundation. The foundation's selection committee believed in the project early on and funded the bulk of my research and travel. The idea that the environmental effects of the military merited an investigation first passed my desk in 1985, during my tenure as editor of a wonderful small (and now defunct) national magazine called *Science for the People*. Stephanie Pollack, an environmental lawyer at the Conservation Law Foundation, was a helpful teacher and an energetic coauthor for my first two articles on this topic and has been a help in numerous ways throughout. Marc Miller, who has edited my shorter work in *Technology Review* for years, pored over an early manuscript and offered immeasurably helpful suggestions small and large. Dan Grossman, a frequent writing partner, also lent his thoughtful comments on many sections of the book and coauthored an article on our local Army facility which made the book's epilogue possible.

Others who offered helpful advice or counsel along the way include Barry Breen, Ralph DeGennaro, Don Gray, Dyan Oldenburg, and Lenny Siegel. I am grateful also to Victor McElheny and MIT's Knight Science Journalism Fellowship for supporting my writing career at a formative juncture, and to my agent, Katinka Matson, who fought hard to find a commercial publisher willing to publish the material. Deanne Urmy and Wendy Strothman at Beacon Press accepted the challenge and have guided the book's development with encouragement and enthusiasm.

In the throes of turning my investigation into a coherent written form, I have been particularly fortunate to have had the outstanding research assistance of Shawna Moos, who provided essential help during this long process, organizing a boatload of unruly documents, tirelessly and cheerfully checking and updating facts and figures, and proving indispensable in compiling the footnotes and glossary. The rigor of the research owes a debt to her, but of course the responsibility for inevitable flaws or lapses is mine alone.

The depressing nature of this topic made the support of many good friends, too numerous to mention, all the more important. I thank them all for their patience with my preoccupation. My extended family, in particular, deserve special note for keeping me from feeling too mired in military toxic waste—from my wonderful grandmothers, Lena Wolf and Frances Shulman, to my sisters Sarah and Jill. As always, my father, Roy M. Shulman, lent support and inspiration. Finally, my wife, Laura Reed, nurtured me and this project in innumerable ways, often to the neglect of her own research. For her unstinting care to both me and the book I am forever indebted.

While no whole sections are excerpted precisely, I feel obliged to mention that for material in a number of this book's chapters I have drawn upon my own earlier articles on the topic (some coauthored), which have appeared in a number of magazines over the past few years, including *The Atlantic, Boston Magazine, Index on Censorship, Nature, Nuclear Times, Science for the People, Smithsonian,* and *Technology Review.*

The Most Toxic Mile

This book was born on the shore of Basin F, a phosphorescent toxic lake on the outskirts of Denver, Colorado. At the time of my visit several years ago, in 1988, this nearly 100-acre basin glowed ominously beneath the majestic Rocky Mountains, the centerpiece of a forsaken tract of land some believe to be the earth's most toxic square mile.

As its prosaic name suggests, Basin F was human-made; three decades before my visit, bulldozers had worked for weeks to scoop a huge hollow out of the surrounding dusty plain. Just as its creation differed from that of a natural lake, so did its contents. Basin F did not contain the kind of toxic pollution that plagues many of our nation's natural waterways, measured often in parts per million or parts per billion; the liquid filling this vast lagoon was concentrated toxic sludge—some of the most deadly chemicals known had been dumped into it for decades. Before me lay nearly 11 million gallons' worth of wastes, including byproducts of the manufacture of nerve gas and mustard gas—chemical weapons whose lethality is normally measured in minute quantities such as milligrams.

Basin F lay almost within sight of Denver's Stapleton Airport, yet nearby residents knew little or nothing of it. It sat hidden within the confines of Denver's Rocky Mountain Arsenal, a U.S. Army installation that sprawls across some 17,000 acres. My access to the site—escorted past the armed guardhouse—derived from my status as a journalist for a well-known magazine. The morning after I first called about seeing the arsenal, an overnight-mail delivery arrived from an Army press office in Washington. I was sent a twelve-page, glossy color booklet about the arsenal contamination called "Meeting the Challenge." A large color photograph inside depicted a young family holding hands, walking together through a lush open field; another showed a handsome deer at the edge of a forest.

During my official visit to the Rocky Mountain Arsenal in 1988, I was told that Boy Scouts use the facility for hiking and picnics several times a year and that military personnel in the area "line up" on the arsenal grounds in the spring and summer months for permits to go sport fishing there. I was even shown a stretch of railroad track the Army had rented to a collector to store the train cars from the 1960s television show "The Wild, Wild West." But the innocuous presentation could not alter the grim reality of the Rocky Mountain Arsenal—a reality that ultimately left a chilling effect that stuck with me and caused me to redirect my work.

Travels for pleasure and on assignment have taken me to many spots around the world where the memory of war lingers with a haunting presence. On the tiny Pacific island of Peleliu, where one of the bloodiest battles of World War II was fought, rusted hulls and bombed-out bunkers left by both Japanese and American troops dot otherwise pristine beaches. No visitor could avoid contemplating the brutal past they conjure up. Other legacies of war abound closer to home. My first view, years ago, of the expanse of Arlington National Cemetery stretching endlessly along the Potomac left me shaken and awestruck.

Few experiences, however, prepared me for the more hidden consequences of war and its preparations at the Rocky Mountain Arsenal's Basin F. David Strang, a fifteen-year employee of the arsenal who then directed its "technical operations division," acted as my escort. As he drove, a little plastic replica of a fifty-five-gallon drum, like those for hauling and storing toxic waste, dangled from the end of his keychain and knocked against the dashboard of the white Army-issue pickup.

Strang drove me to a large gray factory complex. Boarded up and now condemned because of their levels of contamination, the buildings were the major site of U.S. Army production of chemical weapons from World War II through the Vietnam era. Beyond the complex we followed a long, straight road through the middle of the arsenal. Beside the road, stretching ahead to our right, lay the facility's dumping grounds—huge hollows of black, burnt-out earth and other, smaller holes, the only remaining visible evidence of wells where millions of gallons of wastes had been injected deep into the ground.

Strang explained that the row of liquid waste dumps, labeled A through E, reflected the arsenal's history. The earliest ones were simply huge ditches; intermediate hollows had been lined with lime—an effort, as Strang put it, to "neutralize" the toxins. Last in the stretch, hundreds of yards down the road on the other side, we came finally to Basin F, the most recent dumpsite. Because it was lined with asphalt, Basin F, unlike neighboring hollows, still displayed its noxious contents: ninety-three acres' worth of deadly aquamarine sludge. Only at the sight of Basin F did the horror of its empty neighbors come into perspective. Standing before this toxic lake nestled beneath the Rocky Mountains, I began to grasp the extent of the arsenal's mammoth underground nightmare—a plume of highly toxic chemicals nearly the size of the entire twenty-seven-square-mile facility, migrating inexorably northwest, contaminating groundwater on the edge of Denver and threatening the health of many thousands of people. Basin F has since been dredged, but to me its lingering image is more potent than books' worth of data about military contamination.

On the plane ride home, looking down through the clear sky at flat, empty midwestern plains, I could not calm my indignation—or answer my own questions. How could such an enormous toxic lake ever have come to be, especially on the outskirts of a large, populous city? How could the U.S. government, even in the name of national security, have polluted such a vast tract of our nation's land and endangered the health of neighboring residents? And just how many other Basin Fs are there?

At the time I had heard almost nothing about the military's share of pollution. As I used to do, most people associate the problem of toxic waste only with corporate industrial giants like Union Carbide, Exxon, or Du Pont. In fact, the Pentagon's vast enterprise produces well over a ton of toxic wastes every minute, a yearly output that some contend is greater than that of the top five U.S. chemical companies combined.

To make matters considerably worse, the military branch of the federal government has for decades operated almost entirely unrestricted by environmental law. Even today the military routinely sanctions practices that have long been illegal for private firms operating in this country. Billions of gallons of toxic wastes—a virtual ocean—have been dumped by the U.S. military directly into the ground at thousands of sites across the country over the past several decades. And often, even in the face of hard evidence that the pollutants have contaminated the drinking water of nearby residents, the Pentagon has tried to keep the dumping secret and thereby knowingly threatened the health of millions of U.S. citizens.

In all these respects, the Rocky Mountain Arsenal stands as a tragic symbol of the nation's military toxic waste problem. On the edge of Denver, behind a fenced and guarded perimeter, the arsenal's toxic legacy lies hidden from public scrutiny. Similarly insulated from public view is a history of environmental neglect and mismanagement at virtually every one of the thousands of current and former U.S. military installations across the nation and around the world.

As other passengers on my flight home read or dozed, I thought about Beth Gallegos, a quiet but tenacious woman I had met that day. As we sat in the living room of her modest home, a few hundred yards from the fence of the arsenal, Gallegos told me that she was called a "hysterical housewife" in 1985, when she formed a community group called Citizens Against Contamination to address concerns about high levels of solvents and other contaminants in her town's water.

At first, Gallegos's group met opposition not just from the Army, she said, but from the federal Environmental Protection Agency (EPA), the state health department, and the local water board. Many local officials, she told me, were "irate" with her group about the concerns they raised. "At one early meeting," Gallegos recalled, "the head of the local water board drank a big glass of water to try to prove that nothing was wrong." Because she and her group were raising unpleasant questions about an Army facility, they were widely seen as unpatriotic. "For some time," she said, "among my neighbors my name was mud."

Thanks in part to Gallegos and her local organization, the Rocky Mountain Arsenal has received more attention from the local press than has been garnered by most other military toxic waste sites. When a thousand people showed up at a meeting in December 1986, Gallegos said, things began to change. Soon thereafter, Army officials admitted for the first time that they had "contributed" to water contamination beyond the borders of the facility. Bottled water was offered to residents in Adams City, Commerce City, Irondale, and Dupont—towns on the outskirts of Denver—and a water treatment facility was eventually built at the edge of the arsenal to try to catch contaminants before they migrated into the towns' water.

By the time my plane began its descent over the familiar Boston skyline, I had digested a small mountain of documents from the Colorado attorney general's office about the Rocky Mountain Arsenal. Of particular interest was the description of Basin F contained in Colorado's lawsuit against the Army. The suit alleged that the continual releases of "carcinogenic" and "acutely hazardous" wastes from Basin F into the drinking water, groundwater, and soil had caused "irreparable injury to the environment and to the health and welfare of those people who live or work at or near the Arsenal."

"In callous disregard of public health and welfare and the environment," the lawsuit continued, "[the Army] has done little or nothing to stop the hazardous waste leaking from Basin F and has not determined the nature and extent of contamination caused by its ongoing, illegal operation."

Public officials and citizens like Beth Gallegos continue to struggle to ensure accountability in the arsenal cleanup process. Because the Army resists outside supervision of its affairs, it has challenged the jurisdiction of the Environmental Protection Agency and the state of Colorado to oversee the cleanup effort. The long and bitter legal battle continues today.

Also continuing are the military's efforts to obscure its culpability. In May 1991, three years after my visit to the arsenal, I received the Army's latest brochure about the facility, entitled "Basin F: A Success Story." This time the color photographs highlighted the work completed so far to dredge the highly toxic sludge from Basin F into holding tanks. A team of workers toiled for more than a year and a half on this preliminary effort. The materials in Basin F were so highly toxic that the workers wore two layers of impermeable suits; filtering gas masks were not sufficient, so they breathed oxygen from scuba tanks. After each shift, the entire outside layer of the workers' suits had to be disposed of in a licensed hazardous waste facility.

Meanwhile, all the proposed plans now under consideration to treat the arsenal's 432 million cubic feet of contaminated soil are enormously costly and time-consuming; projected costs to restore this one facility start at nearly $1 billion. Even a decision about which methods to use to decontaminate the toxic residue is not expected until 1993—five decades since some of it was generated.

The Rocky Mountain Arsenal I toured on my brief visit to Denver was like a ghost town. Then, as now, only a skeleton crew remained. The facility's military mission—to manufacture munitions to protect the United States against a foreign enemy—has long since been suspended. Ironically, in the name of defending our national security, the Rocky Mountain Arsenal itself created a different kind of threat—to our land, water, and air, and to our health. It is a threat that the arsenal, like the military as a whole, has only barely begun to confront.

PART I

The Threat

CHAPTER ONE

Minefield in the Heartland

Madison, Indiana, has a problem. At the end of a long day, the town's mayor, Morris Wooden, leans back in his desk chair to explain. The federal government, after some consideration, has decided to close the Jefferson Proving Ground, a sprawling Army facility on the outskirts of town. The decision, says Wooden, is part of a fiscal belt-tightening measure mandated by Congress.

Jefferson Proving Ground—JPG, as everyone in Madison calls it—has been a good neighbor and has employed many Madison residents for over a half century. Today it remains one of the town's largest employers, so the economic impact of its planned shutdown is a serious concern, Wooden explains. Madison officials are fighting the congressional order to shut the facility because they want to keep the jobs in their town, and because they think that JPG was unwisely selected for closure.

But there is also another reason. After the military leaves, it is not at all clear what will become of JPG's 100 square miles of land in the lush southeastern corner of the state. The land, Wooden says, is uninhabit-able, a minefield littered with unexploded bombs from decades of Army tests.

Cleaning up JPG, if it is undertaken, will be a mammoth, dangerous, and costly job. Wooden says the Army ignored the issue in its decision to close the base. Now, he reports, the Army admits that there aren't any funds set aside for the job and that none are anticipated. The cleanup costs are so high, in fact, and the work so dangerous, that the Army wants simply to abandon the site. And as things now stand, it is likely that this will happen: the vast installation may well be the first to be fenced off in perpetuity, permanently isolated from human contact, like a quarantined victim with a contagious and terminal disease.

Mayor Wooden's office walls hold framed snapshots highlighting his political career. One shows him shaking hands with a former JPG base commander in happier times. Today the mayor remains on good terms with JPG personnel, but he is livid at the very idea that his town might be saddled forever with a huge abandoned minefield. He calls the prospect "immoral on economic and environmental grounds." The Army's handling of JPG's closure, Wooden says, "is the kind of thing that makes the Pentagon's $600 toilet seats look good."

Heading north a few miles outside of Madison's historic downtown, U.S. Highway 421 begins to hug the fence of the Army's Jefferson Proving Ground. It is beautiful American heartland, this corner of Indiana near the Ohio and Kentucky borders, with miles of rolling pastures and cornfields.

Arriving at this spot by car, the first thing a visitor notices is the fence. It seems normal enough at first for a military facility, an eight-foot-tall rusting chainlink topped with barbed wire. But as it clings unbroken to the road's edge for mile after mile, toward Ripley county, through Belleview and Bryantsville, the fence's length—and the size of the facility it surrounds—begins to sink in. Enclosed behind this uninviting 48-mile perimeter are the 100 square miles of Indiana that Mayor Wooden fears will remain quarantined forever: an area larger than Manhattan and the District of Columbia combined. It is an area that Indiana's Senator Dan Coats has described, probably accurately, as the "largest contiguous contaminated area in the U.S."

Here at Jefferson Proving Ground the Army has tested huge quantities of conventional munitions since World War II. Over the span of fifty years, Army personnel have shot off some 23 million rounds of ordnance, littering the land with more than a million unexploded bombs, mines, and artillery shells which lie on the surface or are buried as deep as thirty feet underground. Some of the buried munitions are white phosphorus shells that JPG officials say are certain to ignite if they are dug up and exposed to air. Other bombs explode unexpectedly from time to time; many more surely would if the Army tried to remove them. JPG is also home to low-level radioactive contamination, toxic sludge, and pesticide residue, but overshadowing all other environmental problems here are the unexploded bombs. And their number mounts daily as JPG personnel continue to test munitions.

If the weather is clear, a driver on Route 421 can immediately hear and feel JPG at work—explosions like huge thunderclaps, but deeper and accompanied by ground-shaking tremors like the aftershocks of an earthquake. At an official briefing during my visit, Colonel Dennis O'Brien, the facility's commander, explained that JPG tests 85 percent of the Army's conventional munitions and currently fires some 80,000 rounds annually—some 40 rounds every hour the facility operates.

Colonel O'Brien is a stocky combat veteran of Vietnam who dons his camouflage fatigues even for office work. The truth about the unexploded ordnance—UXO, as he puts it—is that "nobody has a clue how much stuff we have downrange." Despite O'Brien's frank confession, the Army estimates that 1.5 million unexploded rounds are interred at JPG, as well as another 6.9 million bombs and shells with "explosive potential." Not surprisingly, much of the huge complex is off-limits even to personnel trained in the use and disposal of munitions. The group of officers' quarters and administrative buildings where O'Brien's office is located, in fact, occupies some of JPG's only untainted land. According to the latest estimates, only 2,000 of the installation's 55,000 acres are uncontaminated.

Later, out near JPG's firing range, Ron Jasper, a test director, explains that his specialty is testing FASCAM—the Army's family of sophisticated, scatterable mines. JPG, he says, is the only facility where many of these mines are tested. Most of what the facility does, he says, is "lot acceptance"—quality assurance of samples of munitions.

Jasper has mixed feelings about the fact that the materials he works with daily are "designed to kill someone or destroy heavily armored equipment." Still, he takes pride in his work: "I have a young son, eighteen, who is going into the Army. I like to think that my duty is to provide him with the very best equipment and best armament possible." And, he adds, "we work as safely as we can and with as much care for the environment as possible under the circumstances."

Unfortunately, Jasper's work has left a formidable environmental mess. And to make matters worse, the military's base closure commission overlooked the facility's millions of unexploded bombs in its base closure calculations. The commission budgeted roughly $30 million to shut JPG, which they figured would suffice to cover the decontamination of the facility's buildings. Then, the commission said, the base's land could be sold to nearby farmers for $25 million and the Army would almost break even.

Since the base closure order became final in 1989, however, a dismal picture has emerged. And the response of Hayden Bryan, the base closure commission's executive director, hasn't helped morale in Madison. According to Indiana's Representative Lee Hamilton, Bryan callously dismissed the environmental issue. "If you've got a problem on a base that's going to be closed," Bryan told Hamilton, "throw a fence around it and clean it up later."

JPG has the fence already, but now, it seems, later may be never. A complete cleanup may be too dangerous and destructive to conduct, not to mention prohibitively expensive. To remove all the bombs, most of JPG's wooded and bombed-out land would have to be stripped down to the level of the buried ordnance—as deep as thirty feet below the surface—using special armored bulldozers. Aside from the issue of where to put the contaminated earth, the job is environmentally devastating and almost unthinkable in magnitude. One estimate projects the total cost of such an undertaking at $13 billion. An internal JPG study determined that even a limited cleanup could cost as much as $5 billion and still leave JPG unsafe for unrestricted human use.

To complicate matters further, aging and unexploded ordnance poses a huge and largely unregulated environmental problem. JPG, for example, fails to qualify for cleanup dollars from the federal government's Superfund environmental cleanup program because the EPA, the agency that manages the Superfund, normally excludes unexploded bombs from consideration as hazardous waste. This bureaucratic ruling is unfortunate because such buried aging bombs present many of the same kinds of long-term, chronic ecological threats as do other toxic wastes.

Whatever their designation, the danger of buried ordnance is fatally evident. At a former military artillery range in San Diego County, California, two children were killed in 1985 when an old artillery shell accidently went off a few yards from their home. Fifteen years prior to the incident, the military had sold the land as surplus property to housing developers after completing two separate cleanup efforts at the site.

At the majority of the military's other contaminated facilities, huge quantities of toxic wastes dumped into the ground have seeped beyond the installations' fences and into local groundwater. JPG's explosive contamination is relatively contained on the installation's grounds, but in every other way, JPG's situation could not be more emblematic of the nation's military toxic quagmire. JPG's size, its history of environmental abuse, the extent of its contamination, and the current quandary over its future all parallel the military's broader problem.

The national military toxic burden is a figurative minefield just as JPG is a literal one. Like JPG, the nationwide military toxic waste problem is monumental—a nightmare of almost overwhelming proportion. And like JPG's bombs, the military's toxic legacy is sequestered from public view, waiting, politically at least, to explode.

Largely unfettered by environmental regulations, the U.S. armed forces have contaminated virtually every one of their installations in the United States and undoubtedly hundreds more around the world as well. As top officials at the Pentagon and the Department of Energy (which manages the military's nuclear weapons production complex) are now beginning to acknowledge, the toxic legacy left by our nation's military infrastructure may well constitute the largest and most serious environmental threat this country faces.

The Pentagon's own account now states that dangerous hazardous wastes, stored or disposed of improperly at virtually every U.S. military installation in every state, may currently contaminate more than 20,000 sites on land currently or formerly owned by the U.S. Defense Department. At these locations, millions of tons of toxic wastes have fouled thousands of square miles of soil and polluted the air and groundwater in communities across the country and at hundreds of overseas bases. Sadly, despite recent "waste minimization" programs, the military continues to dump large quantities of deadly chemicals improperly—with little oversight or public accountability.

Corroboration of this dire environmental picture came in early in 1990, when the National Governors' Association, a powerful advocate of the concerns of states, issued a particularly virulent condemnation of the federal government's handling of toxic wastes. In it, the states' executive officers expressed their collective outrage at the federal government's "blatant disregard" for its own environmental laws and at a "hamstrung" EPA, "forced to sit by as basic environmental statutes and regulations are routinely ignored" by military and other federal facilities.

"Virtually every state has within its borders federally owned or operated facilities with environmental violations and compliance problems," the report notes, adding that the U.S. government's facilities across the country operate "at health and environmental standards below the standards it mandates for private firms." The report addresses all federally owned facilities and criticizes the reckless contamination wrought at the nation's seventeen nuclear weapons production facilities run by the Department of Energy. For the breadth of its violations, the report singles out the Department of Defense as the worst federal offender of all.

At JPG, as at every base, the Department of Defense is vested with the responsibility to clean up its own environmental messes. But as several members of Congress have pointed out, the Pentagon's own accounting of its record ranks it "among the worst violators of hazardous waste laws in the country." Out of the roughly 20,000 sites of suspected toxic contamination identified so far by the Pentagon on land currently or formerly owned by the military worldwide, only 404 have actually been cleaned up as of the most recent public accounting.

Finally, as at JPG, a real cleanup of this toxic legacy may not be possible either technically or politically. The obstacles to environmental restoration at military installations are formidable, and not the least of them is monetary. Between the wastes from the Energy Department's nuclear production facilities and those of the Pentagon's bases, cost estimates for the cleanup run into the hundreds of billions of dollars.

As more and more cases of environmental mismanagement have been disclosed, these projections have grown exponentially in the past few years and undoubtedly still underestimate the cost of tackling this toxic heritage. In the carefully considered words of Barry Breen, editor of the *Environmental Law Reporter* and a former environmental lawyer for the Army, the situation ranks "among the most intractable environmental problems we face today."

While the costs continue to mount, one thing is certain: without a concerted political and technological effort, the military's toxic legacy will continue to haunt us, polluting our groundwater, contaminating our land, and damaging our health. To date, not one of the Energy Department's production facilities has been decontaminated, and Pentagon cleanup efforts are complete at less than 2 percent of those waste sites identified on current and former military installations. Some of the remaining 98 percent of the sites, like the Jefferson Proving Ground, already seem destined to become what Michael Carricato, the Pentagon's former top environmental official, has called "national sacrifice zones."

As we tour JPG's firing range the day is bright and warm. Driving east on Ordnance Drive, then north on Wonju Road (named after a battle in the Korean War), we pass a dense array of hundreds of dirty white flags stuck with short spikes into the ground like a field of exotic wildflowers. Placed for a recent visiting delegation, the flags mark the easily visible artillery shells found in the vicinity. Witnessing the dense field of flags, one cannot help but wonder what it would look like if the bombs buried well below ground were included as well.

The car turns onto Machine Gun Range Road, toward the northernmost edge of the proving ground. Although JPG's roads have all been renamed, here and there remnants persist of the towns it displaced in the 1940s. The Oakdale School, one of the oldest stone schoolhouses in Indiana, still stands, but amidst miles of unexploded bombs it offers only a scant reminder of the facility's former life. Some 2,000 residents of this land had their lives altered forever when the U.S. government ordered them to leave their homes within thirty days; even the graves of some 3,500 dead were moved, and within a matter of months of the initial order the facility was up and running. The bombs have been exploding ever since, earning Madison the moniker "Boomville" as early as the mid-1940s.

When this chunk of fertile land was seized in the midst of a war emergency, few expected the military to stay long. But today, as JPG passes its fiftieth anniversary, the impression is widespread that the land here may have been destroyed forever. Horribly polluted by toxic explosive compounds leaching from the buried bombs, and presenting a constant threat of explosion, JPG will need to be isolated from human contact for the indefinite future.

In a macabre way, JPG's scant human population has fostered a strange sort of nature preserve. Indeed, the area may well boast more wildlife today than it did fifty years ago, when it was predominantly farmland. Kenneth Knouf, JPG's resident nature and wildlife expert, says that bobcats, coyotes, red foxes, deer, and even some endangered reptiles, happily make the facility their home—aside from the occasional casualty. "And the bomb craters," he adds, "make for the best frog-breeding areas I've ever found."

CHAPTER TWO

Teaching a Camel to Fly

At ten o'clock on a cool November morning in 1987, Representative Mike Synar of Oklahoma greeted his colleagues and surveyed the crowded room before them. As chair of the congressional Subcommittee on Environment, Energy, and Natural Resources, Synar had presided over many similar hearings in this same room of the marble-gray Rayburn House Office Building on Capitol Hill, but few would prove as frustrating as the one about to unfold. On this day, one month past his thirty-seventh birthday, Synar was beginning to doubt he would ever live to see the Pentagon clean up its toxic legacy.

Things began normally enough, with collegiality and protocol. There was a nice brisk electricity in the air, like that before any performance— lots of anticipatory shuffling and the hum of many hushed, overlapping conversations. This morning the subcommittee was scheduled to receive testimony about the progress the Defense Department had made in addressing its environmental problems.

Synar took special interest in the proceedings. He had staked much of his political career on the issue and had struggled against military recalcitrance for years. He knew the Pentagon's dismal record of environmental abuse; he and his staff had uncovered much of the publicly available information on the subject themselves. Synar also knew that the armed forces could boast some real strides in addressing their contamination problems at Tinker Air Force Base in his home state. He hoped to hear more such reports. While today's hearings might not announce miraculous achievements, the event held some promise. It had been four years since military officials had reviewed the status of their environmental cleanup program before Congress. Synar expected that the normally highly orchestrated procedure of congressional testimony would evoke a good deal of information from the impressive delegation of top environmental officials already in attendance from nearly every branch of the Pentagon.

"It has always been my position," Synar declared in his opening remarks, "that federal agencies should set an example for the private sector." The statement was a simple one, but it was delivered with particular resolve. It was easy to see how Mike Synar could make people proud back home in his rural district. Young and energetic, he brought a populist vitality to his work that showed even in his open, square-jawed American face. Cast Synar back in time about a decade and a half, and one would find a young man chosen as the nation's top 4-H member; the honor came at about the same time Synar's Muskogee family had been named the "outstanding family in the U.S." by an organization called the All-American Family Institute.

Defense installations, Synar continued, "should be held to the same strict standards of accountability for compliance with the hazardous waste laws as are private entities and individuals." He glanced at the military delegation, who were listening politely, unmoved. "Unfortunately, our investigation and hearings to date indicate that all too often this has not been the case. Our purpose today will be to determine how much progress, if any, has been made in solving these problems."

The morning's first testimony came from Frank Conahan, a high-ranking official at the General Accounting Office (GAO), the investigative arm of Congress. The GAO, often at Synar's behest, was virtually the only nonmilitary agency to have compiled a substantial body of information on the military's stewardship of the environment. Despite that assignment, the agency had managed to retain a reputation, even among military personnel, as a credible and nonpartisan source.

Conahan summed up the GAO's latest findings. His statement did not mark an auspicious beginning to the morning for the military. Of the fourteen military facilities his agency had visited, Conahan stated, twelve had been out of compliance with environmental laws. He told the subcommittee that in addition to "storage and disposal problems," the GAO had found "problems in recordkeeping and tracking of hazardous waste shipments, hazardous waste container management and ground water monitoring."

11

Although Conahan didn't give the details at the hearing, the GAO inspection had found that those fourteen facilities had been cited by state agencies for seventy-two separate environmental violations the previous year. Forty-seven of these incidents were "Class 1" violations—the most severe—which, according to EPA criteria, result in "a release or serious threat of release of hazardous waste to the environment."

As for the military's self-advertised program to minimize its output of hazardous waste, Conahan also had few favorable words. The Defense Department had undertaken a program to deal with the issue, he said, "but based on our work, we see very little in the way of installation implementation of that program. We looked at a number of places, and found that they weren't really doing very much." Conahan testified that in the estimation of the GAO the military's hazardous waste program had "a very, very long way to go."

Conahan spoke of "violations" and "problems," but Synar and many others in the room knew that for many of the military's longstanding environmental problems the words were polite government euphemisms.

At the Lakehurst Naval Air Engineering Center in New Jersey, for example, the Navy had estimated as early as 1981 that workers had dumped into the ground more than 3 million gallons of cancer-causing aviation fuel and other toxic substances, endangering the Cohansey aquifer, which serves as the source of tap water for most residents of southern New Jersey. The Navy withheld this information from the public even after three different groundwater tests showed levels of certain substances to be as much as 10,000 times as high as the state considers safe.

In 1984, at the Army's Cornhusker Ammunition Plant in Nebraska, an Army spokesperson had publicly defended the decision of officials at that base not to notify nearby residents that their drinking wells were contaminated with dangerous levels of explosive compounds, levels dozens of times above allowable standards. "We didn't want to get them overly anxious," he is reported to have said. Consequently, the Army waited two years to go public with information about the migration of its pollution, not even measuring contaminants in the majority of endangered private wells in the area until a third round of testing, in 1984, which showed definitively that hundreds of private wells in the vicinity were tainted by the installation's chemicals.

As Synar's congressional hearing would underscore, such serious breaches of public trust were too prevalent in the military's recent history to be simply written off as exceptions. An emerging nationwide pattern marked a patent disregard for the environment by the armed forces. Without doubt the problems were exacerbated by the military's penchant for secrecy, the lack of outside oversight of its practices, and the overarching importance placed on its "national security" mission. The view was characterized in an oft-repeated quip by a Virginia base commander; speaking to a neighborhood group at a 1984 public meeting to address local contamination from his base, he reportedly claimed, "We're in the business of protecting the nation, not the environment."

Following a brief round of questions from subcommittee members, Conahan made way at the microphone for Carl J. Schafer, Jr., then Deputy Assistant Secretary of Defense for the Environment. Flanked by a small legion of top-ranking officials from the various branches of the military, Schafer began the military's counteroffensive with a prepared statement of the Pentagon's official position.

Schafer, in his Pentagon role, oversaw the military's overall environmental status, but day-to-day responsibility for environmental matters was relegated to individuals in each separate branch of the armed forces. Each service—Army, Navy, and Air Force—has a similar structure at the top, but each branch is organized differently, oversees its own installations, and establishes its own separate directives and budget priorities. Two additional armed services, the Marines and the Coast Guard, are much smaller, but add further complexity, falling within the budgetary jurisdiction of the Navy. Finally, a branch called the Defense Logistics Agency (whose representative was also present at the hearing) purchases and transports equipment and supplies on behalf of all of the armed forces.

"Our top priority continues to be cleanup of toxic and hazardous waste," Schafer told the subcommittee, speaking on behalf of all the members of his assembled delegation. "In cases where we discover an existing danger to the public or to the people at our installations, we act immediately to reduce that threat, and then we begin the necessary studies, the remedial investigations and feasibility studies under EPA's nomenclature, to determine the extent and type of contamination and the range of remedies available to be implemented."

Schafer testified that the Pentagon had found 4,611 potentially contaminated sites at 761 U.S. bases. He also reported that representatives from each of the armed forces' separate environmental programs had begun preliminary studies of some kind at the majority of these sites. Although the number of sites uncovered by each branch of the armed services had risen dramatically over previous years, Schafer told the subcommittee that he believed the military had now found most of the polluted lands. As he confidently put it, "We believe we are generally finished with this phase of the program."

Unfortunately, the years since his testimony have proven him badly mistaken. Today Schafer's counterparts make much the same claim. Perhaps now they are more accurate, but events of the decade of the 1980s inspire little such confidence.

Every spring the Pentagon issues a printed volume containing data about its "environmental restoration program." Since Schafer testified before Synar's subcommittee in 1987, the department has issued three such volumes and each year the volumes themselves, like the problems, have grown. The report of fiscal year 1988, enclosed in a plain brown cover, listed 8,139 potentially contaminated sites at 897 installations. The report contained roughly 100 pages. The following year a report with gold writing on a glossy purple cover documented 14,401 potentially contaminated sites at 1,579 installations. That year's volume came to about 150 pages.

The latest report, covering fiscal year 1990, sports a shiny full-color cover with a picture of a bird perched on the bloom of a cactus set against a deep, postcard-blue sky. The report runs about 250 pages. The military now says it has some 17,482 potentially contaminated sites at 1,855 installations—close to four times the number Schafer believed was complete. And in keeping with the Pentagon's accounting practices, none of these figures, including the ones Schafer presented to the hearing, count contamination at sites formerly owned by the military—the Pentagon identifies roughly 7,000 of these—or at U.S. bases in foreign nations. (As for contamination at overseas bases, the information remains largely unavailable—classified as secret "for national security reasons.")

Schafer concluded his prepared remarks by stressing the importance of environmental quality as an "intrinsic part" of the military mission. "I am committed to carrying out our program in full cooperation with the EPA and state agencies," he said, "with public participation and in full compliance with environmental laws and regulations."

Referring to Schafer's claim that "the preponderance" of the sites identified so far by the military consisted of "relatively minor" instances of spills and leaks, Synar asked Schafer, "What do you mean by a 'preponderance'—90 percent, 75 percent, 51 percent?" Schafer's lengthy answer touched, in turn, on the role of the EPA, the large amount of wastes generated by the military, and the San Francisco and Chesapeake bays, where despite the heavy concentration of military bases officials deemed the environmental impact "relatively minor."

"Nice answer," Synar said, rubbing his chin theatrically, "not to my question, but nice answer." And he asked again.

Of the 3,500 sites studied so far, Schafer finally admitted, only 500 had been deemed minor enough to require no further action. "I'm not trying to be disingenuous," he added defensively when Synar reminded him that in his written testimony he had called this a "preponderance" of the sites.

Several minutes later, after similar stiff cross examination, Schafer revealed an astonishing bit of information. Not counting so-called interim removal actions, wherein military personnel had essentially shifted hazardous waste from one place to another, only "seven truly remedial actions" had been completed out of the 4,611 sites being studied—actions, that is, that involved any effort to actually clean up the soil, air, or groundwater.

The hearing room seemed even quieter than usual. Synar asked Schafer—incredulously, rhetorically—"This is the bottom line after ten years of operation of this program?

"At this rate, if the same percentages hold true, Mr. Schafer," he continued, "when do you expect that the task will be completed?"

"Honestly," Schafer responded, "it is a hard, hard issue."

In the course of the hearing, each major branch of the armed services had its turn in the spotlight. Synar, as chair, led the questioning. He asked the Air Force representative, Gary Vest, about reports that Andersen Air Force Base in the U.S. Trust Territory of Guam had polluted the island's main drinking-water supply with toxic solvents. At the time, Vest ranked as one of the Air Force's top people on environmental matters, but his title gave some indication of the issue's low status within the service: Deputy (for Environment, Safety, and Occupational Health) to the Deputy Assistant Secretary of the Air Force for Installations.

According to an investigation conducted by the GAO, officials at Andersen Air Force Base had known since 1978 that some of the base's own water wells had been contaminated with the solvent TCE (trichloroethylene). TCE, a widely used industrial solvent that has been found in small concentrations in as many as a third of all water supplies in the United States, is known to cause cancer in animals when inhaled or ingested and is widely believed to cause cancer in humans as well. Instead of trying to get rid of the contamination, the Air Force attempted to lower the hazardous level of TCE by flooding the contaminated wells with cleaner drinking water from elsewhere.

First, Schafer gave a brief general response to the situation. "We want to fix it," Schafer said, adding, "We are not recalcitrants and we are not anti-environment." For details, he turned to Vest.

"In direct answer to your question," Vest said, "we've submitted our response to Mr. Schafer's office. So I need to defer to him on the final resolution of that."

Synar's response was swift and blunt: "At least we've got all the people who are going to be passing this buck here at one table."

The Navy's representative, Commander Richard Rice, performed no better when subjected to Synar's increasingly exasperated questioning. Rice, a ruddy, balding career officer, sat stiffly in his dark blue uniform, frowning throughout. His strategy seemed to be to say as little as possible about anything, waiting out the hearing stoically, as one might endure an unpleasant appointment at the dentist. Synar asked Rice specific questions about nearly a dozen Navy contamination sites, but Rice gave no answers.

Synar asked about a shipyard at the Norfolk Naval Base in Virginia, where, according to a Navy report from 1983, a 10,000-gallon oil tank had been leaking. The report stated that two monitoring wells nearby had determined that "samples contained more oil than water and as much as 1 million gallons of waste oil could be present."

"Now, as of September 30 of this year—this is 1987—you report no actual construction work underway to correct that problem," Synar stated. "What are you waiting for?"

"Sir," Rice responded politely, "I would have to provide that for the record."

The information he ultimately provided, in the form of a brief written summary, said essentially that the leaking tank had been removed but no cleanup had taken place. The statement read, "Preliminary results show that removing the tank did alleviate the ground water contamination problem. Samples collected from monitoring wells indicate an early reduced oil and grease concentration."

Next, Synar asked Rice about a toxic dump at the same base. At this site, a Navy report had concluded, there was "significant potential" that an estimated 7.8 million gallons of wastes in the soil, including cyanides, degreasers, solvents, and other toxic wastes, could migrate into waterways that feed into the Chesapeake Bay. "When are you going to decide whether that site needs restoration, Mr. Rice?" Synar asked doggedly.

"Sir," Rice responded, "none of them [the Norfolk base's sites] are listed as remedial actions yet because we have not determined what the appropriate action is."

"When?" Synar asked.

"I do not know, sir."

"Mr. Rice, did you not know I was going to ask you about this today?"

"I did not know until this morning, sir."

Synar's indignation was becoming ever more visible. "We've been working with you all down at DOD [the Department of Defense]," he said. "We told you these sites were going to come up today. I mean, this is unacceptable, guys. I've got to tell you. 'We'll supply it for the record. We'll supply it for the record.' I mean, we're talking about a problem here identified in 1983. Nothing has been done as of today in 1987, and you're coming in here and telling me you're going to have to supply it for the record. Why isn't there any construction underway, Mr. Rice? And don't tell me it's a complicated problem. It can't be that complicated to have waited this long."

Rice, unruffled: "Sir, I do not have site specific information."

"Well, does anybody with you have that?"

"No, sir."

At the close of the hearing, Synar told the military delegation of his dismay. He was "very disappointed" in the expert panel's preparations, he said, but "not amazed by the way you skirted around the questions. This is what we found throughout this investigation." As a member of Congress, he said, he found it difficult to ask private industry to meet a tough set of rules and regulations "when at the same time my own government is not meeting those standards and rules and regulations."

Something, it was clear to most of those present that day, was not working. The military, charged with responsibility to clean up its own contamination, simply didn't seem to be doing the job. The situation seemed to frustrate almost everyone present. Even the military delegation appeared shaken; the hearing, it seemed, hadn't gone as smoothly as they might have hoped.

One of the committee members, Matthew Martinez, a Democrat from California, wanted to bring the matter to some higher authority, like the police or the courts, but he didn't seem quite sure where to go; it seemed that under different circumstances he might have suggested calling in the Army. Martinez said he didn't think the Defense Department would ever move on the matter "without anybody policing them." If only someone could threaten some strong "punitive action against them," he suggested on several occasions, then "you'll see how fast they'd clean it up."

Martinez's comments gave vent to the exasperation felt by many at the hearing, but his call for a body to police the military's environmental practices was not taken up seriously at the time. In the years since the hearings, the EPA has stepped up its efforts to regulate federal facilities, including military installations, but the agency still lacks the ability to enforce its rules. Consequently, the armed services remain staunchly in charge of their own toxic problems.

And today, despite a noticeable increase in stated concern about environmental matters on the part of many military personnel, only a handful of the 25,000 suspected toxic sites under the Pentagon's jurisdiction have actually been cleaned up. Many have not even been fully investigated.

Late in the hearing, an infuriated Synar exploded at Schafer, unable to put up with the military delegation's refusal to produce substantive information.

"What have you done?" he asked, almost shouting. "What have you done in this area? Tell me what you've done. Give me some things you've done."

Schafer seemed determined to remain calm. Hunched over the microphone, his voice was deep and steady. "The policies are emanating from my office, and those policies are resulting in derivative policy being issued by the services. Part of the problem is that this program does not fit especially well over the decentralization that is—"

Synar erupted before Schafer could finish. "I don't want to hear that," he said. "What are you doing? Tell me. Tell me what you're doing. Don't tell me about the problems you are encountering. Tell me what you are doing to overcome this problem."

Picking up a report by the Defense Department's own watchdog, its Inspector General, Synar began reading aloud: "'The issues preventing the Department of Defense from achieving the pro-active HM/HW [Hazardous Management/Hazardous Waste] program are: fragmented policies; lack of effective structure management; lack of communications at all levels. Nearly every installation commander and staff visited indicated they believed they were not receiving adequate guidance and support.'" The passages detailed the agency's failure to make hazardous waste cleanup a priority.

"What are you doing?" Synar bellowed again. "Don't tell me about the problems. Tell me what you're doing."

"We are doing everything we can," Schafer offered halfheartedly. "We have issued policies from my office on each and every one of these subjects."

"Policies?" Synar asked.

"Yes, sir," Schafer replied. "That's my function. We are pulling together the policy on these things. We have issued policy." He paused briefly. He seemed, just for a moment, to be at a loss for words. What, after all, could really be said about the department's poor record on the environment and the long litany of toxic atrocities that he had just been hauled through?

"It is easy to say it is fragmented," he exclaimed at last, as though he finally knew how to make Synar understand, "but camels can't fly."

"Toxic Time Bomb"

As Keith Tadewald remembers it, the trouble in Collinsville, California, began on a clear April morning in 1989. Tadewald, a firefighter in nearby Rio Vista, received an unusual request from the county department of health to assist in an investigation of some suspicious-looking fifty-five-gallon drums. An anonymous caller had reported the drums, and an initial inspection had left health officials worried.

Within the hour Tadewald arrived at the specified location—a large abandoned barn on the edge of Collinsville, a fishing village forty-five miles southwest of Sacramento. An odd collection of officials had already assembled. Upon his arrival, Tadewald found the county sheriff and representatives from the health department, the local agriculture board, and the state environmental crimes division. From the start, he recalls, it was clearly much more than a routine investigation.

Tadewald says he recognized the drums' potential as a fire hazard immediately, especially given the drought-ridden weather, but he remembers thinking at first that it seemed like a lot of commotion over just the few barrels that were immediately visible from the outside, even if some of them were labeled hazardous. Like his counterparts from the other agencies, Tadewald had no idea—not even a glimmer of suspicion—that the assembled team was about to uncover one of the largest caches of toxic and explosive chemicals ever found in California.

Tadewald would later conclude that anything could have touched off an explosion in the barn, even the tiny sparks that flew as the team pried open the locked latch on the big doors. Inside, the barn was filled to overflowing with drums of toxic materials. Many of the drums were dented, leaking, and corroded. Side by side were volatile chemicals that are illegal—and dangerous—to store together. As the team would eventually determine, the barn and four nearby trailers contained roughly 40,000 gallons of assorted chemicals.

"So many different hazardous materials were in there," Tadewald recalls, "it was almost unimaginable." The list, when finally compiled, included corrosive and toxic chemicals, known carcinogens, extremely flammable ethers, acids, solvents, paint thinners, lacquers, resins, and pesticides. The officials even found fifteen drums of methyl di-isocyanate, the chemical responsible for the deadly 1984 disaster in Bhopal, India.

A curious fact noticed almost immediately by the team was that nearly all of the barn's toxic contents were clearly labeled with the markings of the U.S. military.

As the story unfolded over the next several months, state environmental officials traced the chemicals' origins. A California businessman named Richard Armor had purchased the massive stockpile from the military over the course of nine years, at auctions of surplus and waste material held by the Defense Department. After leasing the Collinsville land from a large holding company, Armor had stashed the wastes in the barn and subsequently moved out of state.

For decades, state officials learned, the Defense Department had rid itself of dangerous unwanted toxic materials by including them in mixed lots of innocuous surplus goods sold to the public. As a top-ranking Pentagon official confided privately much later, the unofficial policy was essentially this: "If you wanted to buy some used typewriters from the Defense Department, we would throw in some used or expired toxic materials."

The scale of the Collinsville discovery and the publicity surrounding it soon spawned a federal investigation culminating in an unusual congressional hearing on the matter, held in Sacramento in February 1990. Several members of Congress, accompanied by their aides, made the pilgrimage from Washington to hear testimony about the case. At the hearing, U.S. Representative Vic Fazio, whose district includes the Collinsville barn, disclosed that numerous similar cases had been uncovered around the country, including one in Los Angeles that rivaled what he called the "toxic time bomb" in his district.

Like Oklahoma Representative Mike Synar, Fazio was furious at the Pentagon. "The Department of Defense," he declared, "one of the nation's largest generators of hazardous wastes, mismanages the hazardous materials it uses and the wastes it generates at unnecessary expense to the taxpayer and in some instances at substantial risk to human health and the environment." The Defense Department's sale of toxic materials and waste to the public, he said, constituted "nothing less than a fraudulent disposal of hazardous waste in order to avoid the high cost of proper disposal."

Needless to say, Collinsville residents—especially the dozens of families who were evacuated from their homes during the emergency state cleanup effort that ensued—were horrified and outraged. Among other things, Collinsville's "toxic time bomb" offered a rare and frightening glimpse into the hazardous, chemical-intensive practices of the modern military. All too often, behind barbed wire and armed guardposts, military personnel have quietly and steadily dumped hazardous chemicals into unlined pits or nearby creeks and streams. For all these quiet years, the chemicals have seeped steadily, ineluctably underground beneath the installations' guarded borders before being recognized as a problem by community members. As in Collinsville, people throughout the nation have frequently learned of extensive ongoing environmental atrocities at military installations near their homes only when contaminants are suddenly found—often in shocking quantities—in private wells or public water supplies.

Military wastes have turned up in civilian landfills and in civilian backyards. They have also contaminated virtually every one of the military's 1,855 installations around the country: ammunition plants, proving grounds, depots, research and development facilities, manufacturing and maintenance installations, and Navy and Air Force bases, as well as a huge number of forts and other general training and all-purpose installations. Some larger installations have more than 100 separate sites of suspected contamination within their borders.

In Collinsville, a relatively representative sample of the military's toxic inventory had lurked quietly for years. With the barn doors open wide, the military's practices suddenly became subject to the glare of public scrutiny. As Tadewald put it, "Aside from the issue of selling to the public, I had no idea the military even used all those chemicals."

* * *

Just what are the chemicals used for? A figurative walk through the barn reveals much about the military's toxic practices.

At first, a visitor to Collinsville's homemade military depot might find the scale of the inventory overwhelming—hundreds of drums of hazardous materials piled to the barn's rafters. Figures about the armed forces' use of toxic materials have a similar effect. By its own estimate, the Pentagon generates close to 500,000 tons of toxic waste annually—a nearly incomprehensible figure. Each year, in other words, the military makes enough hazardous waste to fill three thousand new warehouses the size of the Collinsville barn—a new barn springing up every three hours around the clock each day.

To put this kind of waste generation into perspective, one must recognize that the Defense Department is a vast industrial enterprise. To begin with, every year the Pentagon purchases nearly 200 million barrels of fuel oil—a toxic material itself. Placed end to end, the barrels used in a year by the U.S. military would wrap around the earth five times. The huge quantity of fuel they would contain is enough, according to the privately funded Center for Defense Information, to run the nation's entire public transit system for more than a decade.

Much of the military's fuel is stored in underground storage tanks just like the rusting, leaking ones that have plagued private industry for years. Officials at Exxon, who oversee one of the largest private collections of underground tanks in the country, say that they have already replaced roughly 70 percent of their 10,000 tanks. Especially in light of the 1990 Valdez oil spill in Alaska, Exxon's image is hardly one of environmental rectitude, but the corporation's efforts look good compared to the Pentagon's. Bill Matney, Exxon's regulatory compliance coordinator, is quick to note that "the military is legally required to upgrade its tanks like everyone else." A study by the Congressional Budget Office, however, estimates that the U.S. armed forces have some 40,000 underground storage tanks, the vast majority of which have never been replaced.

The purchase and handling of fuel are but two examples of the industrial scale of the military infrastructure. Because of the diverse missions of the U.S. armed forces, one can pick a product almost at random and discover that military usage dwarfs that of other large entities. Over the course of the 1980s, for instance, the Pentagon estimates that it purchased nearly 15 million lithium sulfur batteries, most for use by the Army Signal Corps. Their disposal has presented a costly environmental predicament worldwide. The U.S. military is suspected of using more than half of the nation's cumulative total of the ozone-depleting chloro-fluorocarbons (CFCs) Halon and CFC-113—chemicals which until recently were widely used in products like refrigerators and fire extinguishers. One estimate credits these two chemicals alone with responsibility for more than one tenth of the planet's overall ozone depletion.

The truth is, the military generates hazardous byproducts through innumerable facets of its daily work. Huge quantities of toxic waste are generated in the routine operation and maintenance of the military's prodigious collection of vehicles, tanks, planes, ships, and missiles. Producing ammunition—a vast and varied endeavor itself—also leaves behind an enormous quantity of hazardous byproducts, as does the testing and storage of these munitions. And finally, a wide array of industrial practices— ranging from electroplating to milling and machining parts in the military's research and development facilities—creates immense amounts of hazardous wastes.

Each branch of the military has its own characteristic environmental quagmires: the Army has horribly polluted munitions plants; the Air Force continues to struggle with the devastating consequences of its historically indiscriminate use of solvents; and the Navy remains mired in environmental problems, including those resulting from its careless disposal of paints and paint strippers into the ground at shipyards and also into the nation's coastal waters.

In all these cases, the overwhelming majority of these environmental problems are not the result of some devious, errant base commander dumping toxic wastes illegally after dark. Rather, the bulk of the military's toxic wastes originate from decades of standard daily operating procedures. While many practices have been changed to meet environmental regulations, others have not altered since World War II or even earlier.

As was reflected in the contents of the Collinsville barn, the main contributor to the military's toxic waste headache is the sheer volume of solvents used in its operations. Military personnel have poured many millions of gallons of solvents into the ground at installations across the country over the past half century. In this regard, the Air Force is undoubtedly the worst offender. High-ranking Air Force officials freely concede that virtually every one of their bases at home and abroad is contaminated with solvents, most notably TCE—trichloroethylene—seen decades ago as a "miracle solvent" and today strongly suspected to cause cancer. Of the 100 military facilities that sit atop the National Priority List (the Superfund program's listing of the nation's worst polluted lands), more than one fourth are Air Force bases contaminated primarily with solvents like TCE. And the use of solvents remains integral to the Air Force's mission today.

A good illustration can be found at the Wright-Patterson Air Force Base near Dayton, Ohio. This base is headquarters for the Air Force's Logistics Command, whose five facilities generate nearly 90 percent of the Air Force's hazardous waste—a total that exceeded a billion gallons in 1987 alone. Among its other missions, this branch of the Air Force is responsible for maintaining approximately 20,000 aircraft, 53,000 jet engines, and 1,000 ballistic missiles.

Recently retired Air Force logistics commander General Alfred G. Hansen has explained concisely that, "providing this support [to the other branches of the Air Force] often involves large amounts of potentially hazardous substances such as volatile organic compounds used in military coatings and powerful but corrosive agents like acids, fuels and thinners."

Part of the standard maintenance regime at Wright-Patterson, as at virtually every Air Force base, involves spraying planes liberally with solvents to clean and de-ice them. Historically, the runoff has been allowed to seep directly into the ground. In addition, another large-scale misuse of solvents is part of Wright-Patterson's toxic history: for decades, when planes flew in for maintenance Air Force personnel would dip the engine parts into huge vats of solvents to remove grease and grime from them before undertaking repairs; as the solvent baths quickly became dirty, workers would take the vats and dump the toxic contents into unlined pits, letting the chemicals drain into the ground. At Wright-Patterson this routine dumping took place for decades at many of the base's sixty-two unlined waste disposal areas—now identified as toxic waste sites.

Unfortunately, at Wright-Patterson the area's permeable soil has allowed the solvents and other contaminants to migrate quickly. Already some sixty families of base personnel with homes near a base landfill have been forced to evacuate, perhaps permanently. One of the base's numerous toxic problems is TCE at concentrations more than one hundred times safe levels, discovered in the groundwater moving southwest toward the underground supply that the city of Dayton draws upon for drinking water. The imminent threat has forced the construction of what Mark Allen, a state environmental official, calls a "groundwater interception device." Nonetheless, Allen says, low-level contamination has already reached the edges of Dayton's wellfield. General Hansen points to "significant progress toward correcting past mistakes" at Wright-Patterson. But in reality, negotiations with the state and the Environmental Protection Agency over the cleanup effort at this site stalled in 1989, according to the Pentagon's 1991 annual report, and a full study of the problem is not expected to be complete until the year 2002.

While the Air Force may have the most widespread problems associated with solvents, it certainly isn't the only branch of the military that uses them. The Army uses vast quantities of solvents in the maintenance of its fleets of cars, tanks, helicopters, and planes. And by one estimate, the Navy uses nearly half a million gallons of solvents just to clean its torpedoes after test shots.

Strolling gingerly through the Collinsville barn's stockpile, one would soon see that in addition to solvents the inventory bespeaks the large amount of electroplating conducted by all the armed forces. Electroplating, which requires the routine use of acids and degreasers, is a process primarily undertaken to combat rust. Everything from nuts and bolts to large industrial machine parts are routinely plated with noncorrosive metals like copper, silver, or gold. The ensuing wastes include acids, cyanides, and the residue of hazardous heavy metals.

To many U.S. military officials, rust, with its silent and devastating attack, is an enemy that must be taken as seriously as any geopolitical threat. Those in logistics and engineering commands point out that military hardware often sits idle outdoors for long periods but must function flawlessly in a crisis. The argument is used to justify electroplating everything from sensitive aircraft parts to monkey wrenches. Ironically, a visit to the Collinsville barn would reveal that many of the drums—former property of the military—were badly rusted. Some had even begun to leak their contents.

Many of the barn's chemicals—including its assortment of solvents and acids—are relatively common in industrial manufacturing practices in the private sector, like aircraft maintenance and electroplating. But some of the barn's drums contained less well known chemicals. The military uses some of these more exotic compounds in highly specialized procedures for producing, testing, storing, and modernizing its arsenal.

Army munitions plants, for instance, have caused some of the military's worst environmental problems—mostly from explosive compounds disposed of improperly. From rifle bullets to ballistic missiles and artillery shells containing chemical agents, the production of ammunition has devastated the environment at virtually every site at which it has been undertaken. In addition to the twenty-nine Air Force bases listed on the

Superfund National Priority List, sixteen military ammunition plants are also among the nation's top priority sites. Even this number fails to capture the extent of the problem; by the military's own accounting, at least thirty such plants have serious environmental problems.

The Milan Army Ammunition Plant in Western Tennessee offers a telling example. In 1987 the Milan installation received one of the Superfund's highest scores on its hazardous ranking system. At this facility the Army routinely dumped the polluted wastewater from the production of medium-sized artillery shells into eleven unlined lagoons. From there large quantities of toxic explosive compounds (and other wastes, including zinc, lead, mercury, chromium, sulfates, and phosphates) had leached into the region's underground water supply.

At this plant, the Army learned that the water supply was contaminated in 1978 but gave no clear warning to residents in the nearby town of Milan, Tennessee, who had been drinking the polluted water for years. Indeed, the Army continued to use the lagoons for more than three years after the pollution had been discovered before even undertaking further study. Now, some four decades since the plant was built and fourteen years since the Army discovered that its pollutants had made their way into the water supply, the site still awaits Superfund cleanup.

Army officials now often complain that they cannot meet current environmental standards and still produce ammunition. The problem, they say, is the huge volume of toxic "red water," an unavoidable byproduct of manufacturing munitions. This wastewater contains residual amounts of dangerous explosive compounds with exotic names like DNT (dinitro-toluene) and RDX (an abbreviation of "Research and Development Explosive," a name for the chemical hexahydro-1,3,5-trinitro-1,3,5-triazine). Unfortunately, this relatively recent admission by the Army offers little solace to the people in towns like Milan who, often unknowingly, have been subject to dangerous levels of toxics in their drinking water and soil.

According to the U.S. Public Health Service's Agency for Toxic Substances and Disease Registry (ATSDR), workers exposed to DNT have shown increased rates of heart disease as well as effects on their blood and nervous systems. Studies have documented the chemical's lethality when ingested in small quantities by mice, rats, and dogs, and have linked the chemical to nervous system disorders, kidney damage, and liver cancer. The ATSDR maintains, however, that "little dose-response data" is available to judge the chemical's precise effects on humans. Because the chemical is uncommon in the private sector, the agency reports, no studies of DNT are currently known to be underway.

27

The lack of health and safety data is even more pronounced for RDX, an explosive compound which, like DNT, has turned up in water supplies around the country. All information about the chemical had to come first from the military; no other private or governmental agency even knew what the compound was. And RDX is not alone in its obscurity; the Collinsville barn's inventory, for instance, included some chemicals not only unique to the military but designed to serve exclusive and idiosyncratic military purposes. The use of some of these chemicals would be outlawed for private industry, and yet they continue to be required by military specifications.

Several drums in the Collinsville barn deserve particular consideration. They contained a highly corrosive and toxic chemical called Decontamination Solution #2, or DS2, a compound that internal Army memos describe as "nasty stuff." Little health data exists about DS2 (a combination of diethylenetriamine and ethylene glycol monomethyl ether), but the Army says that it is believed to cause central nervous system depression, liver damage, and possibly even birth defects in humans. The substance ignites spontaneously at temperatures around 115 degrees Fahrenheit and explodes on contact with bleach. But perhaps most troubling of all are its corrosive properties: it eats through metal and rubber—and human skin and tissue.

Despite its dangers, DS2 is stockpiled at virtually every Army base in the U.S. and abroad (including hospitals) for use in the event of a chemical war. In such a scenario, soldiers in protective garb are supposed to use DS2 to wash and decontaminate vehicles and machinery.

Like the other chemicals in the barn, the DS2 had been purchased by the businessman Richard Armor at military auctions of surplus material. These auctions are handled by a branch of the Defense Department known as the Defense Reutilization and Marketing Service (DRMS), which has more than two hundred regional offices around the world. This branch of the military receives more than 150 million pounds of hazardous wastes from the armed services every year. In 1989, DRMS officials say, they paid contractors nearly $34 million for shipping and off-site disposal of some 106 million pounds of toxic wastes, but the agency's disposal records don't tell the whole story. The ultimate destination of another 72 million pounds received that year is unclear. The material, DRMS representatives say, was either sold, donated, or recycled.

DRMS officials say that in 1990 some $14 million worth of DS2 was turned in—an amount equal to more than a million gallons at Army prices. It is unknown how much was sold. Unfortunately for Armor, who bought dozens of mixed lots of surplus military goods, including paints, solvents, and other chemicals, he was among the purchasers of this particular chemical. The fact is, there really are no civilian applications for DS2. "There's a joke about it around here that you could use it as fingernail polish remover," says Nancy Dunn, a Pentagon spokesperson, "but you might never see your fingers again."

So far, at least four other cases involving the sale of DS2 to the unsuspecting public have come to light. Some 275 gallons were purchased at auction in 1988 from the DRMS office at the Kirtland Air Force Base in New Mexico. The purchaser later told a federal investigator that he didn't know what he was buying. When he went to pick up the material and expressed concern about the hazard it might present, he was told that he had to take it or be barred from bidding at future auctions.

In the past few years, drums of hazardous wastes sold at DRMS auctions have been found discarded alongside a highway and leaking from a rented storage locker. In one case in Los Angeles, hundreds of drums of hazardous materials purchased through DRMS auctions—including many which were leaking—were illegally dumped in a locked vacant lot owned by the Port of Los Angeles. As in the Collinsville case, the military claimed it bore no responsibility for the discarded toxic wastes.

In one specific response to the 1990 congressional hearings on the Collinsville barn and related matters, the Defense Department has said that—at least in the United States—it will not sell DS2 to any bidders that cannot show their licensed capability to break the material down into its constituent parts for recycling. The Navy and the Air Force have even said that they will stop using the material altogether. Adequate decontamination results, they say, can be achieved with detergent and water.

But military specifications are not easily changed. Despite all the trouble DS2 has caused, the Army refuses to adopt an alternative. Army installations around the country are still receiving shipments of the chemical today. Speaking to a congressional committee several months prior to the Persian Gulf War, Brigadier General David A. Nydam stated unequivocally that the Army "requires the availability of a decontaminant which can effectively be used in an efficient and immediate manner in locations where water may be severely limited in availability."

General Nydam's allegiance to DS2 comes despite the fact (addressed briefly in his statement) that the chemical doesn't even work very well. Army tests from as early as 1984 concluded that applying DS2 to the Army's M1 tanks could make them inoperable. According to the test reports, DS2 "severely damaged electrical components and cables," caused the "rubber road wheels and track of the tank to decompose and damaged the tank's periscopes." Meanwhile, in contrast, the Army tests showed that one M1 tank decontaminated with household bleach twelve times in a row still ran well.

Acknowledging what he called the "definite limitations" of DS2, General Nydam also maintained that "DS2 presents no more of a storage and disposal problem than any other hazardous material used by the Army." Nydam's picture differs from that compiled by others, however. Thomas F. Ward, who headed up one part of a congressional investigation into DS2, reported, "Everywhere we looked, the drums were leaking. We never found any storage sites that didn't look bad." And, as an internal Army report later revealed about the year-long congressional investigation, "every commander they talked to wants it off installation."

After Keith Tadewald and his counterparts discovered the Collinsville barn's military chemicals, the state had no choice but to conduct a massive emergency cleanup effort. Two dozen workers were immediately dispatched to the scene. Some of the material stashed in the barn was so highly toxic that California laws prohibited its transportation; it was exploded on site. The "remediation" took an emergency environmental team of twenty-five workers weeks to complete and ultimately cost state taxpayers more than a million dollars. Dozens of families were evacuated for the duration.

As with all the other hazardous chemicals it has sold to the public, the Defense Department continues to assert that it is not responsible—for DS2 or other hazardous materials sold to individuals through its DRMS program. To date the Pentagon has paid nothing to the state of California to help clean up the Collinsville site. A top-ranking military official admitted recently to the Pentagon's immediate response to the Collinsville incident. "After that debacle," he said, "we learned to take our markings off of all barrels of chemicals we sell." Since the admission, however, Pentagon press officials claim that the idea of removing the military markings was just a contingency plan that was never followed through.

The Collinsville incident offers three important lessons about the military's handling of toxic chemicals. First, unbeknownst to most U.S. citizens, the armed services routinely maintain a tremendous inventory of hazardous materials. Second, their management practices are often questionable at best. Finally, the military's strategy in environmental matters has frequently been to contest its culpability for environmental problems rather than assume its rightful responsibility for the damage.

Not surprisingly, the Collinsville tale and many, many others have hurt the military's image and have incensed many local residents. Collinsville, after all, did get cleaned up; few military sites can make the same claim. Cases like Wright-Patterson and Milan, among many others, have led even such mainstream sources as *Newsweek* to brand the U.S. military the nation's "most pervasive and protected polluter."

To be sure, military personnel today pay more attention to the environmental consequences of their decisions than ever before. But in addition to the Pentagon's toxic legacies of the past, dangerous practices continue. And, sadly, the use of hazardous materials may even be growing. Vice Admiral Stanley Arthur, the deputy chief of naval operations and logistics, has explained clearly why: "As the specifications and pressures of our systems have increased, we've seen ourselves shifting from more naturally achievable materials and fluids to more exotic ones. And that usually means they're more hazardous and toxic."

A Roadside Attraction

In the northeast corner of Maryland, a mile inside the gates of the U.S. Army's Aberdeen Proving Ground, the visitor is confronted by an imposing icon. At first glance, its disconcerting presence calls to mind images of the building-sized doughnuts and hot dogs that occasionally blare evidence of roadside attractions to travelers along American highways. Here at the nation's preeminent ordnance facility, the roadside item is, fittingly, a bomb—not just any bomb, but the largest bomb in the world.

The unlikely totem stands on end, roughly a story tall, its nose cone planted firmly in a pedestal of cement. It is a so-called T-12 "general purpose" bomb (an Aberdeen official explains later), weighing some 43,600 pounds. The attraction it advertises is the U.S. Army Ordnance Museum.

William Atwater, a former marine with a doctorate in military history, presides here as curator of the collection, T-12 bomb and all. The assembled graveyard of military hardware ranges, as Atwater puts it, from "the sublime to the ridiculous." It includes some 8,000 items, foreign and domestic: everything from an assortment of small German-made firearms to an American atomic cannon which, luckily for humankind, was abandoned by its designers before ever being put into service.

Atwater says most of the 200,000 tourists who visit here annually come for the thrill of seeing big bombs and armored fighting vehicles up close.

Behind the squat, one-story museum building lies a vast, manicured open field holding what he calls the biggest crowd pleaser: a twenty-five-acre array of tanks and artillery guns, all shapes and sizes, arranged in dozens of neat rows. The museum describes these attractions as the "Mile of Tanks" and the "Tank/Artillery Park." Not surprisingly, perhaps, the gift shop offers visitors replicas and models of many of the museum's weapons, as well as mugs and tee shirts emblazoned with the insignia of the ordnance corps: two crossed cannons topped by a flaming bomb.

Atwater isn't shy about what he terms the "entertainment factor" of the collection, but he also stresses its archival value. He says he likes to think of the place as "sort of a technical database" offering tangible evidence of the history of military technology. As an archive, in fact, stripping away the tourist-oriented hype, the collection offers many lessons about the history and scope of human obsession with destruction. Each of these thousands of individual weapons, after all, represents its era's most effective and diabolical means of killing people. Many of the foreign weapons here were brought to Aberdeen for hasty study in the midst of major wars—a practice that often played an important role in military intelligence.

A sense of the awesome breadth of the effort to fight and prepare for war comes through strongly here, despite the presiding theme-park aura. But the message is a sanitized one. Not only are the weapons here separated from any mention of their intended purpose, but the neat displays also belie the damage wrought by the production, testing, and storage of these machines of death. This latter fact is especially ironic given the museum's location. Elsewhere at Aberdeen Proving Ground, not far beyond the museum's well-tended lawn and gleaming weapons, a very different picture of the military's history can be found.

Aberdeen's Edgewood Arsenal, to the south of the tank and artillery park, contains an archive of its own. Like the museum, Edgewood also offers tangible evidence of the military's history. But no tourists visit here. In 1985 environmental specialists confirmed the stalwart presence of more than forty dangerous chemicals in Edgewood's soil and groundwater, all in close proximity to two local waterways. Some toxics were detectable at concentrations more than a thousand times greater than the levels considered dangerous by state and federal authorities.

Aberdeen Proving Ground sits northeast of Baltimore and just south of the Susquehanna River, on two squat chunks of coastline that jut out into the Chesapeake Bay. Between these two massive pieces of land, an inlet of the bay cuts deep into the Maryland coast. This estuary, home to a wide variety of waterfowl and woodland mammals, has been designated by Congress as the Susquehanna National Wildlife Refuge.

Because of the coastal geography and because of the extensive pollution here, each half of the 70,000-acre Aberdeen facility has been included separately on the Superfund's listing of the nation's most hazardous sites. Aberdeen is one of few military facilities that can claim to be divided geographically by a nature preserve; it is also one of the few military facilities to be included twice on the Superfund list.

For decades, a site known here as O Field served as the dumping ground for staggering quantities of chemical munitions and other highly toxic materials. An Army study from 1976 showed that O Field was an environmental disaster area. Soil tests in 1985 uncovered astonishingly high levels of dangerous chemicals in the groundwater at the edges of the site: 1,500 times the maximum allowable level of cancer-causing vinyl chloride, hundreds of times the permissible EPA levels of benzene and trichloroethylene, and alarmingly high levels of another forty dangerous compounds. Like O Field, Aberdeen's broader environmental quandary challenges even the notion of "remediation," not to mention its implementation. The Army's feasibility study for the base's contaminated sewerage system, for example, offers little hope. As Cindy Couch, an environmental officer at Aberdeen put it, the study shows quite simply "that there is nothing available to deal with the mess safely." At some of the installation's toxic sites even the use of remote-controlled cleanup technologies has been judged impossible because of the dangerous levels of toxic material the excavations might release into the air.

The severity of the environmental damage here raises obvious questions about the military's historical practices. Exactly how, for instance, did such a dangerous situation ever evolve? Unfortunately, few answers are readily available. Unlike the extensive cataloguing and chronicling of the past that characterizes the Army Ordnance Museum, few people over the course of recent decades bothered even to note what was done with discarded nerve agents, mustard gas, napalm, and a host of other noxious chemicals.

The story of the Edgewood arsenal is perhaps best told by a former employee. Dean M. Dickey, a worker at Aberdeen's O Field, was asked by the Army in the 1970s to recount his tenure working at the dumpsite between 1949 and 1970. The reminiscences that follow were originally contained in an appendix to a 1976 Army preliminary study of potential environmental problems at Aberdeen.

Dickey, who worked at the facility in the late 1940s and then again in the 1960s, offers a rare firsthand look at his facility's brazen, misguided handling of extremely hazardous chemical wastes. His account of walking over extensive piles of explosive bomb parts—bursters, boosters, and fuses—lends a chilling illustration of the military's common practice of burying discarded munitions. For the most part, when Dickey writes of "cleaning up" O Field, he is referring to his efforts to prevent the place from exploding; many of these efforts, important though they clearly were at the time, may well have actually exacerbated the spread of environmental contamination at the site.

Dickey's testimonial could never be construed as representative of standard military practices. Aberdeen, given its mission, was responsible for handling a volume and caliber of toxic material not often found elsewhere—especially the foreign-made chemical weapons procured secretly and brought to the facility for study. But despite Aberdeen's somewhat special conditions, Dickey's matter-of-fact account of the nightmarish scene at O Field is included here at some length because it provides insight into the type of practices that have created the military's woeful environmental quagmire.

"Since there is a great deal of interest in an area known as 'Old "O" field' located on the Gunpowder Peninsula at Edgewood Arsenal and only a few individuals are knowledgeable of the activities there," Dickey writes, "I am recording all the facts that I can remember from 1949 through October 1970."

The so-called Old O Field now sits at the center of the Aberdeen facility's southern Superfund site, a four-and-one-half-acre burnt-out plot, fenced off and pockmarked with numerous pits and craters. Because no cleanup work has yet taken place, the site—above ground, at least—remains much the same as Dickey describes it: littered with explosive material and chemical agents.

It is important to remember that none of the pits or other ground at O Field described by Dickey were lined to prevent the migration of the contaminants dumped there. For many years it was widely believed that wastes would never penetrate the dense layers of clay that underlie the topsoil at most locations. Furthermore, many people also believed that contaminants dumped in the ground would degrade into harmless constituent chemicals before they could do any harm. We know now that both theories were terribly wrong. Heavier than water, many of the contaminants have submerged to the deepest parts of the geological structures below the surface, where groundwater supplies often reside. Here the contaminants have often migrated quickly, spreading a lingering plume of pollution that has posed a threat to human health even in minute amounts.

"I first worked at 'O' Field in September 1949. I was Officer-In-Charge and originally I had a seven man team. I actually walked to the center of the field on 4.2 bursters and boosters and thousands of fuzes [fuses] from artillery rounds. Regardless of how carefully I avoided one fuze or burster I would soon find I had stepped on another. Of course, I consulted with every imaginable 'expert' that I could find. My first task was to carefully screen the top of the field so that I could get equipment, myself and my men into the field without walking or driving over explosives.

"In about three weeks of careful screening (sometimes on our hands and knees) we had cleaned out an area large enough to drive a vehicle into and turn it around without the fear of striking explosives setting off a possible detonation. We placed the fuzes, bursters and boosters into 55-gallon drums, filled the drums with water as a tamping agent and detonated the entire mass. It worked exceedingly well for it left only small fragments of metals.

"Stacked in the middle of Old 'O' Field was a mass of drums contaminated with Mustard [agent], Tear Gas and Adamsite [otherwise known as DM, or diphenylamino-chloroarsine—a chemical agent that has been used in warfare and riot control], barrels of Fog Oil [a smoke agent] and Molasses Residuum [a comparatively benign substance used, according to the Army, to simulate mustard gas in some experiments] which were stored under water.

"I took every barrel of Molasses Residuum that I could find and took them over to the Gunpowder River and after puncturing the top of the lid allowed the Molasses Residuum to float away into the Gunpowder. I saved all the drums. I would estimate approximately 300 gallons of Molasses Residuum were poured into the Gunpowder. I used these, now empty barrels to continue destroying fuzes, bursters and boosters. . . .

"As we began to move some of the items and barrels from the top of 'O' Field," Dickey writes, "we were constantly plagued with White Phosphorous." White phosphorous is a toxic chemical that burns continuously when exposed to oxygen. Shells containing phosphorous are still in the U.S. arsenal today; the bright white smoke they emit is designed to mark the way in emergencies and night maneuvers. Because of its propensity to burn, phosphorous has always been viewed as a hazard; highly toxic, it is currently used as a rodenticide.

As Dickey remembers it, at O Field the white phosphorous "was literally impacted into the soil to the extent [that] if we moved something it would drag chunks of White Phosphorous out and on contact with the air it would immediately begin to sputter and burn. But we did manage to continue removing the fuzes and bursters. As we would uncover a bomb, or other type of munition we would attempt to place like items in stacks. I soon had segregated approximately 1500 M50 magnesium bombs and a lesser number of M69 and M70 Napalm-filled bombs. There were also many yellow smoke and tear gas grenades and FS [another smoke agent]-filled bottles. Someone also had brought glass jars filled with nerve agent and placed them in Pit #1."

Dickey doesn't specify the size or quantity of the jars he found containing nerve agents, but even the least lethal nerve agents known can kill humans in minute quantities when inhaled or ingested. Still, the danger of the chemicals under his purview seemed of less concern to Dickey than the very real threat of dying in an unexpected explosion.

In September 1949, Dickey recalls, "there was an explosion in Old 'O' Field at approximately 1400 hours. We had just entered the field at approximately 1330 when one of the pits exploded. We ducked down behind piles of barrels and bombs until all the fragments had stopped falling. We then left the field and gave it a week or two to 'settle down.' I went back into the field and examined the pit that had exploded. What I saw was a huge hole in the ground lined solid by bombs, some had detonated and some were intact. White Phosphorous was still seeping out of the hole and a strong odor of Mustard [gas] was noticed near the pit. We decided not to bother the pit but to continue in the work area where we were.

"To get more working room I took every barrel that was uncontaminated, hardbacks, metal storage boxes and smoke pot can[s] to the salvage yard as scrap metal. In fact we soon filled many boxcar loads and after two months I could actually see all the way to the back of 'O' Field. Then it became a matter of screening the rest of the field for bursters, boosters and fuzes.

"Approximately at 1100 hours one day in December, 1949, a series of tanks were passing 'O' Field. We were on break time and had gone down to watch the convoy of tanks come by. It was lucky that we did for we had another explosion in the back of Pit 1. We left for the day and closed the road off. On Saturday the pits really exploded and threw munitions everywhere. When I got to 'O' Field it appeared someone had placed a smoke screen down for White Phosphorous was all over the place and some of the woods were burning. All we could do was to see which way the fire was heading and try to keep buildings from being burned down. Decon[tamination] trucks filled with water were used in order to avoid the loss of fire trucks.

"On Monday the policing up began. Munitions were scattered everywhere, and additionally so was mustard agent. I followed the trail of Mustard all the way to Watson Creek and to the Gunpowder River. I am absolutely certain Mustard agent went into the river and the creek. I also suspect that there are munitions still in the river and the creek, thrown there by the detonation.

"We began our clean up by pouring DANC ['Decontaminating Agent Noncorrosive'—itself a highly toxic chemical] and lime on all the Mustard [agent] we could find. The DANC (approximately 1000 barrels) was out there for disposal. We then scooped up the contaminated soil and brought it back into Old 'O' Field. To get the contamination off the tree tops I placed TNT under cans of lime and detonated it. The lime settled on the Mustard on the trees and set fire to the dried leaves and the trees. Incidentally some of the Mustard was not destroyed until January of 1950. The trees died and are now burned."

Mustard gas [chemical name bis (2-chlorethyl) sulfide] is a chemical warfare agent designed to kill and maim enemy troops that has resulted in tens of thousands of combat deaths since World War I. It is also known to cause cancer in humans. Epidemiological studies from at least three separate countries have shown an elevated incidence of lung cancer among factory workers who manufactured the substance. Released as a gas in warfare, it is normally stored as an oily liquid.

"In January of 1950 I tackled more CN [tear gas]-filled drums from Pit 1. We must have recovered 200 or 300 drums which we washed out with caustic and sent to the Edgewood Arsenal Salvage Yard. In March we had made a great deal of progress again and we continued to clean off the top of the field. I found smoke pots, bombs, also 75MM and 76MM rounds filled with Mustard . . . I must have recovered about 2,000 Mustard-filled 4.2 rounds which I placed in Pit 5 and burned. I would lace the bottom of the pit with four or five feet of lumber, place the munitions on top of the lumber and wire WP [white phosphorous] igniters and C4 explosives in series and then pour Napalm all over the entire mess. It made a substantial fire. This is how we destroyed most of the Mustard-filled 4.2 rounds.

"As soon as that was over I directed my attention to the 250 KG and 500 KG German munitions filled with Mustard. I destroyed these in the same manner. Then I incinerated all the Fog Oil and smoke pots. Afterwards I collected all the White Phosphorous rounds and in about six weeks time I had all of them opened and burned. I had several bad moments in dealing with White Phosphorous since some of the White Phosphorous would 'scab' over, smoulder for days and build up pressure on the inside. Once the inside pressure was great enough they would detonate. I was particularly pleased when the White Phosphorous was gone although we still ran into it on occasions.

"My next job was to burn all the 100-lb. M47 Mustard-filled munitions. We did this the same way that we had done the 4.2 (incinerating in pits). Occasionally I would make an error in judgment and place a photoflash bomb on the pit. It would scatter Mustard everywhere when it detonated. I soon learned not to destroy any munition unless I was absolutely positive of its contents. That took some doing for most of the color coding was missing from the munitions body and the munitions were rusty. If the contents shook like water it could be detonated. If it didn't shake, it went into the incinerating pit. To my dismay, I found some filled with high explosives and [they] also scattered my pits. . .

"Old 'O' Field activity was closed for about six months during 1950 due to other emergency jobs. When I returned to 'O' Field I discovered everyone was still using it as a dumping ground. Even though the gate had been locked and everyone had been notified not to dump there any more, I found about 200 Mustard-filled 115-lb. M70 bombs, wing tanks filled with test materiel, and hundreds of small bomblets filled with *Bacillus glopigii* [*sic*, a type of bacteria—most probably *globigii*—used in chemical and biological warfare training]. Someone had also unloaded some M47 100-lb. Napalm bombs on us which I immediately put to good use in destroying the Mustard.

"I was also informed that sheep and goat carcasses which were initially buried in J Field had been brought to the field and buried. I was told that some of the carcasses were slightly radioactive and not to dig near them. Several days later dead horses from experiments were buried in this same area, but in shallow graves. All of the bodies of the dead animals were removed at a later date for animals were digging up the carcasses and several dead foxes and raccoons were found near the shallow graves. I did not ask, nor was I told where the dead animals were taken. I was told that Mr. Jon Roche of Safety Office had requested their removal. . . .

"After two years of daily operation in a hazardous area it was decided to burn the pits and their contents. But first we prepared a site adjacent to Old 'O' Field. It was called 'New "O" Field.'

"Prior to burning the pits, the road was closed and we had to screen the area for loose White Phosphorous. The entire surface area was hand raked and all the fuzes, igniters, bursters and boosters [were] collected from this operation and detonated. Hundreds of gallons of fuel oil were then pumped from tanks into the pits. Then the entire field was sprayed with fuel oil. Forty-five minute time fuzes were placed in the pits and all personnel took cover under the 'Prototype' building at M Field. The operation was a spectacular one. The pits and the entire area burned for two days. One explosion after another for a while and then tapered off to an occasional explosion. Three days later we went back. We had to police up materiel all the way from Watson Creek to the Gunpowder and all the area where new 'O' Field is now located. I didn't have an opportunity to complete the job for I received orders to Korea.

"I returned to Technical Escort in 1965 as Commander. Even though much work had been done in the field and the entire Old 'O' Field area was fenced in there was work left to be done.

"I made Old 'O' Field an Explosive Ordnance Disposal Training area and continued to recover and destroy munitions around and in Old 'O' Field. This work is still going on under present Technical Escort Commanders.

"In my opinion there are still munitions in Watson Creek and in the Gunpowder River in the area near 'O' Field. I would not be surprised to find contaminated soil in and around 'O' Field contaminated with Mustard, Lewisite [a so-called blood agent, akin to mustard agent] and White Phosphorous."

Four hundred miles from Aberdeen, in the lobby of the main building at the Army Material Technology Laboratory, commonly known as the Watertown Arsenal, in Watertown, Massachusetts, an odd treasure is exhibited. Suspended within a glass display case is a dark, encrusted cannonball, roughly 130 years old. Its accompanying plaque proudly explains that the cannonball, made for a Civil War–era cannon invented and produced at the facility, was uncovered on the installation's grounds by accident.

Unlike Aberdeen's extensive museum collection, the lone cannonball at the Watertown installation receives few visitors, even though the facility, founded in 1816, is the second-oldest arsenal in the United States. Undoubtedly among the older pieces of U.S. governmental military waste ever unearthed in the country, Watertown's cannonball stands as a testament to the fact that the U.S. military has been dumping munitions in the ground for more than a century.

In its quiet way, this one excavated cannonball presages the entire story of the military's toxic legacy. And yet, benign and unimposing, it offers little hint of the hazards and quantities of wastes that have been subsequently buried. It is still not clear exactly how much hazardous waste remains nationwide, like the cannonball, to be "uncovered by accident." Judging from Dean Dickey's historical account of Aberdeen's O Field, there is more than ample cause for concern.

Among other things, the sheer horror of daily life at O Field as Dickey describes it makes a mockery of a refrain used by military personnel that current environmental problems can be explained by historical conduct that simply followed the "standard, accepted practices of the day." To be sure, in the 1940s and 1950s chemical wastes generated by the military and the private sector alike were commonly dumped in rivers or burned in the open air. But highly concentrated chemicals *designed* to kill humans had no civilian use, no place in the so-called accepted practices of the day. For these well-known lethal agents, there simply were no disposal practices that could be construed as standard or accepted.

On several occasions in his recollections, Dickey touches upon the issue of culpability for O Field's contamination. His observations give ample evidence that even in 1949 many military officials knew full well of the dangers to human health and the environment presented by the toxic dump. It just wasn't an issue to which they attached much importance.

An EPA official captured this attitude plainly in a recent comment about another military installation—the Picatinny Army Arsenal in northern New Jersey. When it came to environmental matters, noted Robert Hayton, the EPA's project manager for Picatinny, military facilities "took very few notes, especially when they were gearing up for war. Their attitude was to just dump it in a lagoon or toss it away."

As Dickey recounts, O Field was designated in 1943 as just such a disposal spot for dangerous chemicals and munitions. "However, in 1949," Dickey writes, "Colonel Garland White (now deceased) became aware of the unsafe practices and activities at Old 'O' Field and lodged a strong complaint with the Safety Office about the conditions there. He offered to clean up the field provided that it would not be used again and that the new disposal field (J Field) would be monitored to assure a similar condition as 'O' Field would not occur.

"I attended a meeting of inquiry in which Mr. Harry Siler [who was directly responsible for the upkeep and safety of O Field at the time] defended himself by stating that he had objected on many occasions concerning the indiscriminate 'dumping' of every conceivable item imaginable in his work area at 'O' Field. He stated that when he would attempt to turn some of the loaded vehicles back that he was told by his supervisor that he had no other choice but take the items since they couldn't be left at Edgewood Arsenal proper.

"Incidentally, I was at Old 'O' Field on such an occasion. The truck driver after being denied permission to enter the field called back to Edgewood to report that Mr. Siler would not accept his load of munitions. Mr. Siler was called to the phone and told that he would accept the load of munitions. His comment to the truck driver was 'Dump them anywhere you can find the room.'

"The truck driver," Dickey recalls, "did exactly that."

CHAPTER FIVE

The Latest Model

Kevin Doxey, head of a small delegation from the Pentagon, is standing to one side of a large mahogany conference table at the National Academy of Sciences. Before him sit roughly twenty experts, an imposing panel of scientists selected by the Academy to advise Congress on technical policy matters. All eyes upon him, Doxey offers a candid summary of the Pentagon's agenda for today's meeting.

"As far as we're concerned, the key task for the Academy is to add some credibility on Capitol Hill and out there," he says, pointing vaguely beyond the room's dark, paneled walls.

Outside, just a few yards beyond Doxey's outstretched arm, Washington, D.C., is bright and blooming. But here, within the confines of the National Academy, the room is dim and quiet, the mood reserved. This meeting, in April of 1991, marks a milestone in the Pentagon's environmental strategy, but the press has not been invited and few outsiders are present.

Doxey and his aides have come before this small assemblage of prestigious scientists to pedal the Defense Department's latest weapon in its languishing war on environmental contamination: the Defense Priority Model. This elaborate model, more than six years in the making, is designed to help the Pentagon decide which of its tens of thousands of contaminated sites to clean up first.

Although Pentagon officials are normally loath to discuss the matter, Doxey confides to the assembled experts that too many military sites require "environmental restoration"; the job is simply too expensive to conduct all at once. Today, says Doxey, "each state and municipality clamors to have 'my backyard' cleaned up first." Consequently, the Pentagon needs an airtight scientific method to rank the contaminated lands and it needs a model that can be justified to Congress and the public.

To aid this effort, says Doxey, the Pentagon "would be delighted to have the National Academy of Sciences' endorsement" of the Defense Priority Model he is about to present.

Doxey, young and trim, delivers his remarks in a manner befitting his role—a careful blend of deference to the panel members and confidence about his program. Most of the assembled scientists are Doxey's elders: established toxicologists, engineers, and mathematicians from universities and research institutes around the country. On the other hand, few of them are familiar with the details of the military's environmental problems or its priority model. And none of them can claim anything approaching Doxey's weighty role as day-to-day manager of a government cleanup program with an annual budget now exceeding $1 billion.

But while Doxey gives the impression of an official fully in control of a big task, he knows today's assignment is risky. Except during appropriations battles for weapons' systems, the military rarely seeks outside endorsement for its programs—especially from a body as autonomous and unpredictable as the National Academy. To be sure, a vote of confidence from the independent panel will be a strong political asset in the long, difficult cleanup battle ahead. Still, the panel could just as easily reject the model as flawed and thereby jeopardize the entire program.

In his presentation, Doxey appears confident about the caliber of the model itself. Over its long incubation period it has, after all, been reviewed by experts at the Environmental Protection Agency, state agencies, and many separate branches of the military; a prototype has even been tested in the field. But Doxey is more awkward in presenting the scheme's broader summary. He must review for the panel the status of the military's cleanup record to date, and he must defend the need for such a model in the first place.

Although the panel members may not know the specifics of the military's environmental predicament, they are well versed in environmental matters generally. Many will be likely to question the military's intent in its steadfast plan to clean up the "worst first"—a doctrine that serves as the basis for the priority model itself. As these experts well know, the military's selective "worst first" strategy is a luxury that private industry is not allowed. Federal environmental laws are unconditional; enforcement may often lag, but private offenders potentially face stiff fines and even jail sentences if they fail to address any violation as soon as it is discovered—even if the cleanup costs will force the violators into bankruptcy.

Doxey begins to narrate a brief slide presentation projected onto a screen in the corner of the room. "The Defense Environmental Restoration Program was established by Congress in 1984," he says. "To date we have found some 17,400 contaminated sites at 1,850 installations, not including formerly used sites.

"We're finding new technologies to discover sites, and we continue to find smaller sites, but overall the type of problem we're talking about consists of spills, leaking storage tanks, landfills, contaminated fire training areas, and disposal areas. The contaminants include a full range, including some compounds unique to the military."

The room is silent as the scientists scrutinize the graphs and charts before them. Doxey recites the program's funding levels and other vital statistics. Finally, he addresses the status of the cleanup efforts. "We would like to be underway with many remediations going by the year 2000."

Alan J. Goldman, a mathematician from Johns Hopkins University, intrudes upon Doxey's polished address. "To an outsider—a layperson like me—this doesn't sound like a headlong pace."

For now Doxey brushes aside the remark, vaguely acknowledging "systemic, structural problems" in the Defense Department's efforts. He wants to finish his prepared remarks before fielding questions. But before the day's end Goldman's assessment will reemerge in many forms.

In truth, this quiet meeting itself exemplifies the "structural problems" Doxey now leaves unspecified. As critics have long charged, the military often seems to address every aspect of its environmental problems except the actual contamination itself. Many environmentalists and citizens' groups have already complained that the Pentagon's elaborate prioritization model is merely the latest in a long line of bureaucratic obstructions.

Doxey doesn't discuss the issue here, but in many ways the military's failure to keep on top of its environmental problems can be seen as a perverse and unintended outcome of the founding fathers' doctrine of "sovereign immunity"—a notion designed to protect the federal government from becoming an easy target for fines and penalties levied by disgruntled state legislators. The Constitution's framers recognized that the goals of the federal government and those of individual states would often conflict. They believed the federal government needed some immunity to limit the prospect of lawsuits or other regulatory actions against it. Consequently, they drew upon British common law and protected the new government against legal action the way the British Crown had been protected.

In medieval England, after all, the monarch was viewed as having a divine right to define right and wrong. Somewhat later (and more pragmatically) it was felt that English judges—all of whom were appointed by the Crown—could not be asked to rule against the monarch. As Justice Oliver Wendell Holmes remarked in 1907, the related U.S. doctrine of sovereign immunity is based upon "the logical and practical ground that there can be no legal right as against the authority that makes the law on which the right depends."

Naturally, over the years the military has been a great beneficiary of the doctrine of sovereign immunity. It has been allowed to commandeer land in times of national emergency without fear of reprisal. The Pentagon has authorized a host of activities that conflict with state interests, from aircraft test flights near residential areas to the production, storage, and disposal of chemical weapons on the outskirts of cities. Coupled with its penchant for secrecy and its overarching emphasis on its war-fighting mission, the military has used the doctrine of sovereign immunity to bolster its claim to near autonomy in national security matters.

The military's application of the doctrine to environmental issues is exhibited plainly in the text of an article written by two Air Force lawyers in 1986. "One might expect," the authors write, "that due to the unique status of the military in our society, environmental laws would, like the public, stop at the installation gate, leaving the Department of Defense free to concentrate on military matters." Unfortunately, as the authors see it, such an ideal state does not always seem to carry the day.

Richard E. Sanderson, the former EPA director of federal activities, explains one obvious flaw in the traditional military contention that "within the boundaries of their base fences, they were protected by sovereign immunity." Sanderson notes that "pollution doesn't stay behind a fence. It leaks onto state and private lands."

Even aside from the problem of pollution leaking beyond the borders of military installations, the military's alleged right to environmental autonomy on its lands has long been chimerical. The Air Force lawyers quoted above still imagined a "unique status" for the military on environmental matters a full eight years after President Jimmy Carter signed Executive Order 12088, explicitly stating that sovereign immunity did not protect federal facilities from the nation's environmental laws. In theory, at least ever since Carter's 1978 order (and in the case of some environmental laws, much earlier), agencies like the Energy Department, the Federal Bureau of Investigation—and the Pentagon—have been subject to the law like everyone else.

"The head of each Executive agency is responsible for compliance with applicable pollution control standards," President Carter ruled. Lest there be any uncertainty, he appended to the order a lengthy list of the pertinent environmental laws of the day. The order states that for federal agencies, including the military, "applicable pollution control standards means the same substantive, procedural, and other requirements that would apply to a private person."

The language of the executive order, like that of Congress in most of its environmental legislation, could not be much clearer. And yet the military continues, even today, to fight what it sees as an erosion of its right to immunity from the laws of the land. Despite the vast environmental debacle the U.S. military has caused, the Pentagon insists on running its cleanup program entirely on its own, resisting outside regulation and oversight at every chance.

In many ways, Doxey's priority model is a case in point. In Doxey's presentation at the National Academy of Sciences, the Pentagon parades its own priority model regardless of the fact that the Environmental Protection Agency has created, and implemented for a decade, a functionally identical ranking model. The EPA has used its "Hazard Ranking System" widely and successfully to select sites for the National Priority List—to help judge, in other words, which contaminated lands are eligible for inclusion in the Superfund program. All the military services have already used EPA's model to rank the severity of environmental damage at hundreds of military installations.

But the military has long held that it must be treated differently from other polluters. Presumably in this case the Pentagon believes that its polluted sites need to be judged by a slightly different set of criteria. Pentagon officials say their model will offer more information, which will be helpful to rank all their sites rather than just the most severely polluted ones ranked by the EPA's system. The argument is technically valid, but underlying such a view is a long tradition in which the military has argued that the armed services differ from private entities. Along these lines, one standard refrain is that the armed forces cannot pass environmental costs on to consumers the way private industry can. Or, as Captain Michael J. Carricato, former Acting Assistant Secretary of Defense for the Environment (and a predecessor to Doxey's current boss), complained quaintly, unlike private firms the Pentagon "can't go out and raise the price of dropping a nuclear bomb on someone in order to raise the money to clean up the environment." Again, the argument may be technically accurate, but it holds little weight; taxpayers foot the military's cleanup bill anyway.

His slide presentation complete, Doxey introduces Marcia Read, a Pentagon official whose task is to explain the mechanics of the Defense Priority Model. The panelists listen intently. "We must prioritize our sites," she says, "and we need to carry out our goal of 'worst-first' nationwide." To Read, the goal seems unflappably simple. "We want the best model we can have," she asserts.

As Read explains it, the model contains 75 separate inputs (it has since expanded to over 100) that installation personnel can enter into a software program that runs on a desktop computer. "It's like doing your taxes," she tells the panel. Once the military completes a preliminary environmental investigation at an installation, base personnel are asked to calculate the amount of known pollution at the installation according to the major pathways through which it can travel—air, soil, or water. Personnel also add factors that take into account differences in the mobility of the pollutants, such as the difference between fast- and slow-moving groundwater.

The model has been designed in such a way as to minimize the effects of normal variation in individual reporting. Interestingly, from Read's talk it appears that the Pentagon has been relatively sanguine about the prospect that officials might neglect to report pollution on their base. Rather, Read says, a primary concern of the model's designers was that installations would try to exaggerate—to overreport pollution—to receive cleanup funds faster.

As Read describes it, after all the inputs have been entered by the base official, the tricky part comes in the way the Defense Department model weighs the different variables to arrive at the installation's general score. Potential threats to humans (either base personnel or nearby residents) count heavily. "Without a human threat," Read says, "a site could never be ranked among the top 10 or 20 percent."

The panelists begin to do what they do best—ask tough, probing questions, many of which seem quickly to deflate some of Read's more enthusiastic claims. One panelist wants to know how the Pentagon defines its basic unit—the site—upon which the model bases all of its comparisons. "You have tens of thousands of sites of contamination you are comparing. But what is a site?" he asks.

"Well," Read says, pausing briefly. "That's a good point. A site can be a small spill, or a very vast area of contamination." She says that the model tries to take into consideration both the quantity and potential hazard of the chemicals present, but it remains unclear how it would compare a large, relatively benign problem to a smaller, more hazardous one.

Another panelist points to the model's failure to account for regional and cultural differences in human behavior, like diet ("how much fish a given population might eat") or bathing and showering habits ("a surprising amount of contamination is absorbed through the skin"). Such differences can change the hazard presented by a given amount of contamination. Read reminds the panelists that the model is a comparative tool, "not intended as a risk assessment." The point, she says, is not to calculate the risks from a given site in a thorough or precise manner. "We want to be as accurate as we can," she says, "but we have to weigh how much additional information will benefit the precision of the score."

Finally, with the next several questions, Read and Doxey acknowledge some striking shortcomings. Several panelists want to know exactly how toxics and other environmental dangers are tallied by the model in the first place, noting that a model is only as good as the inputs that go into it. Read and Doxey acknowledge that the model does not address unexploded ordnance—which has killed innocent victims and possibly permanently devastated tens of thousands of acres at many military installations. Rather, it appears, such ordnance will be shunted to the bottom of the military's priority list.

Dangerous and contested undertakings, like the military's plan to burn most of its chemical weapons stockpiles, are also excluded from consideration. Read explains that the model focuses only "on past activities." Finally, the panelists learn, bases that are slated for closure are also excluded from the model; the priority of the cleanup efforts at these contaminated sites will have to be decided through some other means.

These shortcomings clearly frustrate some of the panelists. One member questions the entire undertaking, saying the model looks increasingly like nothing more than a "process of getting numbers to derive more numbers to go to a table to get a further number all in an effort to rationalize a comparison of apples and oranges." Ultimately, perhaps, such comparisons cannot be made on a "scientific" basis, but are simply policy choices.

What one is left with, the panelist maintains, is a simple and possibly unanswerable question: "Is my airborne contamination in California worse than your groundwater contamination in Utah?"

As the afternoon wears on, Doxey fields questions patiently. Once more he stresses the rationale for the model. According to his figures, some 4,000 sites now under study will soon need cleanup action. The Pentagon anticipates that "many sites will enter the high-cost 'remedial action phase' simultaneously," he says, a prospect that puts the program in a difficult and controversial position.

When he is asked about it, though, it turns out that the Defense Department is really in such a position already. In the entire history of the military's cleanup program of its active bases, only 296 "remedial actions" are listed as complete. Doxey tells the panelists that many of these are actually "interim actions"—activities that often diminish but do not redress existing environmental problems. Many other sites are listed as "underway," but this designation most often means only that some preliminary study has been undertaken.

As far as cleanup is concerned, the vast majority of the military's contaminated sites are listed in yet another category—a fact not lost upon the panel. One panelist asks what all the Fs listed on one of Doxey's charts mean. Doxey explains that the designation in question is known by the military as the future category. All told, more than 7,000 sites are currently listed in this manner.

"The future category," Doxey explains, "means that cleanup at that site is not now underway, but we know we have to do it."

In light of Congress's explicit language and President Carter's 1978 executive order, how can so many thousands of sites idle in this vague "future" category? Certainly, the perceived urgency of the Pentagon's military mission goes far to explain its historical free reign in environmental matters; for decades, the military maintained that it had too many important and pressing obligations to be hampered with strict environmental regulations. And for many of those years the doctrine of sovereign immunity offered the Pentagon strong protection against interference in its affairs by other governmental agencies.

Despite this history, though, it is still baffling that the Pentagon managed to blatantly ignore the specific waivers of sovereign immunity Congress wrote into the major environmental legislation of the 1970s and 1980s. Certainly by the time of President Carter's order in 1978 no doubt remained: federal facilities were required to adhere to the nation's environmental laws.

For at least the past thirteen years, the applicability of the nation's environmental laws to the federal government has been all but indisputable. But until recently, and to a lesser extent still today, the Pentagon has largely ignored these laws, and—what is perhaps even more puzzling—the rest of the federal government has failed to enforce them.

To some extent, the situation can be explained by government inertia and ineptitude. Historically, the military has been particularly reluctant to comply with environmental laws that might force it to change mission-oriented activities like training exercises and weapons tests. Meanwhile, the beleaguered EPA—the nation's environmental enforcement agency—has long been unsure of its jurisdiction over sister branches of government. Besides, it had more than it could handle in the private sector.

More important than ineptitude and inertia, however, politics explain the military's failure to observe, or be made to observe, the nation's environmental laws. By the mid-1980s, congressional demands for oversight of federal facilities had reached a crescendo. In response, the EPA finally laid plans to boost its enforcement activities toward the military and other federal scofflaws. But before it could act to enforce the law, it was instructed otherwise.

CHAPTER SIX

Eastern Europe at Home

The government's failure in recent years to enforce environmental laws at military bases stems directly from a doctrine concocted by the Reagan administration in the mid 1980s. Fighting regulation and thwarting the Soviet Union through a military buildup were ardently pursued, overarching goals of the Reagan administration, and the "unitary theory of the executive," a notion the administration advanced, was quickly seen to be of use toward both aims.

In keeping with this new doctrine, Reagan penned Executive Order 12580 about environmental cleanup at federal facilities, exploiting an enforcement loophole in Carter's 1978 ruling. Reagan's order, signed in 1986, limited the EPA's jurisdiction by saying that the federal Department of Justice must approve any enforcement actions undertaken by EPA against federal facilities. In keeping with the administration's unitary theory of the executive, though, the Justice Department held that one body of the executive branch may not sue another. With so many military bases overtly and repeatedly violating pollution regulations, the order, then, dealt a severe blow to the EPA's already limited enforcement abilities. As Representative Mike Synar put it, "Justice has tied EPA's hands."

Like Synar, many other members of Congress were outraged. They took the Reagan administration's unitary executive scheme as an infuriating affront. In hearings immediately following Reagan's order in the spring of 1987 (about the same time Representative Synar's subcommittee was taking the Pentagon to task for its environmental record), a separate subcommittee tackled the enforcement issue.

Representative Dennis E. Eckart, a Democrat from Ohio with a long record of involvement in environmental legislation, seethed as he addressed a Justice Department official testifying on behalf of the Reagan administration's unitary theory. In hearings before the Subcommittee on Oversight and Investigations of the House Committee on Energy and Commerce, Eckart began, "Mr. Chairman, whoever came up with this unitary executive theory ought to be nominated for a Pulitzer Prize for fiction."

"I wrote Section 120," Eckart continued, referring to a section of the recently reauthorized Superfund program legislation. Holding up the document, Eckart read aloud the law's requirements for federal facilities: "[They] shall be subject to and comply with this act in the same manner and to the same extent, both procedurally and substantively as any nongovernmental entity."

Eckart told the committee that by limiting the EPA's ability to take enforcement action against federal polluters like the military, the unitary executive branch theory defied the law and the intent of Congress. During the drafting of the law, Eckart said, no one, including the representatives from the Department of Justice who were involved in the process, had ever indicated that the EPA's authority would be different for federal facilities than for private industry.

Pleading the administration's case before the subcommittee was Assistant Attorney General for Land and Natural Resources F. Henry Habicht III. Eckart addressed him directly.

"I cannot find under any stretch of the imagination, Mr. Habicht," Eckart declared, "what language in any of these documents you believe can serve as a basis for your imaginative, convoluted repudiation of specific statutory law."

By way of response, the Justice Department's Habicht explained that the issue of whether there should be a unitary or a pluralistic executive "was the subject of very, very extensive debate in the constitutional conventions of 1787."

Eckart's quick retort captured both his exasperation and disbelief. "I was not there," he snapped. "I was in the Superfund conference."

Sharing Eckart's exasperation at the hearings was Hubert H. Humphrey III, then attorney general for the state of Minnesota, who testified about environmental contamination at the Twin Cities Army Ammunition Plant in New Brighton, near Minneapolis–St. Paul.

Minnesota's Pollution Control Agency, Humphrey said, believed this Army installation to be "the major, if not the sole source of contamination of regional groundwater aquifers in the northern suburbs of Minneapolis and St. Paul." Trichloroethylene and other volatile organic compounds from the base were believed to be spreading from the base toward these populous urban areas in a gigantic underground plume possibly exceeding thirty miles in diameter.

In the case of the Twin Cities Ammunition Plant, the Army had been aware of pollution problems for years, but had never notified state or federal environmental officials. Despite the fact that the Army had issued an internal assessment of past disposal practices in 1978, Humphrey testified, Minnesota state officials did not find out about the spreading pollutants until 1981, when a citizen provided the state environmental agency with a copy of the 1978 Army report obtained through the Freedom of Information Act.

Now, Humphrey said, Reagan's Executive Order 12580 had resulted "in agonizingly slow cleanups at federal facilities and an increasingly high level of frustration on the part of many states."

The extent of the military's refusal to comply with the law was often dramatic, as a GAO report showed in detail for just one unexceptional Air Force Base. From 1985 to 1987, the aging wastewater treatment plant at Beale Air Force Base, just east of the town of Marysville in northern California, was known to be discharging unsafe levels of cyanide and many other chemicals into a nearby creek. But despite intervention by outside agencies, military officials at Beale repeatedly and blatantly failed to comply with water pollution laws.

The state of California sent Beale officials repeated notices of their violations during this period. The letters complained not only that the base was discharging illegal amounts of pollution, but that it was deficient in its sampling, reporting, and monitoring of its water quality. Environmental reports required by the state were issued late if at all, lab results were missing, and the required documentation of water sampling was incomplete.

Finally, in May 1988, the state of California threatened that the base would be forced to "cease and desist" its activities if it was not in compliance with water pollution laws by August of that year. Even such dramatic action by the state yielded little or no result. The base continued to pollute nearby waters illegally. Its self-monitoring reports for July and August of 1988 were once again sent late and incomplete. And, with no federal backing from the EPA for the state's enforcement efforts, the issue languished. Today, several years later, the Pentagon reports having completed no remedial action at the base.

The story of Beale Air Force Base is not particularly unusual. In December 1988, the GAO reported that military installations were twice as likely to violate the Clean Water Act than their counterparts in the private sector. Nearly half of the military violators were discovered to have remained in noncompliance for a year or more. With such a record, the importance of direct enforcement powers for the EPA becomes abundantly evident. After all, the examples above chronicle the military's problems with just one of numerous environmental laws—laws that regulate not only water pollution, but air pollution and the disposal and handling of toxic materials and wastes.

To be fair, things on the water pollution front have improved considerably over the past few years as the military has sought publicly to make its current environmental practices conform more closely to the nation's laws. But none of these changes has affected the military's ability to clean up the legacy of its past. And the Environmental Protection Agency still lacks enforcement powers.

A special task force dispatched by the governors and attorneys general of every state in the country assessed the situation this way in 1990:

> Under federal environmental statutes, federal agencies are directed to comply with federal and state environmental laws to the same extent as private facilities, but many have failed to do so. Although the Environmental Protection Agency is aware of numerous violations, its enforcement powers have been crippled by a Department of Justice policy prohibiting EPA from filing lawsuits or issuing unilateral enforceable orders against its sister agencies. Hamstrung by the Justice Department's "unitary theory of the executive," the nation's chief environmental watchdog is forced to sit by as basic environmental statutes and regulations are routinely ignored at federally owned facilities.

A related battle is currently being fought in the courts over the Army's contamination of the Rocky Mountain Arsenal. In this case, which for years has focused upon the cleanup of Basin F (see Preface), the state of Colorado has refused to relinquish the right to set final cleanup requirements at the installation. Testing the limits of federal powers, the state maintains that it doesn't trust the EPA to force the military to adhere strictly enough to environmental requirements in the installation's cleanup.

The Army currently maintains that the state has no enforcement authority over the facility, even though the federal district court judge who presided over the case in 1989 ruled in favor of the state, writing:

> I conclude that the E.P.A.'s potential monitoring of the Army's Basin F cleanup operation . . . does not serve as an appropriate or effective check on the Army's efforts. As long as both of these federal agencies are represented in the [Rocky Mountain] Arsenal CERCLA [Superfund] actions by the same Justice Department lawyers who have professed that they have no conflict of interest, even though one of their clients is a plaintiff and another a defendant in the same consolidated action, there is no vigorous independent advocate for the public interest.

Meanwhile, in Washington, D.C., Congress continues to fight to make federal facilities comply with the environmental laws it has passed. When it updated the Superfund legislation in 1986 with SARA, the Superfund reauthorization act, Congress dramatically expanded communities' "right to know" about toxic chemicals used or stored near them. The disclosure of the new information filed by industries across the country has recently been compiled by the EPA into a computerized public database called the Toxic Release Inventory, which provides communities with enough data to prepare for potentially dangerous releases. Despite the EPA's urging, the Defense Department refuses to submit data about its releases of toxic materials into the air, water, and land. As the law is written, the Pentagon is not legally required to submit data to the Toxic Release Inventory, but several members of Congress have now called for this loophole to be redressed.

In a related and even more comprehensive effort, the House of Representatives has twice overwhelmingly passed a bill (sponsored by none other than Representative Eckart) giving the EPA the authority to enforce hazardous waste laws at federal facilities. But a similar 1990 bill in the Senate—the Federal Facilities Compliance Act—never made it to a vote. This Senate bill may soon pass, but given the realities of the Pentagon's situation (as illustrated, for instance, by the Defense Priority Model), it is not clear how large or swift an impact a new compliance bill could have.

For its part, the Bush administration has done little to change the Reagan administration's policies on the issue, despite a strong campaign pitch by then Vice President Bush, running to become "the environmental president."

Speaking at a campaign stop in 1988 in Seattle, not far from the horribly polluted Hanford Nuclear Reservation, Bush pledged that as president he would "insist that in the future federal agencies meet or exceed environmental standards." As Bush apparently believed then, "The government should live within the laws it imposes on others."

One of the ironies of the U.S. military's environmental quagmire is that throughout, the situation was perpetrated in the name of the Cold War. The Pentagon's longstanding actions, and even the more recent efforts of the Reagan administration, were all informed by a sense that defense against the Warsaw Pact nations took precedence over other concerns. Today, with the dissolution of the Warsaw Pact, it is clear that similar priorities were in operation on both sides of the iron curtain.

In fact, the environmental situation in Eastern Europe offers an instructive perspective upon the U.S. military's problems at home. In particular, the environmental problems encountered by the recently unified nation of Germany have much in common with those confronting the U.S. military.

At the close of 1989, when the Berlin wall crumbled and the path was opened for the reunification of Germany, celebration was the order of the day for the country's citizenry. Tens of thousands of jubilant demonstrators flooded the streets by Berlin's Brandenburg Gate, cheering and singing for several nights on end. The opening of East Germany, however, like similar events unfolding in neighboring countries in Eastern Europe, brought into clear view for the rest of the world the horrendous environmental degradation that had been perpetrated for decades in the East bloc.

Rumors had circulated for years, but the West was shocked to learn the specific consequences of unchecked industrialization. In the Leipzig area of East Germany, the West learned, drivers need to turn on their headlights in the middle of the day because the air pollution is so dense. Nearly half of East Germany's forests are dead or dying. More than 60 percent of the region's rivers are badly contaminated. German officials quickly assessed that it would cost hundreds of billions of dollars to bring the industries of Eastern Europe to a level of environmental management considered acceptable under West German law.

Given the many diverse and overwhelming ramifications of the changes underway in Germany, environmental matters have not been at the top of the agenda. But there is no doubt that Germany has inherited a two-tiered environmental system. The new nation might have one set of environmental laws, but at least for the foreseeable future, they will be applied and enforced differently. In the western half of the country, environmental regulation rigorously limits the discharge of pollutants. These regulations now apply to the east as well, but to date their existence has had little tangible effect; the entire region is almost hopelessly out of compliance.

In the discussion and debate over Eastern Europe's environmental problems, several commentators have looked for the roots of these problems, trying to understand how the former East-bloc governments could have allowed industrial pollution to proliferate to such an extreme extent. One such analyst is Dennis L. Meadows, director of the University of New Hampshire's Institute for Policy and Social Science Research. Speaking in the spring of 1990, Meadows declared that the environmental outcome in Eastern Europe was almost predictable.

"When you have vested in one authority the strong pressure to increase production, the responsibility for the environmental impacts of that production, and the ability to keep things secret," Meadows stated, "the circumstances are ripe for raping the environment."

Meadows recognized that the conditions he described were similar to those existing for the U.S. military. "On a narrower scale," he said, "the same thing occurred in the U.S. around nuclear facilities." At the time of his comments, public attention in the United States was riveted upon revelations in the press about the Department of Energy's blatant disregard for public safety and the environment in its nuclear weapons program. But Meadows might just as accurately have stated that the same problem exists at virtually all U.S. military facilities—ammunition plants, depots, air force bases, and naval shipyards.

Like the problems in Eastern Europe, the U.S. military's environmental practices have been shrouded in secrecy for decades. Like the former governments of Eastern Europe, the U.S. military both produced vast quantities of pollution and took sole responsibility for handling this contamination, allowing for little outside oversight or accountability. Both situations resulted in a devastating legacy that will be exceedingly expensive and difficult to address.

Equally telling are the ways the Pentagon's situation differs from the one currently faced in Germany. In the United States, no single border line delineates more and less polluted regions, as the former border between East and West Germany does. Far from being contained in one region, like the pollution in Germany, the U.S. military's contaminated lands lie scattered throughout the country. Behind thousands of fences around thousands of properties, the military's pollution taints pieces of every state in the nation.

The U.S. government did not suddenly inherit official responsibility for its military's contamination, as did the West German government for East Germany's problems once the Berlin Wall came down. The U.S. military has been in violation of the nation's environmental laws for at least a decade, far longer in the case of certain sites. And yet the U.S. government has allowed the situation to continue unabated in clear and blatant disregard of federal environmental regulations.

Overshadowed by the Cold War's commanding external peril, the U.S. military's legacy of environmental contamination was simply ignored. In a fateful twist, our external enemy has evaporated. But the threat at home looms larger than ever.

PART II
Secret Legacies

CHAPTER SEVEN

Lakehurst, New Jersey: "The Dark Years"

Inland from the aging beachfront towns of southern New Jersey, the Pine Barrens blankets nearly one million acres with thick evergreen woodlands. The region is an unusually secluded pocket amidst the populous and polluted sprawl of one of the nation's most industrialized states—a largely undeveloped amalgam of isolated, poor rural towns, state forests, and other vast wooded tracts.

Long recognized as one of a dwindling number of wild and untamed spaces in the northeastern United States, the Pine Barrens has only relatively recently received the recognition it warrants for its ecological importance and fragility. In 1978 Congress designated the area as the country's first National Reserve—then a new federal classification designed to protect the area but allow local communities some flexibility in their establishment of environmental and resource management regulations.

But most of the action here takes place underground. Even more precious than the uninterrupted miles of thick pine forest of the newly named New Jersey Pinelands Preservation Area is the huge groundwater supply below. The Cohansey aquifer, which flows freely in the shallow, porous layers of gravel and rock beneath the region's soil, is the largest known source of potable freshwater in the Northeast. It is believed, in fact, to be one of the largest groundwater supplies in the country, holding an estimated store of more than 17 trillion gallons. If the Cohansey were on the earth's surface, it would be larger than Utah's Great Salt Lake, covering some 2,000 square miles to a depth of more than thirty-five feet.

Today everyone in southern New Jersey depends on the Cohansey aquifer for their drinking water. And its bountiful reserve has not gone unnoticed by larger municipalities in the vicinity. Officials in both Philadelphia (some forty miles to the west) and New York City (seventy-five miles to the north) have discussed tapping into the Cohansey supply during periods of drought in the past and continue to covet the aquifer's water, but New Jersey's management plan prohibits this.

Interest in the aquifer stems not only from its size but also from the nearly ideal geology southern New Jersey provides. Rainwater readily replenishes the groundwater, which lies close to the surface, because the area's sandy soil swiftly drains new moisture into the subterranean flow. But these same geologic features heighten the Cohansey's vulnerability. The shallow groundwater and permeable soil also mean that pollutants dumped into the ground reach the aquifer quickly, before their potency can be filtered or absorbed. In addition, a solid layer of bedrock below means that contaminants in the aquifer are likely to become trapped, threatening the quality of its water for decades, even centuries.

After a brief explanation of the region's geology, Lucy Bottomley steps around her desk and motions toward a large aerial photograph in her office at the Naval Air Engineering Center in Lakehurst, New Jersey. The poster-sized black-and-white photograph depicts her domain: the 7,400 acres she oversees as head of the installation's environmental team. The Lakehurst facility has long been a key location for the development and evaluation of technologies for Navy aircraft. For decades, among other projects, Lakehurst personnel have pioneered the use of catapults and special landing gear to allow Navy planes to shoot into flight off aircraft carriers and to land safely upon their return.

The Environmental Protection Agency ranks the Lakehurst facility high among the nation's most desperately polluted sites, but Bottomley blames its elevated rank primarily on the base's location at the northernmost tip of the Pine Barrens. Geologically speaking, she explains, there is nothing underground to stop the flow of the installation's pollutants into the Cohansey aquifer. "Below us," she says pointing to the photograph, "there are 17 trillion gallons of drinking water we could wreck."

Bottomley's rugged, sincere demeanor suggests a deep commitment to the base's environment. But her candid assessment of the threat posed by her facility, accurate though it may be, tells only part of the story. The size and vulnerability of the Cohansey aquifer certainly contributes to Lakehurst's toxic ranking, but the Superfund program does not determine its priority cleanup efforts based merely on an area's sensitive ecology. The truth is, Lakehurst's past practices—and the way they came to light—would present more than sufficient cause for alarm in even the most hardy ecosystem.

When questioned about them, Bottomley describes her early experiences at Lakehurst as "the dark years." She came to the base in 1979, armed with a degree in mechanical engineering and previous experience as an engineer at a company that manufactured forklifts. She had also spent ten years raising a family and serving as president of the local school board. When she was hired at Lakehurst—initially as a civil engineer in the Public Works Department—the base's environmental problems had just begun to attract attention.

At the same time that Bottomley came to Lakehurst, on the eve of the enactment of the federal legislation that created the Superfund program, officials at the base decided to investigate the extent and nature of the facility's toxic contamination. Navy documents from this period indicate that the investigation was at least partly motivated by the prospect of public scrutiny. A memo that winter from the Navy bureaucracy in the Pentagon to Lakehurst and other naval installations cited the "environmental emergency" that had taken place at Love Canal in western New York State.

With some obvious trepidation, the memo noted that in the case of Love Canal, "chemical wastes buried 30 years" had returned to haunt the town—ultimately requiring "the relocation of families and abandonment of homes, and result[ing] in suspected health problems including birth defects and miscarriages." Summing up the situation, the memo from the Naval Command in Washington suggested a course of action:

> In the past few years there have been reports in the media of harm to property and public health caused by improper handling of HM [hazardous material] and disposal of HW [hazardous waste]. . . . In view of . . . the Navy's extensive involvement, the need to protect people from HM, and the high level of public concern, it is prudent to develop a Navy program for the control of HM and HW.

What is noteworthy about this memo, aside from its admirable attention to environmental issues, is the Navy's clear recognition of its "extensive involvement" with hazardous substances—and the absence of any overall program prior to this time to manage its prodigious use of toxic materials at hundreds of bases throughout the world. This deficiency had first attracted the attention of high-ranking Navy officials in February 1980—a full twenty-five years after the federal government's passage of the Clean Air Act, eight years after passage of the Clean Water Act, four years after the nation's major toxic waste legislation, and two years after President Carter specifically directed federal facilities to comply with all of the above.

As Bottomley recalls, the problems she inherited at Lakehurst gave concrete meaning to the Naval Command's assessment of "extensive involvement" with toxic materials at its facilities. The investigations at Lakehurst would ultimately document that personnel at this ecologically fragile base had dumped into the ground an estimated *3 million gallons* of contaminated aviation fuel, solvents, hydraulic fluid, and dozens of other highly toxic chemicals over the previous several decades.

For the first year after Lakehurst officials uncovered troubling information about their past practices, however, the local public at risk would learn nothing of the problem. In fact, one year after Lakehurst's initial environmental investigation, neighboring residents learned of the situation only when news of the story was leaked to the media by a disgruntled employee. Even then, Lakehurst officials hid the full extent of their knowledge about contamination at the base from the public and from outside agencies for another three years, during which time internal studies uncovered a steady stream of worrisome information about environmental contamination at the base. During this period, secrecy and deception prevailed at the installation as the Navy moved only haltingly to address the situation.

Outside Bottomley's office, the landscape is dwarfed by the ungainly presence of Hangar One, an imposing reminder of the base's lengthy and eventful history. The gargantuan building, completed in 1921—the same year Lakehurst was commissioned as a naval air station—and "camouflaged" on the exterior with a patchwork of garish multicolored panels, is now recognized as a national historic landmark. Despite the Navy's highest ambitions for it and despite numerous successes here, the hangar, like the base itself, will forever be associated with disaster.

The enormous Navy hangar, the pride of the Navy's "lighter-than-air" World War I zeppelin program, was the ultimate destination of the famous German-built passenger zeppelin, the *Hindenburg*, on its maiden voyage in 1937. The *Hindenburg* was designed to inaugurate a grand new way for passengers to cross the Atlantic, but its flight ended in tragedy when it burst into flames while landing at a nearby airfield on the Lakehurst base.

Today the Navy still boasts proudly that the entire population of the state of New Jersey—some 7.3 million people—could stand together inside Hangar One. The building's interior has been known to develop its own weather patterns; Navy literature documents that warm fronts have occasionally caused rain to fall inside Hangar One while the sun shone through clear skies outside.

The truth is, Hangar One will always be remembered as a symbol of the *Hindenburg* conflagration—a disaster that killed not only dozens of travelers but the future of an entire mode of transportation. But while the *Hindenburg*'s demise was the first and most notorious environmental tragedy in Lakehurst's history, it would not be the last.

A few miles west of Hangar One, a parched, empty plot of dusty earth spreads out for hundreds of yards in every direction. The site, originally cleared as a parachute jump circle, was among the very first to alert Lakehurst officials to the severity of the base's toxic waste problems.

Nervous about outside scrutiny over the base's environmental problems, officials at Lakehurst began in earnest in the fall of 1979 to investigate the legacy left from past practices at the base. The immediate overall findings were alarming, but the parachute jump site attracted the greatest initial concern. The first hint of trouble was a warning sign found near the jump site: "Materials Containing Tetraethyl Lead Buried Here, April 1966."

Upon investigation, Navy officials would soon determine that between the years 1950 and 1970, workers at this specific location dumped approximately *2 million gallons* of aviation fuel into this site's porous soil— enough fuel to fly a full Boeing 747 jet around the world more than a dozen times. The Navy's initial study calculated that the routine dumping at this one location alone was responsible for depositing more than ten tons of tetraethyl lead—designated by the EPA as an "extremely hazardous substance"—into the soil, not to mention other toxic fuel constituents and additives. Initially, however, Lakehurst officials notified no one— including nearby residents—of the potential threat posed by this site at the edge of the installation.

Navy documents emphasize repeatedly that this toxic dumpsite was "discovered" in 1979, but in truth many people at the base were aware of its existence long before this date. Several employees, when questioned later, were even able to offer details about the standard dumping procedures at the site. And, as the sign itself documented, Navy personnel at the base were concerned enough about the place even in 1966 to warn posterity about the contaminants buried there.

A high-ranking Lakehurst official justified the dumping procedure to a congressional subcommittee in 1980 by explaining, "Fuel wasn't worth much in those days. The environment wasn't such a concern." Consequently, the Navy's routine practice, as Lucy Bottomley describes it, was to "defuel" planes after landing. Workers would pump the leftover fuel, which could possibly be tainted with oil or other substances during the flight and thereby undesirable, into tanker trucks and then drive them out to the parachute landing area. There in the forsaken clearing they would open the valves and drive around in circles until the unwanted fuel was drained.

While it is no longer the practice to dump fuel like this, it remains unclear whether anyone at the time of the dumping considered the threat this practice posed to the shallow Cohansey aquifer underground. Bottomley says that officials during this period were more concerned that sufficient fuel was applied to rid the parachute jump site of grass and other vegetation so it could be easily spotted from the air.

It seems that Lakehurst officials, confronted with the disturbing information they initially uncovered in 1979 about past practices at the base, simply didn't know what to do at first. The first environmental accounting found some twenty-nine potentially toxic sites like the fuel disposal area at the base, but little or no action was undertaken to address any of them. As Bottomley concedes, "During this period, we were sitting on our duffs."

Then in November 1980, a full year after the contamination was formally discovered, the Lakehurst base was forced into the glare of intense public scrutiny. A disgruntled employee at Lakehurst leaked word of the installation's initial environmental findings to the press. Neighbors discovered pollutants in their wells and some accused the base of being responsible for the contamination. But while reports in the *New York Times* and local newspapers captured the essence of the suspected problems, they failed to uncover the complete story. Several of the articles, for example, charged with alarm that the facility had dumped some "20,000 gallons of aviation fuel" at the parachute jump site—a hundred times less than the Navy's ultimate assessment.

Amidst the onslaught of public attention, several former employees came forward with damaging information; in one dramatic episode, a former worker escorted officials from state and federal environmental agencies onto the base to show where he had personally dumped hundreds of drums of chemicals into the sandy soil. Among the chemicals dumped, the worker contended, were suspected carcinogens like carbon tetrachloride and trichloroethylene.

At the instigation of Representative James J. Florio of New Jersey, congressional hearings quickly ensued at the end of 1980 to review Lakehurst's plight. Unfortunately, however, the hearings were dramatically inconclusive. Top-ranking Defense Department officials capitalized on the fact that the disaffected personnel had gathered little hard data about Lakehurst's environmental practices over the year since they had "discovered" the problem. One such official lobbying on Lakehurst's behalf, was Deputy Assistant Secretary of Defense (Energy, Environment, and Safety) George Marienthal. "You should note," Marienthal told the congressional subcommittee in November of 1980, "that while newspaper accounts indicate 20,000 gallons of aviation gas were dumped, we are unable to verify that quantity or, for that matter, any quantity."

Sadly, despite this outside scrutiny and criticism at the end of 1980, Lakehurst officials continued to withhold information from the public. In February 1981, for example, just two months after the congressional hearings, Lakehurst officials found dangerous levels of chemicals in water samples taken from one of the facility's water pipelines. The test found levels of methylene chloride (a known carcinogen) at 870 parts per billion—a level known even at that time to be dangerous—but the test's findings were never officially reported to outside regulators.

James Gardner, supervising environmental engineer for the Naval Air Engineering Center (and Lucy Bottomley's boss at the time), later defended the secrecy by stating that "single results are not conclusive." As Gardner put it to a *New York Times* reporter, "One day you come up with nothing, the next day, you find enough to kill somebody. It's a long, time-consuming process."

By April 1981, however, Lakehurst officials were sufficiently concerned about the situation to have undertaken three separate tests of its water supply. Taken together, the results were dramatic, revealing enormously elevated levels of at least eight cancer-causing chemicals contaminating the base's wells. The levels of some of these chemicals exceeded federal safety standards by many orders of magnitude. One suspected carcinogen, a chemical called acrylonitrile, used as an additive in aviation fuel, was found at more than 35,000 times the maximum levels allowed by the EPA.

Despite this evidence, however, Lakehurst officials took no action to protect the neighboring public, or even their own personnel housed near the base. Instead they contracted to conduct more tests and to hire a consultant to try to explain their problem. Privately, though, the situation clearly had them worried. Gardner, for instance, began to lobby internally for the Navy bureaucracy at the Pentagon to send out a team of environmental specialists on a priority basis. In a memo about the matter which he wrote in July 1981, Gardner described the "extensive program" Lakehurst had undertaken to analyze the quality of the base's drinking-water systems.

As Gardner stated to his superiors, "The [Lakehurst] Environmental/Utilities Branch had suspected that the testing would show traces of chemical pollutants in the drinking water. The test results, however, indicate extensive pollution, both in the number of chemicals involved and their concentrations." Despite the alarming results of the three separate tests, the memo brazenly confirmed the intent of Gardner and other Lakehurst officials to withhold the information about the contamination until yet another consultant could study the data. Until then, Gardner wrote, "the test data will not be disclosed to [the Navy's] Northern Division, NAVAIR or NEESA [both Navy agencies], nor to the EPA or NJ Department of Environmental Protection."

In response to the base's appeal, a special Navy team did agree to study Lakehurst's problems in the fall of 1981. Their work culminated in a report finally issued in the fall of 1983. Finding a total of forty-four potentially contaminated sites at Lakehurst, the team's report advised that the base implement an extensive groundwater monitoring system, but the report revealed no alarm at the possibility that the contamination in the ground beneath the base posed an immediate threat.

Despite the known toxic plumes migrating through the soil at numerous locations at the base, Lakehurst officials took the opportunity at this time to convince the public and base personnel that the base's water presented no hazard. "Drink up!" read a headline in the base's newsletter in April 1983. In the article James Gardner is quoted as saying, "We test for every known chemical pollutant that's ever been found in a drinking water supply in New Jersey, *even though there's no reason to suspect any such pollutants would be found here* [emphasis added]." Gardner's comment came the same year that his base reported generating some 240 tons of hazardous wastes.

The Environmental Protection Agency, when it was finally apprised of the Navy's report on Lakehurst in 1983, strongly disagreed with Gardner's misleading contention. The Navy's report, EPA officials complained, "takes the position that none of the problems reviewed represent an immediate threat to human health or the environment." Unfortunately, the EPA reviewers said, "the information presented . . . does not support this conclusion. Testing of drinking water from the three water systems at the base has indicated extensive system-wide contamination. In addition, the water supplied to off-base Navy housing units by the Lakehurst Municipal System exhibits contamination."

The EPA reviewers noted that the Navy's report had found "that the levels of Acrylonitrile; 3,3 Dichlorobenzidine; Benzene, and Chloroform all exceed established EPA water quality standards *by as much as 5 orders of magnitude* [emphasis added]. All of these compounds are carcinogenic and their presence in such high amounts represents a concern for human health." Because each water supply system tested at the base exhibited some high readings, "there appears to be contamination throughout the aquifer," the EPA maintained, concluding that "in any case it is apparent that the drinking water is contaminated and presents an immediate threat to human health."

A tour of the base with Frank Montarelli, Lakehurst's bright, loquacious press officer, yields several surprises. After passing the parachute jump site, Montarelli points out a plot of land where Lakehurst officials dug up several dozen buried bombs and artillery shells. Oddly enough, in this case the Navy can fairly blame Russia for at least some of the explosives exhumed.

The grounds of Lakehurst, it turns out, were used in 1915 by the Eddystone Chemical Company to test ordnance manufactured for none other than the imperial Russian government. Of course all of the buried ordnance did not stem from this unusual source. Lakehurst, Montarelli acknowledged, was used for testing munitions throughout World War II, including chemical weapons. Even today the existence of buried munitions is prevalent enough that the base requires that builders sweep for explosives before any construction can begin.

Montarelli stresses the pride Lakehurst personnel take in the installation's mission, calling many of the base's facilities the "most advanced in the free world." At one location, workers strap jet engines onto weighted railcars, shooting them down miles of track to test the engines' capabilities. Nearby, a huge airfield simulates the upper deck of an aircraft carrier, complete with a hydraulic catapult to launch planes into flight. Another, newer facility, with a roof that rocks back and forth, tests equipment that helps helicopters land on listing ships.

Unfortunately, Lakehurst's worthy accomplishments must be considered alongside its egregious environmental legacy. An ample illustration comes in a quick visit to a "fuel farm" at a far corner of the installation. The site consists of a vast, cylindrical fuel tank connected to a smaller distribution tank where trucks can load up with aviation fuel. The smaller tank is surrounded by a jumble of barbed wire, chains, and padlocks.

Montarelli explains the security measures by saying that officers at the base believed for years that someone was stealing fuel from the facility. All the while, however, a leaky valve in the smaller tank was draining its toxic contents into the soil below.

In a similar case in 1981, base officials realized that 3,000 gallons of aviation fuel had spilled at a larger fuel farm at Lakehurst. To its credit, Lakehurst's environmental team, including Lucy Bottomley, conducted a speedy cleanup by digging a well and pumping out the fuel from the soil. The effort, like many others at Lakehurst, won the team an award from the Navy. Disturbingly, however, the spill recovery process came up with more than 10,000 gallons of pure fuel—more than three times the amount documented as having been dumped into the ground during the incident. The Navy's study several years later would explain why: at this site, as many as 400,000 gallons of contaminated water mixed with aviation fuel had likely been dumped or leaked in past years, when Lakehurst officials routinely "bled" the tanks directly into the ground.

The fact that efforts at Lakehurst were frequently touted as a model and honored with awards by the Navy stands as a sad testament to the Navy's status nationwide in the environmental arena. Self-congratulation amidst unfolding environmental tragedy, as it turns out, is a hallmark of the base's recent history.

In one example, also from 1981, the base was nominated for a special citation from the Secretary of the Navy for its environmental program, including its "good neighbor policy." When the nearby local police department of Brick Township discovered 12,000 foil packets of phenol (a caustic and toxic chemical) scattered in the woods, a team from Lakehurst retrieved them. Less mention was made in the award nomination of the fact that Lakehurst's Defense Reutilization and Marketing Office (part of the same organization responsible for the toxic contents of the Collinsville barn) had just recently sold the surplus phenol to a private citizen in the first place.

Lakehurst's most recent recognition from the Navy for its handling of environmental matters came in 1989—a decade after this base's contamination was first investigated—when Lakehurst finally signed an "interagency agreement" with the Environmental Protection Agency to allow the Superfund cleanup to proceed at a scheduled pace that stretches beyond the year 2000. Astonishingly, Lakehurst was the first Navy installation ever to reach such an agreement with the EPA.

Meanwhile, Bottomley says, "the immediate challenge is to change people's attitudes." Despite all, Bottomley's energy and dedication offer more than a glimmer of hope. But the task is not an easy one. As Bottomley's assistant in Lakehurst's environmental branch, Carol Uhrich, puts it, "We bring it to the people's attention that they can't pollute anymore. . . . Believe it or not, it's something you really have to push on the people."

CHAPTER EIGHT

Grand Island, Nebraska: "Overly Anxious"

Chuck Carpenter, a weathered forty-five-year-old junior high school science teacher, wistfully remembers the day in 1978 when he and his family bought a house in the northwest corner of Grand Island, Nebraska. The houses in this area, called the Le Heights district, were a little further apart than those downtown, he says, and it felt more like being in the country. Plus, the home Carpenter and his wife chose was situated near the local public schools, elementary through high school—it would be convenient for their four children. "I think we had heard that the Army had a big ammunition plant a few miles away, but we just didn't think a thing about it," he says.

Carpenter says he tries not to be bitter, but his dealings with the U.S. Army over the past decade have been a nightmare—one he hopes is finally behind him. Through no fault of their own, Carpenter and his neighbors fell victim to pollution from the U.S. Army's Cornhusker Ammunition Plant.

Because of the perennial threat posed by seeping toxic chemicals and because he believed the military contaminants threatened his family's health, Carpenter says, he knew by 1986 that he couldn't let his family continue to live near the Cornhusker installation. But with the local publicity about the pollution in his neighborhood, he couldn't sell his house, and the Army offered no compensation. So, after living in the Le Heights district for eight years, Carpenter was forced to declare bankruptcy and walk away from his home. He and his family began anew, moving initially to a rented apartment across town. His house was finally sold by a bank at auction for roughly $25,000—a fraction of its former value.

But Carpenter says that perhaps the worst part of the entire saga is the way the Army treated him and his neighbors. Years ago he told the local press it felt like being a guinea pig, but today he puts it a little differently. "We were treated like mushrooms. The Army kept us totally in the dark."

In 1978, when the Carpenter family first moved into their Le Heights home, the Army's Cornhusker Ammunition Plant languished quietly in a "standby" status. Probably because of the plant's low profile at the time, Carpenter and his family overlooked Cornhusker's history as a major site for the Army's production of conventional bombs. Just several years earlier, though, the plant had been bustling, building virtually every 1,000-pound bomb used in the Vietnam War. The installation had, in fact, contributed firepower to every major conflict in recent U.S. history prior to the Persian Gulf War. And below ground contaminants from the weapons' production lingered and spread.

The nineteen-square-mile Cornhusker installation is nestled in the Nebraska farmland of the Platte River valley, just outside Grand Island, population 33,000. The town grew as a railroad junction at the turn of the century, but now it relies more on nearby Interstate 80—its exit marks the midway point between the Atlantic and the Pacific.

Shortly after Cornhusker opened in 1942, the plant packed explosives into munitions ranging from 105-millimeter shells to 1,000-pound bombs. TNT (trinitrotoluene) and other explosive compounds arrived by train from several locations around the country. At the base, the explosives were kept in hundreds of so-called magazines—bunkers that bulge like oversized anthills out of Cornhusker's largely flat terrain. A long line of magazines held source materials, and another equally long line held the final munitions; both lines were designed to be conveniently accessible to the railway lines.

Workers at the installation were arranged in lines as well: five separate assembly lines, some more than a half-mile long. At these "load lines," contained within extended rows of linked warehouse buildings, workers mixed the TNT, aluminum flakes, and other compounds and poured them into a huge vat from which the final explosive mixture would be packed into the casing of bombs, shells, and mines.

In a 1984 interview, Charles Fisher, then-plant director, recalled the intensity of the plant's most recent production schedule. "Those lines worked six days a week, full blast, when we had 5,100 people here for the Vietnam buildup." Fisher also noted the reason the plant didn't run seven days a week—so that the large quantities of toxic, explosive dust generated during production could be washed down. "You don't want a lot of that explosive dust accumulating."

The weekly cleansing procedures undoubtedly kept the plant from igniting, but unfortunately the dousing also proved to be responsible for polluting groundwater. Workers called the thousands of gallons generated from the weekly rinsing "red water"; high concentrations of TNT gave it a distinctive pink tint. This wastewater ran off into a network of more than fifty cesspools and leaching pits.

An internal Army report in 1980 stated that given the "high permeability" of Cornhusker's soil and the "rapid groundwater flow" beneath the installation, "a potential exists for contamination migration at CAAP [Cornhusker Army Ammunition Plant]." The assessment is not surprising; cesspools and leaching pits are designed to allow contaminants to filter out and migrate through the soil. Army documents say that the contaminants in these pits underwent "percolation and evaporation." The truth is, however, that little evaporation occurred. Instead the compounds seeped, or "percolated," straight into the soil and groundwater. The explosive compounds are volatile only in the popular sense of the word, not in a strict chemical sense; unlike most fuels and solvents, they do not readily turn to gas.

There were other sources of red water at Cornhusker. Each load line had a "change house," where workers would shed their work clothes—often thick with explosive dust—after every shift. Contaminated clothing from the change houses, the Army reports, was cleaned at the installation laundry, and the wastewater from this procedure flowed into an underground sump where at least some of the silty explosive residues were caught in burlap-like sacks and routinely removed to be ignited.

In 1970, during the height of production for the Vietnam War, the Army actually kept track of the laundry's wastewater, estimating that the procedure generated a daily outflow of approximately 473 cubic meters (roughly 100,000 gallons) of water contaminated with explosive residues. As the Army's 1980 report on Cornhusker graphically describes, the laundry's contaminated wastewater "meandered to the north section of the installation where it terminated in a marsh."

Even as early as 1970, Army officials knew of the looming environmental problems at the plant. Citing threats to the groundwater, the Army contractor at Cornhusker appealed to higher-ups to construct a toxic-wastewater treatment facility on the plant's grounds. But the base's production cycle soon ended as U.S. involvement in Vietnam waned, and the facility was never completed.

As Carpenter remembers it, the first he ever heard of the explosive compound RDX was in 1982, when he saw a story in the *Grand Island Daily Independent* revealing that the Army had discovered the substance in the base's groundwater. He says the story didn't seem like cause for concern—a Cornhusker official was quoted as saying there was no evidence that domestic wells even on the plant's grounds were contaminated. At about that time, Army specialists also confidently told the public that it could take more than a century for the compounds to reach the town's outer limits.

In truth, however, an Army report from as early as 1980 documented that "significant levels of TNT and RDX exist in the groundwater." "Furthermore," the report states, "the contamination may be migrating across the installation boundary." The same year the Army estimated that groundwater underneath the plant could be moving toward Grand Island at a rate approaching three meters per day; at this rate, the plant's contaminants could reach town in just four years. By May 1982 the Army had confirmed explosive compounds at levels of potential danger in test wells on the base and had strong reason to suspect that the chemicals had migrated beyond the installation's boundaries. Concentrations of RDX, a little-known explosive compound, were discovered at levels eight times higher than even the Army's proposed limit.

With more tests that summer and continuing through early 1984, Army officials verified their earlier finding of high levels of RDX. But for almost another full year, while a vast, highly toxic plume migrated swiftly from the Cornhusker Army Ammunition Plant toward Grand Island, the Army said nothing to the public.

In April 1984, four years after the off-base migration of RDX was suspected and two years after the Army confirmed elevated levels of RDX in nearby wells, Army officials at Cornhusker finally called a public meeting. The Army released a summary of the environmental data it had gathered at the installation in lengthy tests over the previous two years. Rather than testing residents' wells in 1980, when they strongly suspected contamination, the Army waited. Only now, at this 1984 meeting, did they reveal their findings to the public: more than half of the 467 private wells the Army tested in the Le Heights and Capitol districts of Grand Island had extremely elevated levels of RDX. The Army's underground contamination, in other words, had already migrated more than three miles from the edge of the facility.

At the time neither the Nebraska Department of Health nor the federal EPA had established a standard for safe levels of RDX in drinking water. But the Army knew that the levels it had found were disturbingly high. Army officials had already accumulated evidence of the chemical's effects upon the human nervous system, often resulting in seizures and unconsciousness; there was evidence of effects among World War II munitions workers and among Vietnam-era soldiers who inhaled chemical fumes when they burned a compound containing RDX to heat their meals. Based on studies in rats, mice, and monkeys, the EPA has now listed RDX as a possible carcinogen. At the time, though, it had issued no recommended standard, accepting by default the Army's contentions that levels of RDX below 35 parts per billion presented no danger to human health.

Carpenter recalls resentfully that when the dramatically elevated levels of RDX were found in initial tests of residents' wells, the Army refused to release the results—even to the people whose wells were tested. The Army's Toxic Assessment Program chief, Andrew Anderson, defended the base's decision. "We didn't want to get them overly anxious," he told a newspaper reporter from the *Sacramento Bee* in 1984.

Anderson accounted for the Army's long delay by explaining the procedure the base followed. "First, we sampled and found [contamination] at the plant boundary," he said. "So we sampled again a mile further out, figuring we would get beyond it. But we found it again. So we had to sample a third time before we got what we felt was accurate data."

"The plume," Anderson added, "was moving in more of an easterly direction than we thought."

Today Chuck Carpenter still vividly recalls his concern when he first learned that he and his neighbors were threatened by the Army's pollution. "We were stunned, disoriented," he says. "We didn't know quite what to do—we weren't told exactly what the dangers of these chemicals were."

Disoriented or not, Carpenter says he knew he wasn't going to "take the situation lying down." Before the end of 1984, Carpenter founded a citizens' group called Good Neighbors Against Toxic Substances (GNATS). Drawing upon his background in science, he began to try to find out more about the hazard presented by the contamination. In 1984 the GNATS group filed a lawsuit against the Army, charging that the Cornhusker plant was responsible for contaminating GNATS members' wells. The case sought compensation for damages to their homes and health and for their plummeting property values.

The group's research uncovered similar cases of contamination at numerous military bases around the country. Researching the history of Cornhusker, GNATS found material documenting that from the day the plant opened in 1942, workers were always required to bathe and change clothes after working with the explosive chemicals. The Army itself, however, would provide GNATS with little information. At an early meeting in 1984, Carpenter remembers, the Army "said the contamination levels would cause 'no harm to the public.' " Army officials told residents that their safety standard of 35 parts per billion had a built-in 100-fold "safety factor"; in light of this, Army representatives claimed that the levels found at the time should not be cause for alarm.

In these discussions, Carpenter remembers, his group held its ground. A representative from the Sierra Club spoke on GNATS' behalf and criticized the Army for providing little access to data about the contamination. "We charged that the Army had been covering up a lot," Carpenter says.

The Army responded that winter by offering people in the affected districts an opportunity to receive a newsletter about the evolving situation. As small an offer as it was, Carpenter says, the only issue he ever received was one he picked up at a meeting. "In all these years since the contamination was made public," he says, "I don't recall getting any information sheet mailed to me regarding the base, despite the Army's promises."

Meanwhile, GNATS research seemed to turn up more questions than answers. The group appealed to the Environmental Protection Agency for help and advice, but the EPA had no information about RDX; at the time the agency simply relied on the Army's standards. In addition, the EPA's regional office for the area was headquartered in Kansas City, some 200 miles away. "They pretty much avoided our situation like the plague," Carpenter says.

In addition, GNATS members, testing their own well water, found numerous other contaminants besides RDX, including disturbing levels of the solvents dichloroethane and trichloroethane. Despite the fact that there were few other possible sources and that the solvents were found in the same contamination pathway, showing up along with the RDX, the Army refused to admit responsibility for any contaminants but the one indisputable explosive compound. Little matter that their past practices included the dumping of a variety of hazardous materials; the Army has only recently accepted culpability for contaminants other than RDX that have shown up in wells near its borders.

Meanwhile, Carpenter became convinced in 1984 that RDX was responsible for a variety of odd health problems he had noticed in himself and his children. He had seen the doctor, for instance, about splitting headaches he would get in the morning, sometimes lasting through lunch. His doctor had never determined a cause, but Carpenter realized that the ailment would always start after he showered. Over the course of the next year and a half, Carpenter's nine-year-old daughter developed a serious digestive problem, and other family members suffered from skin rashes.

To make matters worse, for the summers of 1982 and 1983 the water table was unusually high. Carpenter's home, like many in Le Heights, had at least an inch or more of contaminated water sitting in the basement for most of the year. When Carpenter brought the matter to the Army's attention, he was told that traces of RDX would remain in the basements even after the water was gone. That fact pushed Carpenter over the edge.

Carpenter describes the first year and a half after he knew about the contamination in his groundwater as one of the most difficult periods in his life. Before he left his home in Le Heights, the Army argued first over who in the area was entitled to free bottled water. Then, he recalls, the Army "haggled with the city over how much it would pay toward extending city water mains to the affected areas"; finally, the Army agreed to pay to hook up homes with unsafe water, as well as those similarly threatened in the vicinity—a total of roughly 900 homes in all. The job ultimately cost more than $5 million.

Meanwhile, the abnormally high water table complicated the extension of the town's water line. The Army proposed to address the problem by "de-watering"—pumping huge quantities of the contaminated groundwater into nearby Silver Creek. Not surprisingly, local farmers downstream, who fished in Silver Creek and used its water to feed their livestock, objected vehemently to the plan; but the Army prevailed, arguing successfully that in the rapid flow of the creek the RDX concentrations—by their estimates up to 60 parts per billion—would be low enough to be of little concern. "It was a case of the old rule that 'the solution to pollution is dilution,'" Carpenter quips.

Finally, on a gray day in 1986, Carpenter made the two-hour drive to Lincoln, Nebraska, to seek legal advice about his personal situation. He was determined and distraught. The value of his house had already dropped by almost two thirds, and he still owed a great deal on his mortgage. Upon hearing his story, his attorney advised him simply to "get out of there" and worry about the financial side later. Carpenter acted on the advice immediately, moving his family to an apartment on the far side of Grand Island. He formally declared bankruptcy later that same year.

Ultimately, the Cornhusker case turned on an odd technicality that worked in the Army's favor. Army officials did not contest the fact that Cornhusker personnel had polluted the groundwater during the installation's production cycles from World War II through the Vietnam War; nor did they deny that no water treatment facility had ever been built at the plant or that little effort had been made to minimize the hazard presented to neighboring communities. Army officials did argue, however, that the case should rest on the question of how fast the groundwater pollution was migrating.

The Army argued that the contaminants causing the problems at the edge of Grand Island probably resulted from weapons production during the Korean War era or earlier. During this period, the Army argued, the waste products Cornhusker generated were legally permissible—an accepted practice of the time.

The Army's legal argument ignored the obvious fact that pollutants from this earlier time made up only the forward-most part of the toxic plume that today continues to migrate northeast from the plant. The argument also neatly avoided the fact that Army procedures at the plant explicitly violated the law after 1965 when President Lyndon B. Johnson directed the Pentagon to monitor and treat wastewater at its installations.

Nevertheless, toxicologists and hydrologists hired by the GNATS lawyer were unable to prove that contaminants dumped since 1965 could have migrated all the way to Le Heights. Expert estimates placed these more recent contaminants at least several hundred feet short of Chuck Carpenter's well. And since the Army had already acted to provide municipal water for the affected residents, the lawyer advised GNATS to drop the case. Carpenter says that the group wanted to continue to fight the Army in court, but that it didn't have the money to cover high legal costs, especially if there were a chance the group would lose and be required to pay attorney's fees for the Army. "Normally, I'm not one to give up a fight," Carpenter says, "but in this case we bailed out. We didn't get anything out of it."

Since the case closed in 1990, Carpenter says, Cornhusker's contaminants have been discovered another two miles further from the plant, potentially polluting the wells of dozens more families further to the northeast of Grand Island—an outcome the GNATS group predicted and warned the city about several years ago.

In addition, in 1988 the EPA's Office of Drinking Water finally established an advisory safety standard for RDX. The agency determined that the Army's long-proposed standard of 35 parts per billion was more than seventeen times too lenient. A new interim standard, now agreed to by the Army, the state of Nebraska, and the EPA, says that 2 parts per billion is the maximum concentration of RDX allowable in drinking water.

The strict new standard does not bode well for the Cornhusker cleanup, despite its current status on the Superfund National Priority List. It bodes especially ill for the health of residents who, unlike Chuck Carpenter, remain in the Le Heights and Capitol neighborhoods.

Over the past several years, an environmental contractor for the Army incinerated roughly 40,000 tons of soil on the grounds of the Cornhusker installation. This high-temperature incineration was intended to stem the tide of new contaminants seeping into the plume. However, it only treated soil down to the level of the water table, and it failed to clean up the contaminants to the agreed-upon EPA limits; the equipment the Army used could not detect RDX at 2 parts per billion, let alone decontaminate it to that level.

Meanwhile, a decade since the Army first discovered the RDX contamination, no water treatment has yet been undertaken at Cornhusker, and the installation's contaminants continue to spread. As Carpenter puts it, "After all they put us through, they never did anything with the underground plume of polluted water."

Sacramento, California: "Moving Target"

Eight miles northeast of downtown Sacramento, a highway strip of fast-food restaurants and car dealerships is eclipsed by a different land-scape. Through a massive gate, a thoroughfare called Peacekeeper Way stretches to the center of an entirely separate city. Suddenly the signs and billboards that shape the chaotic jumble of strip architecture are sup-planted by huge, anonymous hangars, barracks, warehouses, and admin-istrative buildings. A tall steel water tower stands motionless against the skyline, but everything around it seems to move. Cars, trucks, buses, planes, and people on foot all give the surroundings a busy, industrious feeling.

In all of northern California, only the state government employs more people than the bustling McClellan Air Force Base. The installation qual-ifies as a small city by almost any measure, one in which everything is underwritten and operated by the federal government. The base has its own post office, library, gas station, and clothing, food, and liquor stores. Many of the 17,000 people who work here each day also make use of McClellan's movie theater, gymnasium, museum, and bowling alley.

Over more than half a century, McClellan Air Force Base has served as a major point of departure for the U.S. Air Force's projection of America's military might in Asia. When the Japanese attacked Pearl Harbor in 1941, McClellan was the only Air Force depot on the West Coast. Base person-nel, hearing word of the attack on a Sunday morning, rushed to work to dispatch planes and equipment immediately to the scene. Until the war ended McClellan bore the brunt of air logistics to the Pacific. By June 1943 its employee count topped 20,000.

As part of the Air Logistics Command, headquartered at Wright Patterson Air Force Base in Ohio, McClellan's main function is to repair and maintain aircraft. The base played this role during the Korean War in the 1950s and again during the Vietnam War, when it pioneered a program that sent teams of highly trained maintenance personnel to Southeast Asia to fix aircraft in the midst of the war zone. Today the base serves as the central management and maintenance facility for a number of the Air Force's most sophisticated models of aircraft, including the new F-117A Stealth fighters used in the Persian Gulf War.

Longstanding industrial activities at McClellan have conspired to create one of the most challenging and dangerous environmental problems in the country. Air Force documents reveal that the base's total of 170 separate potentially polluted sites result from the routine dumping of toxic liquids, sludges, and solid wastes, from accidental spills at various locations, and from leaks in underground storage tanks and industrial waste lines. The range of contaminants dumped here includes solvents, electroplating wastes like cyanide, caustic cleaners, and degreasers, paints, waste oils, phenols, chloroform, acids, and oils contaminated with PCBs.

Aside from the size of its problem, though, McClellan is notable as one of the first bases where the community actively confronted the military's pollution. Aggressive local and state involvement brought the extent of McClellan's groundwater contamination to light and forced the closure of a municipal well which fed a system serving tens of thousands of people. The community's involvement also prompted the construction of a vaunted water treatment facility at McClellan, designed to remove contaminants and thereby forestall their migration beyond the installation's borders. Despite the community's many small and precedent-setting victories, however, the Air Force says it has completed cleanup effort at only one of McClellan's 170 toxic sites, and has completed final studies of only 17 sites.

A bland, low-lying building marks the headquarters for McClellan's environmental management team. Inside, the office, like the base itself, is bustling, honeycombed throughout with partitioned offices for the environmental team's fifty workers. Deep within the building lies the windowless office of Mario Ierardi, the energetic director of McClellan's Installation Restoration Program.

Ierardi, just thirty-four years old, oversees one of the most daunting cleanup projects ever conceived, but the weight of the problem he must face daily does not discernibly faze him. Clean-cut and neatly dressed, Ierardi has an efficient, professional air. He seems to approach the base's toxic legacy as a straightforward problem that can and will be solved. Even his office lacks any visible signs of his job's prodigious demands; his desk, notably lacking stacks of forms to file or papers to sign, is virtually empty.

Ierardi explains casually that the installation has made great strides in recent years but still faces a nearly overwhelming environmental cleanup problem. A significant portion of the land beneath the base is polluted, Ierardi says—so much, in fact, that the delineation into separate "sites" is of little use. Instead of grappling with individual sites of contamination, McClellan's environmental team has conceptually divided the installation's land into eight sizable polluted areas, labeled A through H. The group hopes eventually to design a separate, thorough cleanup plan for each one, but even this planning effort is not expected to be finished until after the turn of the century.

Like so many military installations, Ierardi explains, McClellan had a difficult time coming to grips with its contamination problems. Its case was so stormy, in fact, that it is still referred to within the military as the "McClellan Experience." Today Ierardi and his environmental co-workers talk about the period of the early 1980s much the way rehabilitated alcoholics might discuss their erstwhile drinking habits.

Joining the base in 1983, Ierardi missed the start of the base's protracted confrontation with city, state, and local officials over their pollution problems. But he says he had more than a taste of what it was like. He compares his early experience at the base to "walking the plank."

A recent internal advisory document, which Ierardi passes across the desk, proselytizes for reformed thinking to base personnel. "Even if the news is bad," the advisory reads, "it's not like fine wine—it will only get worse with age. If the perception exists that you are hiding something—especially in the emotionally charged area of environmental compliance—then you won't be trusted." This, Ierardi says, referring to the withholding of bad news, is what happened at McClellan: "We failed to be responsive to the community's needs. We learned that the key thing is taking ownership of the problem. But we learned the hard way."

Ierardi's boss, Colonel Keith Findley, McClellan's director of environmental management, sums up the base's new-found *glasnost*. "The good news is, we know we have a problem," Findley says, underscoring a significant change in the base's handling of environmental matters over the past few years. "The bad news is, it's a big problem."

At its core, the infamous "McClellan Experience" stems from decisions base officials made over the course of several years to try to withhold information about contamination in wells on the base and even beyond its borders. During this formative period, which began in 1979 with the first known tests that showed contamination on base property and beyond its borders, officials at McClellan routinely withheld environmental reports for upwards of a year at a time, pending the Air Force's internal review. On several occasions, base officials made the environmental information public only after legal action was threatened by the state or by other regulatory agencies.

The press and many members of the public in the Sacramento area were rightfully outraged at the base's secrecy and arrogance, especially given the breadth and scope of the contamination at the base. Readings of excessive concentrations of solvents in some of McClellan's more than 100 groundwater monitoring wells continued for years. For example, in 1985 TCE was detected at 22,600 parts per billion, more than 4,500 times the maximum level allowed by the EPA. Concentrations of arsenic, barium, cadmium, chromium, and lead were also found to exceed EPA's drinking-water standards.

Since 1979, solvents have also been detected in public and private wells to the west of McClellan. Numerous wells have been forced to shut down due to TCE contamination, including the municipal well mentioned above, which was part of a system providing drinking water to 23,000 residents. Several wells were closed during the early 1980s, and the base provided bottled water to nearby residents. In one of the first arrangements of its kind, in 1987 more than 550 homes were linked to an alternative public water supply system at the Air Force's expense.

Ierardi explains that the base's major contamination problems stem from the former use of TCE, as well as other volatile organic compounds like the known carcinogen perchloroethylene. In addition to aircraft maintenance, Ierardi says there is evidence of even more widespread and frivolous use of these solvents. "We used to use TCE as a weed killer," he confides.

TCE, which has caused lingering contamination at many U.S. military installations, has been detected in the water supplies of 133 cities in the United States. It is believed to be present in trace amounts in as many as one third of the nation's water supply sources. According to the Agency for Toxic Substances and Disease Registry of the U.S. Public Health Service, animal studies have shown that ingesting or breathing even small amounts of TCE can cause nervous system changes; liver and kidney damage; effects on the blood; tumors of the liver, kidney, lung, and male sex organs; even leukemia. Some studies in mice have also shown that TCE exposure to either males or females can lead to birth defects in offspring.

To make matters even worse, Ieradi notes, the suspected carcinogen TCE breaks down into other chemicals, including vinyl chloride—an extremely hazardous chemical that is definitively known to cause cancer in humans. At McClellan, data show that bacteria in the soil have frequently stripped away a chlorine atom from TCE—forming the similarly hazardous 1,2-dichloroethylene, or DCE. As early as 1982, DCE was found at the base in concentrations as high as 63,000 parts per billion. Fluctuations in concentrations of contaminants often prove such extremely high concentrations to be anomolous, but at McClellan—at least in the highly polluted "Area D" in the base's northwest corner—shockingly high levels are endemic. One study found the *average* level in monitoring wells throughout this area to be 11,687 parts per billion.

Unfortunately, high levels of contamination are not confined to the base's property. When state regulators in 1983 found wells near the base contained levels of TCE and DCE exceeding state action levels by dozens of times, McClellan officials initially denied responsibility and refused to act to redress the situation. "We weren't responsive," Ierardi admits.

Soon thereafter, in 1984, a group of citizens brought a landmark lawsuit against the Defense Department under the name of MESS—an acronym for McClellan Ecological Seepage Situation. The MESS group sought the enforcement of existing environmental laws and claimed that the Air Force should be required to pay penalties if it failed to comply. But, in a narrow, limited interpretation of the law, the federal court ultimately upheld McClellan's sovereign immunity in 1986, ruling that meeting the environmental demands of the local community would be tantamount to shutting down the operation of a vital federal installation.

"I've stayed in the fight since 1984," says Chuck Yarbrough, a Sacramento resident and electronics mechanic at McClellan who sits on the base's cleanup review committee as the city's representative. "They have called me a gadfly, but I'm just interested in upholding people's right to know about information that pertains to their health." Yarbrough's outspoken persistence led, in 1986, to a well-publicized effort by McClellan officials to oust him from the review committee. Yarbrough's overwhelmingly strong backing from city and state officials, however, caused McClellan's efforts to backfire; he remains an influential member of the committee today.

Also a member of the MESS group, Yarbrough is involved in the legal case against the base as well. MESS attorneys are currently appealing the case based in part on several recent court decisions that have run counter to—and even explicitly criticized—the 1986 McClellan district court verdict. Yarbrough stresses that with so much contamination at the base, the bulk of the cleanup effort still lies ahead, but, remembering the base's tactics in the mid-1980s, he sighs heavily. "Those early days were horrible."

Eventually, though, Ierardi says, the years of confrontation between McClellan and local residents like Yarbrough led to changes at the base. He proudly cites the fact that the Air Force now regularly describes McClellan as its most environmentally farsighted installation. Ierardi's coworker Paul Brunner explicitly credits the base's trial by fire for their current environmental resolve, noting, "Crisis forced change." Without the "McClellan Experience," Brunner says, "the needed radical change probably would not have occurred."

Today McClellan boasts numerous examples of their new environmental thinking. The base was the first Air Force installation to develop an environmental management program (in 1985) and to allow the program to have a say on a wide variety of decisions, including procurement and planning. Today the environmental team advises other departments of the environmental consequences of proposed actions.

McClellan officials have also cut the base's output of hazardous wastes by many tons per year over the past several years. Ierardi says that slowly but surely McClellan personnel have also awakened to the fact that properly disposing of products like batteries or cans of spray paint can cost up to ten times as much as purchasing them in the first place. In the autumn of 1990, McClellan even became the first base in the country to switch to JP-8, a cleaner-burning jet fuel that produces less smog.

Activities like these have won the base numerous awards, many of them well deserved. Unfortunately, as Ierardi readily admits, the base's new enlightened attitude about the environment has come too late to alter the realities of its existing toxic legacy. For all their efforts to date, no one knows how long it will take or what it will cost to restore McClellan's natural resources. Paul Brunner talks in terms of decades and billions of dollars, and Ierardi agrees. Official estimates now begin, in fact, at $3 billion to clean up the base; McClellan's top-ranking environmental official, Colonel Findley, said recently that the total cleanup cost will likely top $10 billion.

"Costs are coming due on our past waste practices—the principle and years' worth of compounded interest," Ierardi contends. "Our problem took forty years to create," he adds quietly. "I hate to tell you this, but it's probably going to take that long to clean it up."

Ierardi explains why the job is such a big one: "We've got several billion yards of contaminated soil up to a depth of 100 feet. One of the deepest contaminated wells we have even shows contamination down to a depth of 400 feet." Meanwhile, he says, pointing his index finger downward in an animated gesture, "there are 10 billion gallons of water down there—enough to serve Sacramento's needs entirely for years. And you've got to remember, McClellan is out west. Water is gold."

At McClellan, even the scale of the problem may be dwarfed by its complexity. Decades after the dumping of a formidable variety of dangerous chemicals, the job of redressing the extreme levels of contamination found at McClellan requires Ierardi's team to operate in nearly uncharted territory. Cleanup technologies and procedures have rarely been tried on a scale like the one required here. California's strict environmental regulations limit the decontamination methods that can be used and permit few options for the legal disposal of toxic residues generated in the cleanup process. And despite Ierardi's best efforts, much still is not known about the existence and movement of contaminants underground. In many ways, Ierardi says, "the situation is like a moving target."

First, he says, "it's easy to miss things"—a prospect he admits has given him nightmares. "I can't say I know everything that happened here over the past fifty years. There are few records to help. But I'm out there trying to find out."

Even more important, though, are the intense difficulties involved in every step toward redressing the base's contamination. For instance, he points out, monitoring wells can actually exacerbate a groundwater problem. To monitor levels of contaminants, workers must drill holes deep into the ground; but if the wells are not constructed correctly, such drilling can facilitate the migration of contaminants even deeper into the ground.

Ierardi says that this frightening prospect may have already occurred at McClellan. "We learned," he says, "that until recently we hadn't been screening the wells right. At the time we didn't understand how to do it properly."

* * *

Exiting Ierardi's cool office into the heat of a sunny August day, our small delegation heads east across the base toward McClellan's environmental crown jewel—its new, multimillion-dollar water treatment facility.

The tour is led by Doug MacKenzie, a ruddy young environmental engineer who personally oversaw the construction of the treatment facility. En route MacKenzie points out the remains of a former electroplating facility. Work here ceased in 1980, but the building remained so contaminated that its very existence violated California's environmental laws. For decades at this site toxic byproducts from electroplating had flowed into the ground through trenches dug in the floor. They had also seeped into the foundation of the building itself.

All that remains to be seen here is an empty lot dotted with a small collection of doghouse-sized structures that cast little square shadows beneath the strong California sun. MacKenzie explains that the structures are part of a cleanup design that physically caps the foundation of the razed building. The foundation, he says, was too dangerous and costly to remove.

The removal of the building itself was an expensive and taxing job. In 1986 and 1987, decontamination crews with impermeable moonsuits and oxygen tanks had to seal the building, cover all openings, and dismantle the entire place from the inside out. All material from the job was carted in special trucks to a licensed hazardous materials landfill.

Ierardi says the story of the electroplating building is a good example of McClellan's former failure to count environmental costs. The old electroplating facility cost $500,000 to build in 1957, he says, but it cost roughly $3 million to take down. And even that cost removed only the building—not the contaminants that have now seeped deep below ground.

Several hundred yards beyond the electroplating complex, McClellan's water treatment facility rises from the installation's dry and dusty expanse. Its densely packed industrial tanks, incinerators, and other machines spread over nearly an acre. As MacKenzie explains, this "pump and treat" facility is one of the first of its size and type in the entire country. Its design and construction required the concerted effort of a specialized outside environmental engineering firm working with McClellan's environmental staff for more than two years.

Dwarfed by the treatment facility's huge components, MacKenzie proudly spouts its vital statistics: 200 gallons of McClellan's polluted groundwater are pumped here every minute from more than one hundred feet below ground. When it comes out of the facility, he says, the water should be clean enough to drink. Plus, he notes with obvious satisfaction, the effort even won an award from the Sierra Club.

MacKenzie yells above the din as he walks alongside the process to explain its workings. First, he begins, the water pumped to the facility is heated and sent into an "air stripper" unit—a large, cylindrical structure several stories tall that looks like a vast grain silo. Inside, air is blown through the heated water at a high velocity to remove the volatile organic compounds. These compounds—now in the form of gases—are sent into an incinerator that reaches temperatures of 1,800 degrees Fahrenheit. At such high temperatures, the hazardous gases break down into constituent chemicals such as carbon dioxide and hydrochloric acid. The acid is sent to a "scrubber," or air-filtering unit, where it is "neutralized," or turned into a combination of water and common salt before being vented through a smokestack.

Following another set of pipes, MacKenzie explains that the ground-water—now cleaned of the bulk of its volatile organic compounds—is sent to a biological treatment unit, where a special film absorbs further contaminants. From here the water travels through a set of six large charcoal filters to remove other organic compounds and trace metals like lead. Finally, the water is pumped back into the ground. Should anything go wrong, MacKenzie adds, the whole area is surrounded by a plastic-lined moat.

Ierardi says that this plant alone cost the Air Force $8 million and will carry a yearly price tag of close to $1 million to operate. To date ground-water is being pumped here from only two of McClellan's numerous contaminated areas, but in the future the facility may treat water from other parts of the base as well. Unless new technology is developed that is cheaper or more effective, the Air Force anticipates that this facility will run constantly for decades to come. So far it is working well; the treated water is tested weekly and is reportedly free of elevated levels of contaminants. The incoming groundwater, however, continues to contain high levels of pollutants.

Understandably, Ierardi, MacKenzie, and other Air Force officials at McClellan take great pride in their water treatment facility—the first of its kind the U.S. military has commissioned. Their sense of accomplishment, though, may well be exceeded by that expressed by their higher-ups in Washington. Air Force documents, articles, and speeches point repeatedly to the water treatment project at McClellan as tangible evidence of the Air Force's commitment to clean up its environmental problems. A glossy full-color brochure about the project concludes that "the

Air Force has learned the importance of environmental management and is proud to be a leader in its implementation in the industrial world."

In an even more extravagant effort, the Air Force recently sent a special mailing to every member of Congress. The cover letter from Gary Vest, the Air Force's top environmental official, explains that the information enclosed is intended to apprise the members of the Air Force's "accomplishments in the environmental field." Featuring McClellan's water treatment complex among other projects, the mailing spares no opportunity to promote Air Force environmental efforts. "We are part of the Earth and it is part of us," the material gushes. "Air Force people are making the Earth a better place. They are being responsible environmental stewards."

Standing before the noisy industrial maze of pipes and tanks, though, the Air Force's excessively positive message about the facility is undercut by the plant's very size and complexity. Faced with the scale of this technological tangle, it is hard to imagine that it won't have more of a sizeable impact on the base's environmental problems; unfortunately, the hundreds of thousands of gallons of groundwater pumped through here daily literally constitute only one clean drop in the vast sea of McClellan's woeful heritage of water pollution. And even over the course of decades, under the most favorable of circumstances, this facility will treat only a small piece of the base's overall contamination problem—the billions of cubic yards of contaminated soil, for instance, will still remain.

In this context, the Air Force's glowing hyperbole about the project rings hollow. The scene is captured better in a comment Ierardi made earlier in the day. "It doesn't take much to cause an environmental problem," he said, shaking his head. "But it takes a whole lot to fix one."

Hanford, Washington: "Sacrifice Zone"

On a spring day in 1989, John Burnham stepped up to the podium in the spacious Olympic Room of the Seattle Convention Center. Burnham, an energetic retiree from the nuclear industry, relished his chance at the microphone—a chance made possible by a group of environmental scientists at the University of Washington who had organized an unusual two-day symposium. Gathered before him were participants from virtually all the parties involved in the environmental debacle at the Hanford Nuclear Reservation, representing such diverse constituencies as the federal bureaucracy, the academic scientific community, the nuclear industry, and affected neighbors of the troubled nuclear installation.

Burnham was vice president of the Tri-Cities Development and Economic Council, which served the now overlapping cities of Richland, Pasco, and Kennewick, bordering the Hanford installation. He had been a longtime supporter of the U.S. military's nuclear program. He had worked at Hanford for three decades and had raised a family in the area.

Burnham's efforts to keep the nuclear reservation alive had been assiduous, but he must have long seen the tide run against him. Hanford's current fate was foreshadowed as early as the 1960s, a decade during which six of its nine nuclear production reactors were permanently shut down. By 1989 all of the installation's hulking nuclear reactors had been closed, but their toxic and radioactive byproducts, and those from the vast processing plants nearby, all remained.

"We heartily support ongoing DOE [Department of Energy] missions," Burnham said, speaking for the Hanford-area commerce organization. "Furthermore, we believe that there is a correlation between the level of operations and the level of cleanup at the facility. What we are worried about—we don't really like to talk about it—is that a shutdown in activities at Hanford will cause a default by DOE on its cleanup obligations."

The audience was silent. To be sure, the concern Burnham was expressing was not new. Years earlier, government officials in the military and the Department of Energy had broached the possibility of "national sacrifice zones"—areas of the country where environmental contamination could prove too costly and remote from human contact to merit restoration. It was known that byproducts from Hanford's processing plants, like the unstable radioactive isotope iodine-129, present a hazard to human health that will linger for more than a million years. As antinuclear activists often and quite nearly accurately assert, "plutonium is forever."

Rarely, however, had a prominent member of the Hanford area's business community publicly discussed the possibility that the nuclear reservation's toxic and radioactive legacy might simply be abandoned by the government. The conference's participants differed widely on many points about Hanford's future; but most agreed that Burnham's ruminations were a grim indicator of Hanford's precarious and deteriorating situation.

The Hanford Nuclear Reservation, in the southeastern corner of Washington State, was established in 1943 as a top-secret installation to manufacture material for the Manhattan Project's atomic bomb. Almost overnight, the U.S. government relocated two rural communities of a few hundred homesteaders and imported some 20,000 employees from around the country—virtually none of whom had an inkling of the project's overall mission. Laboring at a furious pace at this sagebrush desert reservation half the size of Rhode Island, these workers soon produced the world's first significant quantities of plutonium—the earthshattering and deadly ingredient used in the bomb the United States dropped on Nagasaki, Japan.

Today, nearly fifty years since it opened, Hanford represents one of the most daunting environmental catastrophes the world has ever known. The Hanford installation, like the rest of the United States' nuclear production complex, is run by the Department of Energy—not by the Pentagon—an outgrowth of U.S. efforts at the dawn of the atomic age to place nuclear weapons technology squarely under civilian control. The Department of Energy, in fact, is a direct descendant of the Atomic Energy Commission that oversaw the Manhattan Project *and* Hanford's construction. From the start, Hanford has had an unmistakably military mission; any account of the military's environmental legacy would be lacking without full consideration of the nuclear weapons production complex.

Seventeen major facilities make up the core of the United States' fifty-year effort to amass its huge nuclear arsenal. At these large secret installations, nuclear material has been produced and processed, weapons have been built and tested. Some of the facilities—like the weapons laboratories Los Alamos in New Mexico and Lawrence Livermore in California—specialize in research and engineering. Others, like Hanford, supply the plutonium or enriched uranium—the materials that fuel the weapons' devastating explosive power. Today all of the government's nuclear facilities are polluted—possibly beyond repair. Many of these facilities have been forced shut due to the environmental dangers they present. But none matches the scale of the problems at Hanford.

In an unparalleled environmental nightmare, at least 750,000 gallons of deadly, high-level radioactive waste are believed to have leaked from Hanford's underground storage-tank "farm" over the past few decades. These liquid wastes, byproducts of the process of splitting uranium atoms to make plutonium, are among the world's most dangerous and highly radioactive substances. Within the first decade of Hanford's operation alone, installation officials also knowingly released nearly half a million curies of airborne radioactive particles—secretly exposing more than 10,000 residents to dangerous levels of radiation. By comparison, the well-known 1979 accident at the Three Mile Island nuclear reactor in Harrisburg, Pennsylvania, released less than thirty curies.

Burnham, like most Hanford-area residents, says he wants the government to clean up the nuclear facility. But, as a representative of the region's business community, he is intensely concerned about the economic effects on the community if the government were to clean up—and formally close down—the installation. "If everyone is working on cleanup, you're working your way right out of a job," he said. "It's like digging your own grave—what do you do for an encore?"

To his credit, Burnham's speech broadly outlined his preferred solution to Hanford's current quandary. "We're interested in seeing a center for waste management in the Tri-Cities—to build expertise in both radioactive and hazardous waste handling and disposal." He looked up from his prepared text. "After all, we have plenty over there to practice on."

* * *

The mighty Columbia River carves its way through the Cascade Mountains of the northwestern United States, dividing Washington and Oregon. Standing on its bank, one cannot help but feel humbled. Every day the Columbia irrigates 7 million acres of land and delivers a steady surge of electricity to the entire region, as well as to parts of Los Angeles, nearly 1,000 miles away. But even such impressive facts cannot convey the overwhelming scale of the river set against the open, untamed countryside that surrounds it.

U.S. military planners chose the location for Hanford largely because of its proximity to the Columbia River. To produce material for their nuclear weapons, they needed a huge and steady source of cold fresh water to cool the reactors. They also needed large amounts of electricity, which the river also provided. In 1942, just a year before the Hanford program was initiated, the Grand Coulee Dam was completed 100 miles north of the site—one of the largest hydroelectric projects of its kind ever built.

At lunchtime on a hot and dry Wednesday prior to Burnham's speech, about a hundred Tri-Cities residents stood scattered on a bluff overlooking a gravel-strewn dock along the edge of the Columbia, not far from Hanford's main gate. The bystanders, including some newspaper reporters and camera crews from the local television news, awaited the arrival of a barge bringing a large shipment of low-level nuclear waste to be buried at Hanford. The well-publicized shipment contained an entire reactor core discarded from a nuclear power plant in Pennsylvania, which had recently been dismantled and floated some 8,000 miles (through the Panama Canal and up along the West Coast) to be dumped at Hanford.

Notably, especially in an era of heightened local environmental activism, the crowd had not gathered to protest the shipment but to welcome it. Among the onlookers, Marilyn Druby, a Tri-Cities native and a public affairs officer for the Westinghouse Corporation, explained the impromptu welcoming committee. "We're a very gung-ho area," she said. "You see the wide open spaces here. Hanford's big. There's plenty of room for one more shipment here. And Hanford's been a good neighbor."

It is understandable that Tri-Cities inhabitants take pride in the reservation where so many of them work. Around here, just about everybody or their parents or grandparents was involved in the major war effort that the Hanford Reservation initially represented. But driving down Richland's Proton Avenue or past Pasco's Atomic Foods and the nearby Atomic Laundry, it is also easy to see why outsiders call the place "nuclear city," and often claim that the area has taken it all too far.

Revelations in recent years of radioactive releases from Hanford have been disturbing to many in the area. To date, however, they have made little dent in the allegiance the local population demonstrates for the nuclear reservation.

In 1988, for instance, a group of students at Richland High School formally proposed that the school change its emblem—a mushroom cloud emblazoned on the helmets of the football team, depicted in the floor tiles of the school's entrance, and painted billboard-size at the end of their home playing field. The students argued that it was inappropriate for the school's emblem to glorify nuclear weapons. Some teachers agreed, noting that the insignia had caused particular embarrassment several years before when a group of Japanese students had visited their school. After a bitter battle that engaged teachers, parents, and alumni, however, the students' proposal was overwhelmingly rejected, and the mushroom cloud remains today.

Meanwhile, new findings continue to surface that Hanford officials covered up releases of radioactivity that seriously threatened the health of the installation's workers and neighbors. In one of the most dramatic cases, documents released in 1986, after a court battle, show that Hanford officials knowingly and purposefully released enormous amounts of radiation into the air without warning or notifying anyone in the area.

In the aftermath of the national press coverage of the releases, a special independent panel was established by the Energy Department in 1988. After panel members reviewed a total of nearly 60,000 pages of documents from Hanford, most of which were previously classified, specialists concluded that the most dangerous airborne releases occurred between 1944 and 1947, when Hanford officials knowingly allowed some 400,000 curies of radioactive iodine-131 to spew into the atmosphere.

The 1940s releases, the largest known to date, took place during the reprocessing of uranium, when radioactive fuel rods were dissolved in acid to extract plutonium for use in nuclear weapons. Although the process continued at Hanford for decades, subsequent changes in the technology and filtration systems used prevented further releases of similar magnitude.

Using a combination of investigative and statistical techniques, the panel's experts studied the releases to reconstruct the dose received by people in the area. Although iodine-131 decays to harmless levels within a few months, the panel determined that it would have been consumed by residents in milk from cows that grazed on contaminated grasses in the vicinity of the Hanford installation. According to the panel's findings, over this three-year period roughly 5 percent of the 270,000 residents living in the vicinity accumulated doses of radiation in excess of 33 rads.

Much of the radioactive iodine-131 consumed by people in the area affected their thyroid glands, because the thyroid is an organ that needs iodine to function. When radioactive iodine-131 is absorbed and deposited in the thyroid, however, it irradiates the organ and surrounding tissue, possibly leading to thyroid cancer. The panel's experts estimated that some small portion of the area's infants and children accumulated doses of radiation to their thyroid glands as high as 2,500 rads during the same three-year period.

To put these figures in context, the current level of airborne radiation considered safe by the U.S. government for civilians living near nuclear facilities is 0.025 rads per year. Workers in nuclear power plants in the United States are limited to 5 rads exposure per year to their entire bodies. In addition, some studies show that the absorption of even the tiniest amounts of radiation by the thyroid gland can raise the risk of thyroid cancer. All told, the Energy Department has now officially acknowledged the panel's assessment that more than 13,000 people living near the Hanford Nuclear Reservation received "significant" doses of radiation as a result of these secret airborne emissions alone.

Jack Geiger, medical professor at the City University of New York Medical School, studied Hanford's contamination as part of a task force on the matter assembled by the national organization Physicians for Social Responsibility. Geiger says that Hanford's airborne releases "were not made out of ignorance." As he explains, "You don't have to be scientifically sophisticated to understand that 400,000 curies might be dangerous." Rather, he says, "the exposures were the result of policy decisions that gave nuclear weapons production, at any cost, priority over the lives of the citizens whom the bombs were supposed to protect."

Geiger and many others fault Hanford officials' "irresponsible" judgment at the time. But perhaps most unforgivable is the government's suppression of the information for four decades. Geiger goes so far as to say that the case compares unfavorably to that of the devastating nuclear releases at the Chernobyl plant in the Soviet Union. Chernobyl released more radioactivity, but as Geiger points out, its cover-up lasted a few weeks, while Hanford's went on for four decades. In addition, he says, "Chernobyl was an accident. Hanford was deliberate. Chernobyl was a singular event, the product of faulty reactor design and human error. Hanford was a chronic event, the product of obsessive secrecy and callous indifference to public health."

Inside the gates of the 560-square-mile Hanford Reservation, well past the guardhouse at the entrance nearest town, Bill Klink, a public relations official at the installation, reports that a specially trained police force here is armed with submachine guns and attack helicopters to protect against terrorists. The remark points up the grim seriousness of Hanford's business, but somehow too it seems a jarring and dissonant reminder amidst the quiet emptiness of the expanse of land at Hanford's center.

The day is hot. Klink stops at a tall bluff—one of only a few elevated vantage points in the entire reservation. In the distance, the discarded Pennsylvania reactor core can be seen creeping to its final resting place, hauled by a convoy of huge trucks. Otherwise the view is serene, filled with scrubby, grey-green flatland—miles and miles of it.

In the spring of 1989, Washington's governor, Booth Gardner, and officials from the Department of Energy signed a landmark cleanup agreement for Hanford. The agreement is laudable in its intent, but if it did anything it dramatized for the world the extent of Hanford's environmental woes. The cost of the thirty-year cleanup program is estimated at a staggering $57 billion. This enormous sum reflects the amount of waste involved—an estimated 30 million cubic feet of nuclear waste and perhaps as much as 100 times that amount of contaminated soil. Some 200 billion gallons of radioactive wastewater are estimated to have been poured into the ground here, creating a plume of radioactive groundwater that stretches at least six miles to the Columbia River. Already, levels of highly radioactive strontium-90 have been found to contaminate the massive river at levels 500 times federal standards. From my perch surveying the vast, open scene, the facts and figures weigh heavily, but seem incomprehensible, otherworldly.

During the 1940s, the team at Hanford initially built three plutonium production reactors, three chemical processing plants, sixty-four underground storage tanks, and a complete town with 4,000 new homes. The government spent some $350 million on the entire effort. Restoring this facility today, if it is actually undertaken, will cost taxpayers roughly 100 times the price of the installation's initial construction, even accounting for future inflation.

Despite the cleanup agreement with Washington State, it is unclear whether Congress will apportion the full amount over the coming decades; the sum dwarfs that requested for almost any other single project. The price tag to clean this one remote location is almost double the U.S. government's annual expenditure for public education, more than three times greater than the entire Energy Department's yearly budget. The Bush administration did not inspire confidence in this regard when it announced in early 1991 that the year's appropriation would fall more than 25 percent short of the amount the Energy Department said it needed to begin to clean up the nuclear weapons complex. Particularly disturbing about the Bush administration shortfall is the fact that the Energy Department projects its annual cleanup budget to increase substantially in coming years.

Even aside from the astronomical costs involved, though, much of Hanford's cleanup effort remains plagued by organizational and technical problems. The Office of Technology Assessment (OTA), a research arm of Congress, issued a report in February 1991 that sharply criticized the Energy Department's overall cleanup effort. The plan, OTA contends, "is being hampered by a paucity of data and qualified personnel, lack of ready technical solutions, and public skepticism." The report concludes that "the effective cleanup of the nuclear weapons complex in the next several decades is unlikely unless aggressive policy initiatives are taken."

Seven more miles into the reservation, Klink stops near Hanford's underground tank farm. Here, above ground, lie row upon row of thousands of black drums of transuranic waste, long-lived but slightly less radioactive than the high-level waste material in the tanks below. Sadly, even this seemingly endless array of drums gives little hint of the threat and scale of the underground tanks' contents. Only four places in the United States hold such deadly high-level liquid waste. Of them, this is by far the largest.

Ironically, Hanford's tank farm was intended to provide only temporary storage for the highly radioactive liquid wastes generated from the processing of plutonium. In the nuclear weapons program's early years, no one was quite sure what to do with the unwanted fragments of uranium left from the manufacturing process. As plutonium is produced, these fragments become radioactive isotopes, unstable elements such as cesium-137, strontium-90, and iodine-129. These byproducts emit large amounts of radiation as they try to regain a more stable form. Forty years after the government began to dump these wastes in Hanford's tanks, however, no permanent solution has been found to the disposal problem they pose.

The Energy Department began to build one-million-gallon double-shell tanks below ground starting in the 1970s. The agency acknowledges today that nearly half of the 149 single-shell tanks built prior to this time have breached. The tanks' leaks represent a piece of the cleanup quandary that remains unresolved. The entire area surrounding the underground tank farm is devastated and dangerous, and the single-shell tanks themselves are still filled with corroding, highly radioactive sediment. Even if the leaching wastes could be contained, no permanent dumpsite yet exists for high-level nuclear waste.

Of all the travesties that have recently come to light about the handling of radioactive materials at the Energy Department's facilities around the country, Hanford's underground tanks may be the most egregious, but they have much competition. At the Savannah River Plant in South Carolina, some 30 million gallons of radioactive liquids were dumped into the ground every year until recently. At this facility, strontium-90—a known carcinogen—has been found in surface water at levels 43,000 times above federal government drinking-water standards. Drinking water in Atlanta, Georgia, is also threatened by the Savannah River site.

To name just a few other examples: Cincinnati's water supply is known to be contaminated by leaching uranium from the Feeds Materials Production Center in Fernald, Ohio; plutonium, one of the most carcinogenic substances ever created, has been dispersed by the Rocky Flats Plant over broad areas and water reservoirs near the Denver metropolitan area; at the Idaho National Engineering Laboratory, some 16 billion gallons of waste water containing 70,000 curies of radioactivity are reported to have been dumped into the Snake River aquifer between 1952 and 1970, through injection wells.

At Hanford, though, the problem has recently taken a new and ominous twist. DOE officials now think that gases trapped within some of the millions of gallons of highly radioactive wastes stored in underground tanks at the facility could cause the tanks to explode, spewing large quantities of airborne radioactive particles throughout the region. Government documents unearthed by Congress show that Energy Department contractors knew of the existence of flammable hydrogen gas in at least one tank at Hanford for thirteen years, but did not notify higher authorities or attempt to remove the danger until the spring of 1990.

A special advisory committee on nuclear facility safety, chaired by John F. Ahearne, former head of the U.S. Nuclear Regulatory Commission, described the potentially exploding tanks as constituting "a serious situation, if not an imminent hazard." The consequences of such an explosion at Hanford's tank farm, the committee said, could be grave, owing to "the magnitude of the radioactive inventory available for dispersal."

The problem at Hanford is that a crystalized crust has developed on top of the liquid waste in some of the storage tanks. The crust, which can be as much as two or three feet thick, is believed to have been caused by chemicals that were added in the late 1950s and 1960s to newly produced liquid wastes at Hanford in order to reduce their volume. Hydrogen gas, which is known to build up in the liquid wastes, is now trapped underneath the hardened crust, and according to the report, could be detonated by heat generated inside the tanks or by a spark or shock from the outside. The chemical explosion would spread long-lived radioisotopes, including cesium-137 and strontium-90, into the surroundings.

It is not clear how imminent the danger of explosion actually is, but what is certain is that hydrogen trapped in some of the tanks frequently causes "tank belches," in which the tank's crust moves upwards, sometimes as much as a foot, as it vents the trapped gas. Senator John Glenn of Ohio, who chaired a Senate hearing on the problem in August 1990, released information documenting that at least three "major steam explosions" have already occurred at Hanford's tanks. One explosion, in 1965, lifted a tank six feet off its underground foundation and sent a geyser of radioactive steam fifty feet into the air.

Publicly, Energy Department officials have tried to allay local concerns about the tanks, but privately, inside sources say, they are "frantic" about the problem. Hanford officials have confirmed that at least one tank, known as 101-SY, has been declared off-limits to workers for over a year because of fears that activity could touch off an explosion. They say the tank belches hydrogen almost continuously.

Near the tank farm, Klink points out the spot where the Pennsylvania reactor core will soon be buried. A small plaque marks the spot as "trench number 14 218-W4C," and a metal chain ropes off the area, dotted with several small hanging yellow signs warning of radioactive surface contamination. Klink briefly explains the plans under consideration to clean up the tank farm, but his discussion is overshadowed by the fact that radioactive waste from around the country continues to be shipped here for permanent disposal.

For reasons of cost, technical complexity, and organizational incompetence, all signs point to the fact that Hanford's problems will never be effectively redressed. But if Hanford is to become a "sacrifice zone," few have yet said so publicly. "Hanford is not a dumpsite," Marilyn Druby had stressed firmly the day before, at the edge of the Columbia River. "It's a burial site." A wooden sign at the edge of the trench takes Druby's euphemism even further. Here the sign sprouting from the parched, dusty gravel terms the vast radioactive trenches the Hanford "burial garden."

CHAPTER ELEVEN

Between the Cracks

Lakehurst, Cornhusker, McClellan, and Hanford have much in common. In each case, the government agencies involved—the Navy, Army, Air Force, and Department of Energy, respectively—have struggled to come to grips with an enormous and frightening toxic heritage. All of these military agencies initially kept their problems hidden from the public—even from those endangered—and each was slow to start cleaning up the contamination that had been dumped over the course of decades. By now, however, all of the above installations have budgeted funds for cleanup and have assigned employees to address environmental matters on a full-time basis.

Regrettably, some pieces of the overall military environmental predicament lack such attention. The widespread contamination that plagues the U.S. military's formerly used lands in this country and its overseas bases has largely fallen through the bureaucratic cracks; the Pentagon has taken little action to address these problems. At the lands formerly used by the military, a disorganized and inept program has yet even to study most of the sites of suspected contamination, and with regard to its overseas bases, the Pentagon continues to cover up the problem at home and in the host countries involved.

From his office in Washington, D.C., Thomas Wash directs the military's program to clean up contamination at old and forgotten military dumpsites. Wash works for the Army Corps of Engineers, but through a bureaucratic fluke he oversees the cleanup of lands formerly used not just by the Army but also by the Navy and Air Force. (The Department of Energy has its own program.) Scattered around the United States at some 7,000 locations, these polluted sites under Wash's jurisdiction make an odd collection.

In Novato, California, outside of San Francisco, a polluted former Air Force base has languished since 1974, its chain-link fence warning away visitors. Cleanup lags despite the willingness of a large corporate firm to purchase the valuable land; the military cannot legally sell it because of its contamination. Near Boston, in Watertown, Massachusetts, another valuable lot, overgrown with grasses and weeds, sits along the Charles River, discarded by the Army but still technically owned by the federal government. Army workers dumped and burned toxic and radioactive wastes here for decades, but now the only visible remnant of the activities are the lingering yellow and black signs warning of radioactive contamination. The 15,000-acre former Weldon Spring Ordnance Plant outside of St. Louis, Missouri, is so badly contaminated with explosive compounds that it earns a spot on the Superfund National Priority List—one of a dozen former military sites included on the list to date.

Wash's program oversees cleanup at each of these sites; he was also called in when a stash of military wastes turned up recently in a mine shaft in Nevada and when beachgoers in 1988 discovered unexploded ordnance poking up through the eroding dunes on Martha's Vineyard. "We've got bombing ranges, training fields, ammunition plants," Wash says. "I think we're even responsible for cleaning up a former World War II–era internment camp."

The Pentagon, with its penchant for acronyms, calls the diverse assortment of polluted lands under Wash's purview FUDS—formerly used defense sites. Their prospects seem particularly grim. Relatively new to the job, Wash is a refreshingly candid and accessible official, but his comments do not auger well for the FUDS program. When asked about the severity of the contamination problems at the 7,000 lands he oversees, Wash says he simply doesn't know. "After all," he volunteers, "there are some 3,000 to 4,000 that we haven't really looked at yet."

Wash even professes ignorance of the status of the sites already surveyed. He cannot say, for instance, how many of the lands are owned privately and how many are still owned by the military or other governmental agencies, and he is not sure whether the figures are available. "We don't have good, effective data," he confides. "We're still trying to get our act together." By almost any measure the Army Corps' learning curve has been slow: the FUDS program is currently moving into its sixth year.

In fact, Wash goes so far as to say that he is "scared to death someone from Congress will come by and ask what we did with the $247 million we have received since we got this program started. I really couldn't tell them in any specific sense." The current cost estimates to complete the job also give Wash pause. The Pentagon has estimated that all these lands can be cleaned up for $2.7 billion, he says, adding plaintively, "Who knows if that's in the right ballpark?"

But while Wash is reluctant to commit himself to projections about what lies ahead, others outside the program have gone on record. A 1990 report from the Congressional Budget Office estimates that nearly half of the 7,000 FUDS properties are likely to require "large, costly cleanups of landfills, burial sites, and gasoline tank farms at former arsenals, ammunitions plants, and depots." Cleanup of another several hundred of these sites, according to the report, will necessitate the removal of unexploded ordnance and explosives manufacturing wastes. New information indicates, though, that buried explosives could be far more prevalent than previously imagined. Wash says that a new estimate from the Army Corps branch in Huntsville, Alabama, projects that as many as a thousand of the military's formerly used lands could be contaminated with unexploded bombs, including, in certain cases, unexploded chemical munitions.

What is clear, according to Pentagon figures, is that preliminary inspections have been completed at only 2,369 of these abandoned lands as of 1991. Of these, roughly two thirds—some 1,500—have been found to be eligible for inclusion in the FUDS program: the military had direct control of these sites at one time and may have contributed to contamination problems. More than three quarters of these polluted lands have been found to require some kind of cleanup action—a total cleanup docket approaching 1,300 so far. Meanwhile, the Army Corps of Engineers has completed only 108 such "remedial actions" to date—many of which have been relatively minor projects to haul away drums, tanks, or small quantities of contaminated soil.

Whatever the program's problems, Wash explains, they are not a question of money. In a recent internal presentation, he termed the FUDS program "dollar rich, plan poor": its annual funding has grown rapidly, jumping by nearly 50 percent in each of the past two years, but until this year, the Army Corps has been unable to spend the money allotted to it. Instead, the FUDS program has returned unused funds to the parent Defense Environmental Restoration Program (DERP) annually, despite the extent of the problem that lies ahead. Complicating matters further, Wash says, the Army Corps often operates "in the dark." It frequently lacks access to information about past practices at sites used by Navy or Air Force personnel. Often little or no documentation about such practices even exists.

Given their unimpressive track record in environmental cleanup, one cannot help but wonder how the Army Corps ever got saddled with responsibility for all the formerly used lands in the first place. Longtime employee Noel Urban explains that the Army had a head start over the other services on environmental cleanup in the mid-1970s, establishing a small "installation restoration program." The Army Corps also had some experience cleaning the residue from military activities in Alaska in the early 1980s. In its official report on the Alaskan cleanup—much of which involved simply gathering together discarded radar equipment left in remote areas of the Alaskan wilderness—Army Corps personnel drafted what Urban calls a "broad overview" document, one that established criteria for how to undertake the cleanup efforts. It was this general language about the project, he says, that caught the eye of key Pentagon officials.

Soon thereafter, with the passage of the Superfund Amendments and Reauthorization Act (SARA) in 1986, Congress ordered the military to address its contamination problems through a centralized program. With little expertise and few options, Pentagon officials determined that the Army Corps was the military agency best prepared to handle pollution at formerly owned sites. The officials presumably weighed the Army Corps' construction experience building bridges and dams for over a century, and the fact that the Corps had bought and sold real estate for the Army and the Air Force for decades. It was a matter, Wash quips, of "being at the wrong place at the wrong time."

The Army Corps' FUDS program may suffer from neglect and mismanagement, but the military's 395 overseas bases have no integrated program at all. The foreign bases receive a hefty portion of the annual defense budget and represent a key component of the U.S. military's efforts to project force around the world. The Pentagon estimates, for example, that approximately one quarter of all active-duty personnel are currently stationed outside of the United States. And yet the environmental status of these installations overseas largely remains secret. There is little reason to imagine that their contamination problems differ substantially from those at U.S. bases at home. But under the guise of national security concerns, the Pentagon has failed so far to disclose even aggregate data about environmental contamination at its bases overseas.

Several years ago, an inspection team from the Defense Department's Office of the Inspector General conducted a worldwide investigation of U.S. military environmental problems, visiting thirty-three facilities in Hawaii, Guam, and seven foreign countries. The team's 1986 official report offered a scathing overview but few details. It concluded that the United States was not in compliance with environmental laws and regulations at home or abroad and that management of hazardous wastes was ineffective.

"The Department of Defense overall management of hazardous materials/hazardous waste is unsatisfactory," the Inspector General's report stated. "Policy, guidance, and technical implementation are fragmented, conflicting, and almost nonexistent at installation level. Communication . . . is generally poor."

Even with such harsh criticism from a branch of the Pentagon itself, however, the department has still not established a program to manage overseas cleanup. No funds are specifically earmarked for the purpose. The Defense Environmental Restoration Program, which underwrites the military's cleanup at home, including the military's formerly used lands, does not cover overseas bases.

Technically, U.S. foreign military bases have been required to adhere to at least "host country" environmental laws ever since 1978, when President Jimmy Carter signed Executive Order 12088, explicitly applying domestic environmental laws to governmental agencies. As Barbara Blum, former deputy administrator of the EPA in the Carter administration, has explained, the intent of the directive "was simple and straight: all federal installations, not just the ones at home" are subject to the nation's environmental laws.

But because the Pentagon has frequently held that its foreign bases must obey only the laws of the host country and not those of the United States, little protection is afforded against the heavy usage of toxic materials by the U.S. military. Especially in some Asian and Third World countries, existing environmental laws are often extremely lax or even nonexistent. With scant oversight from the Pentagon, few inspections, internal or by outside agencies, and virtually no public scrutiny, the environmental situation is grim for many such bases. The excessive secrecy surrounding the Pentagon's handling of environmental matters at its outposts abroad hinders its incentive to adhere to the law—or to clean up past contamination.

In 1986, the year of the Pentagon Inspector General's report, the GAO undertook the first detailed nonmilitary investigation of contamination at overseas bases. GAO officials visited thirteen military installations in seven countries. Upon completion, however, the GAO report's information was classified as a state secret by the Pentagon and thereby withheld from public scrutiny. Until recently, a similar fate befell a more recent 1990 GAO study.

At the congressional hearing in 1987, Representative Mike Synar confronted Carl Schafer, the head of the Pentagon's environmental program, about the secrecy surrounding the initial GAO study. Synar noted the far-reaching critique levied by the Pentagon's Inspector General and asked why the Pentagon had classified the more detailed GAO report.

"The reasons for classifying reports," Schafer responded, "are generally based upon the judgment that release of the totality of the information would jeopardize our relationships and especially our programs. The data individually is not all that outstanding." Unsatisfied with such bureaucratic jargon, Synar questioned whether the information was withheld for national security reasons or not. Under this additional questioning Schafer testified that the report had indeed been "classified because of national security interests." Synar continues to question this justification, however, viewing the Pentagon's decision as one designed merely to avoid embarrassment, not to protect legitimate security interests.

As Synar pointed out at the hearing, by law federal agencies are required to respond to the recommendations made by such reports. Synar asked whether the Pentagon had in fact responded. "I believe we have," Schafer said. "If I might add, sir, the substantial findings in that GAO study have been corrected."

"You mean I have to take your word for that?" Synar asked.

"Trust me," Schafer said.

"Oh, trust you," Synar retorted. "You all have such a good record in this area."

Despite the Pentagon's efforts at secrecy, the overseas environmental situation presents a problem that is simply too large to conceal completely. Under pressure from the U.S. press and from some host nations, a picture of the situation has begun to emerge. According to the *Los Angeles Times*, for example, the U.S. Air Force admits to having polluted soil and groundwater at every one of its airfields in Europe. The Air Force's Gary

Vest said in a separate interview that the Air Force expects to find between 10 and 20 contaminated sites at each of its foreign installations.
And while the U.S. Army has yet to begin a formal investigation of contamination abroad, it has already identified more than 350 contaminated
sites in Germany alone.

More details have recently begun to surface. Germany, which is home
to the lion's share of U.S. military overseas bases—more than 200 in all—
has, not surprisingly, been particularly concerned about the matter. A
German newspaper reported in 1990 that twenty-six known Army sites
alone will require cleanups costing more than a million dollars each. In
just one example, at the Army's Mannheim base, TCE and other solvents
used for cleaning military vehicles have leached into the ground. German
authorities discovered the contaminants in the nearby town's water supply
during a routine drinking-water surveillance program. Cleanup costs for
this site alone are anticipated to exceed $10 million.

In another example, at the Rhein-Main Air Base, German authorities
discovered that 300,000 gallons of toxic jet fuel from the base had leaked
from underground piping into the major groundwater aquifer supplying
drinking water to the city of Frankfurt.

Perhaps the most detailed information of all, however, comes in reports
about the Pentagon's pollution at bases in U.S. trust territories. Because
of their special relationship to the United States, the Pentagon seems to
have been unable to suppress information about the plight of these bases.
On Guam, the self-governing U.S. territory in the Pacific, for instance,
U.S. bases take up half of the nation's real estate. An unclassified 1987
GAO report cites dozens of environmental violations on Guam's bases.
According to the report, workers and military personnel at eight separate
facilities at the island's Andersen Air Force Base have dumped toxic
chemicals into the ground and into storm drains, contaminating Guam's
principal aquifer—the source of drinking water for the majority of the
island's population.

Given the U.S military's record at home and mounting public evidence
from around the world, Guam's predicament is widely believed to offer
an early glimpse of the type of U.S. military contamination overseas that
is virtually certain to surface in numerous other locations as well.

In addition, some details about practices at foreign installations can be
surmised by comparison to domestic bases with similar functions. Clark
Air Force Base in the Philippines, for example, can be compared to large
domestic air bases; as the home base of the Thirteenth Air Force Division, the Third Tactical Fighter Wing, and units of the Pacific Air Forces,

Clark was a large base that conducted a good deal of aircraft repair and maintenance.

Oklahoma's Tinker Air Force Base—a major repair depot—offers a comparison. Tinker is known to produce more than seventy types of hazardous wastes, including a million gallons daily of contaminated wastewater. The facility's industrial wastewater treatment plant has been in violation of environmental permit standards since the day it was built in the 1960s. Pollution from Tinker has created an underground plume of contamination nearly half a square mile in area, requiring the closure of three drinking-water wells. Clark's Crow Valley Bombing and Gunnery Range can likewise be compared to domestic proving grounds that have been rendered unusable by unexploded ordnance and the toxic byproducts of military explosives.

After the eruption of the Mt. Pinatubo volcano in June 1991, the U.S. Air Force evacuated Clark Air Base permanently, leaving it under a foot of volcanic ash and soot. The current situation almost certainly precludes the possibility that the United States will ever redress the base's environmental legacy, leaving it to threaten the Filipino population for generations to come.

The Pentagon has recently announced that it will close two dozen facilities overseas and downscale activities at another eighty-five foreign installations. Further belt tightening in U.S. "force projection" is almost a certainty in the years to come. With the prospect of closing bases abroad, a troubling question emerges: when the U.S. armed forces relinquish pieces of their vast global real estate holdings, what environmental legacy will they leave behind in these host countries?

As things now stand, the Pentagon's position seems to be that it would rather not know. An internal memo to the assistant secretary of defense about the Air Force's environmental status in Germany highlights the dilemma. "The AF [Air Force] has been hesitant to identify and investigate sites because of the potential political ramifications," the memo states. "If they identify sites, do nothing, and the Germans find out, they have problems. If they don't do anything and the Germans identify [that] the pollution exists, they have problems."

Interestingly, despite the lack of oversight or an integrated Pentagon program, personnel at individual bases abroad have begun in earnest to request funds for pollution abatement. The Pentagon has not announced the fact, but it has come to light because the agency is required to file submission forms with the EPA outlining the cost of any proposed environmental abatement project. Compiling these hundreds of disparate funding requests, the EPA offers the astonishing fact that the Pentagon expects to quietly spend over a billion dollars in overseas cleanup efforts in fiscal year 1992 alone.

Meanwhile, late in 1990, in its 1991 Defense Authorization Act, Congress called upon the Department of Defense to develop and explain "a policy for determining applicable environmental compliance" at overseas military installations and to determine how much such compliance might cost. Already there are indications in many locations that the Pentagon is planning to try to foist the bulk of these costs upon host countries. As Mayor Hermann Weyel of Mannheim, Germany, predicts, "The bases in Germany will be cleaned up when the U.S. leaves, but it is increasingly clear that it will be the Germans who pay for it."

In many ways, it seems obvious that the U.S. military's current efforts to cover up the environmental debacle overseas will in the long run only bring the nation further political embarrassment and scorn in the international community. But the secrecy continues nevertheless.

In 1991, after a protracted fight, several U.S. reporters who appealed to the Pentagon under the Freedom of Information Act won access to the suppressed 1986 GAO report. But the report's release marked a hollow victory: the Pentagon released it only in a "sanitized" form. Echoing the language of the Pentagon's Office of the Inspector General, the tenor of the GAO report comes through, even in its expurgated edition.

"We identified actual or potential pollution," the report states, "resulting from the inadequate hazardous waste management practices followed at 11 of the 13 installations visited [in seven countries]. These included waste being dumped down drains, poured on the ground, and stored indefinitely . . ."

Sadly, though, much of the report's detail remains censored. In the sanitized public version, information on nearly every page has been carefully eliminated; even the names of the countries visited by GAO inspectors continue to be suppressed. Four pages at the heart of the report tell the whole story: here, where the GAO presumably outlines some of its specific findings, the contents have been excised in their entirety, the empty leaves marked only by the report's page numbers and, ironically, the word "unclassified," stamped routinely across the top and bottom prior to their release.

PART III
Facing the Future

CHAPTER TWELVE

The Pentagon Gets Religion

Early in September 1990, a crowd of 500 filled every seat at dozens of round tables in the ballroom of a large hotel near Washington, D.C. The scattered uniforms stood out at once; shoulders and lapels throughout the room gleamed a shiny gold beneath the ballroom chandeliers and gave tangible meaning to the term "top brass." Addressing the meeting was U.S. Secretary of Defense Dick Cheney.

"A decade ago," Cheney began, "it would have been difficult to imagine a gathering like this." The remark was more a statement of fact than opinion. The watershed gathering was the first ever to bring together top Pentagon officials, environmental activists, government regulators, and representatives from industry to discuss the military's environmental problems. Initiated by a branch of Cheney's office, the meeting was billed as the inauguration of the "Defense and the Environment Initiative."

"Defense and the environment is not an either/or proposition," Cheney told the crowd. "To choose between them is impossible in this real world of serious defense threats and genuine environmental concerns.

"The real choice is whether we are going to build a new environmental ethic into the daily business of defense—whether we will make good environmental actions a part of our working concerns, from planning to acquisitions to management."

Cheney could not have outlined the challenge before the military more clearly. But it is a challenge not easily met. Several months prior to Cheney's speech, the Defense Department's Office of the Inspector General, which answers directly to Cheney, had issued a new report on the Pentagon's environmental cleanup program. Its findings underscore just how far the department currently stands from the vision championed by Cheney. The report's summary offers a litany of failure: "lack of DOD directives to implement public law; lack of supplemental and detailing instructions for the DOD components; late funding, which caused programs to lag; poor relations with states and the EPA; poor information flow—up, down, and laterally; poor cooperation among DOD components, although they share the same problems; no program consistency among DOD components; inconsistent personnel practices among the components; inability to set consistent priorities for cleanup." The list faults almost every aspect of the military's cleanup program.

If anything, the failings outlined by the Inspector General make Cheney's plea for a new environmental consciousness all the more noteworthy. Achievable or not, Cheney's environmental agenda marks the first time in U.S. history that a secretary of defense has made the issue a priority. Until recently, such rhetoric itself was virtually unheard of within the military.

Cheney's environmental campaign had begun eleven months earlier, in October 1989, with the release of a landmark memorandum to the military departments under his dominion. Just five short paragraphs, the memo was unequivocal. "This administration wants the United States to be the world leader in addressing environmental problems," Cheney wrote, "and I want the Department of Defense to be the Federal leader in agency environmental compliance and protection."

Cheney, a former Republican representative to Congress from Wyoming, could never be characterized as an ardent environmentalist, but he grew up in Casper, Wyoming, in the foothills of the Rocky Mountains—as good a spot as one could find to nurture an appreciation of unspoiled wilderness. In addition to his congressional work in military intelligence, which earned him his current post, Cheney served on two subcommittees that addressed the concerns of his rural state, one overseeing the country's national parks and one with jurisdiction over public lands and water resources.

Whatever his environmental proclivities, Cheney has finally provided leadership within the Pentagon to confront the military's pollution problems. Largely because of his high-profile efforts, a change in attitude is emerging within the mammoth military bureaucracy. Officials at installations around the country commonly refer to the Cheney memo as proof of the Pentagon's newfound belief in environmental stewardship.

Nonetheless, Cheney's directive came only after much prompting. He issued the memo on the eve of the twentieth anniversary of Earth Day, against a backdrop that could only be construed as a fever pitch of national concern about environmental issues. One poll in the spring of 1989, for instance, showed that for the first time ever Americans ranked "global environmental problems" ahead of even the prospect of a nuclear war as the "top-priority threat" to U.S. security. The same year, Cheney and his staff had watched as forceful newspaper reports about the abysmal state of the government's nuclear production facilities prompted a public and governmental outcry that resulted in a virtual shutdown of the Department of Energy's nuclear production operations. Many officials undoubtedly feared that to some degree the same could happen to the Defense Department.

Cheney's memo itself reflected the public mood: "Federal facilities, including military bases, must meet environmental standards. Congress has repeatedly expressed a similar sentiment. As the largest Federal agency, the Department of Defense has a great responsibility to meet this challenge. It must be a command priority at all levels. We must demonstrate commitment with accountability for responding to the Nation's environmental agenda."

Congress and the public, in other words, demanded a change. Environmental laws had been on the books for more than a decade. The DOD's Office of the Inspector General had emphasized the problems for years. "The Department of Defense's overall management of hazardous materials/hazardous waste is unsatisfactory," it declared flatly in 1986. Even then, four years before Cheney's current campaign, the Pentagon's watchdog office had called for top-level leadership, warning that "the Department of Defense will never be able to achieve a proactive position [toward its environmental problems] without formalizing the structure, minimizing fragmentation of effort and by [sic] placing management in the hands of . . . the Secretary of Defense."

According to Cheney's office, the answer to all of this pressure from inside and outside the Pentagon is the Defense and the Environment Initiative. The fledgling program is supposed to chart an environmental strategy for the military, to reach out to patch up the military's environmental image, and, as one military document puts it, to "provide the foundation for increasing the environmental sensitivity of DOD's day-to-day operations."

In keeping with such an agenda, Cheney told the assembled generals, admirals, and assorted others at the inaugural meeting of the Defense and the Environment Initiative that he wanted them to "serve as the scouting party—to go before us, if you will, to find new areas for prevention and stewardship, and then, working with the entire department, help us move ahead. We don't want to leave any stragglers behind."

Unfortunately, though, the scouting party remains deeply divided about its role. Many of the military officers in attendance at the meeting were frustrated about environmental issues. They decried the difficulties posed by complicated regulations and lack of guidance, and expressed the belief that environmental matters conflict with their military missions. They even expressed fears about their personal liability for the environmental problems they might inherit at the bases they oversee.

The speaker who followed Cheney to the podium articulated the frustration. Admiral David E. Jeremiah, Vice-Chairman of the Joint Chiefs of Staff, second highest ranking military official in the country, pledged *pro-forma* support for military leadership on the environment, but he barely concealed his disdain for the event. For his part, the admiral managed to undercut almost everything Cheney had said.

"In many cases," Jeremiah asserted, the environment "is used as a screen to mask hidden political agendas"—agendas which, he said, could often be characterized as "anti-military." Environmental regulators must recognize the fact that war and its preparations are inherently destructive, Jeremiah told the audience; as a result, environmental programs must always take second place to fighting and winning in combat.

Only minutes earlier, Cheney had declared that the Pentagon's military mission "is no excuse for ignoring the environment. Nor is it something the department needs to abandon to be a leader in the environmental arena." But Admiral Jeremiah dissented; from his perspective, environmental demands were stifling and thwarting the military's mission. Obliquely likening environmental critics to Iraqi dictator Saddam Hussein, who had just recently taken American citizens hostage in Iraq, Jeremiah asserted, "We can't hold our program ransom to a few local demagogues."

The different positions on the environment expressed by Cheney and Jeremiah underscore a profound internal fight underway in the military.

Cheney seeks to impose what amounts to "new religion" upon the military's traditional treatment of the environment, but the change will not come easily. The most stubborn obstacles may be the most intangible. The new environmental program marks a steep increase in funds and personnel earmarked for environmental issues, but as Jeremiah's position suggests, the program has yet to win the hearts of the ranking military core.

One obstacle is generational. By the time Cheney finished his graduate studies at the end of the tumultuous 1960s, Jeremiah had been a commissioned officer since 1956, had served on five Pacific Fleet destroyers, and was already the executive officer of one. Unlike younger colleagues who grew up with Earth Day and the intensifying public preoccupation with environmental degradation, older career officers like Jeremiah rarely consider environmental restoration a priority. Environmental issues were never a significant part of their military training; overtly or covertly, many continue to view them as an overblown irritant.

There is a further gap between civilian and career-military sensibilities. Cheney, in his preeminent role as secretary of defense, is a civilian. Jeremiah, on the other hand, is a career military officer. The tension between civilians and military officials can be seen clearly at the installation level, where the majority of the in-house environmental workers are civilians. Some are environmental professionals, holding advanced engineering or managerial degrees. No matter what their level of expertise, nearly all of the jobs held by these workers focus explicitly on environmental cleanup and compliance—a fact which often pits them against their military counterparts, who are responsible for a variety of military activities that can conflict with environmental priorities.

Consider Jeremiah's own career. He worked his way to the top in the same way most of his fellow officers did, by performing military missions. He commanded a destroyer squadron and oversaw the capture of the Egyptian airliner carrying the hijackers who had seized the Italian cruise ship *Achille Lauro* in 1985. During operations in the Gulf of Sidra between January and March of 1986, Jeremiah directed an operation that sank two Libyan warships and destroyed an anti-aircraft missile site. At best, Jeremiah's action-oriented military record has little to do with environmental issues; the personal attributes historically favored in the combat arena can well be seen as antithetical to those required to promote and maintain environmental stewardship.

At the Defense and the Environment Initiative gathering, the distinction between military officers and their civilian counterparts within the armed forces was heightened by the unfolding geopolitical situation. The meeting was held early in September of 1990. Iraq had just recently invaded Kuwait and the United States had responded swiftly with Operation Desert Shield—a massive deployment of military hardware and soldiers. To many attending the meeting it did not seem right for a roomful of top military officers to sit around talking about the environment in the midst of a major military campaign.

In this context Cheney's presence was all the more significant. Civilian or not, within the rigid military hierarchy Cheney was the superior of the officers present. His attendance, taking time away from Operation Desert Shield, made an important statement about the priority he attached to the issue. The Persian Gulf conflict highlighted the military's vital primary mission, Cheney told the audience, but even the ongoing conflict did not mean the department could ignore its environmental responsibilities.

As one would expect, Cheney made an effort in his remarks to highlight the fruits borne of his commitment to the issue. The examples were carefully chosen, but they also indirectly showed the incipient program's severe limitations. Cheney spoke of "an integrated multimedia pollution prevention plan," developed at Langley Air Force Base in Virginia, that would serve as a model for other bases. Translating for his uniformed audience, Cheney quipped, "In military terms, I guess that would be a coordinated land-air-water assault on pollution." The analogy was dramatic, but it obscured the modest status of the effort so far: cleanup was actually underway at only two of Langley's thirty-six toxic sites and was complete at none.

Similarly, Cheney noted that Jacksonville Naval Air Station in Florida had won a prize for its recycling program, but he failed to mention the base's standing as a Superfund priority site or the lingering presence of many contaminants in the groundwater at the base. Trichloroethylene, for instance, had been found in the groundwater at one location on the Jacksonville installation in concentrations 30,000 times higher than acceptable levels.

Cheney repeatedly stressed that things were changing at the Pentagon. "This year alone we are spending over $600 million on cleanup efforts in the Department of Defense," he said. In a similar vein, Deputy Assistant Secretary of Defense (Environment) Thomas Baca—the military's new top environmental official—pointed out later in the morning that the military collectively employs some 5,000 people to work on environmental issues—a figure that he claimed rivaled the number of active environmental workers at the EPA. In fact, Baca termed the military's environmental program "probably the largest such effort in the world."

As grand as Cheney and Baca made the achievements sound, they must be judged within the context of the scale and complexity of the military infrastructure. With almost 5 million people and a budget approaching $300 billion annually, the Pentagon's environmental effort begins to look smaller by comparison. Cheney's dollar figure represents just two tenths of a percent of the Pentagon's overall budget; Baca's personnel figure similarly represents only one tenth of a percent of the Pentagon's total workforce.

The fact is, the U.S. military is so huge it could make almost anything seem small. The Pentagon receives nearly a quarter of all federal dollars and roughly two thirds of all federal allotments for research and development. The Pentagon also ranks among the nation's largest landholders, with jurisdiction over some 27 million acres in the United States—a total area five times larger than the state of Massachusetts. On these many acres sit nearly a half million buildings, scores of airports, seaports, factories, hospitals, and housing. As Pentagon officials frequently suggest, the numerous installations must be seen as comparable to small cities.

In combat all of the disparate forces within this military behemoth are organized through an elaborate, clearly defined hierarchy. Several so-called unified commands oversee and coordinate the interactions of all the branches. Such a technique, for instance, allowed Army General H. Norman Schwarzkopf to head up U.S. military operations in the Persian Gulf despite the fact that all the major armed services participated in the effort. In peacetime, though, less interservice organization can be found. Some interservice coordination is handled by a branch of the Pentagon called the Defense Logistics Agency, which purchases and transports equipment and supplies—and often deals with hazardous waste—on behalf of all the services.

Against this backdrop, then, the looming Persian Gulf War offered another, subtler lesson in contrasts. The conflict, halfway around the world from the United States, illustrated how effectively the Pentagon can synchronize its different forces. Even aside from the added complexity of allied military efforts, the Pentagon's daily planning for the Gulf War entailed thick computer printouts orchestrating the movements of a prodigious array of personnel and equipment. The precision and alacrity displayed by the military in the Gulf conflict, though, make the Pentagon's actions on environmental issues seem all the more inept by comparison.

Almost overnight the military had moved huge numbers of people to the scene, transported tanks and planes, built entire outposts, complete with runways, barracks, and kitchens that somehow managed to feed everyone involved. But in more than a decade its Environmental Restoration Program had only cleaned up some 400 toxic sites out of a festering pool of tens of thousands.

The Pentagon's ambivalence and disorganization on environmental issues surfaced even in the planning of the Defense and the Environmental Initiative meeting itself. The meeting's Pentagon sponsors originally announced that they hoped to invite 150 environmentalists, 150 Pentagon representatives, 150 government contractors, and 50 people from other government agencies. But the group, run out of the Office of the Secretary of Defense, had trouble setting a date. When a date was finally set, the organizers did little outreach and attracted few grass-roots registrants. About a week before the event the Pentagon realized that they had signed up pitifully few environmentalists—a fact that badly undercut the meeting's intended purpose.

At the last minute, staffers at the Denver-based Keystone Center, an organization that specializes in environmental dispute resolution, convinced military officials that they could attract a credible number of environmentalists from local groups concerned with military pollution if the Pentagon offered to pay airfare and expenses. Just days before the event Pentagon officials agreed, and with the frantic, eleventh-hour help of several environmental groups, they managed to recruit some forty environmental representatives from small local groups around the country to attend the meeting.

Given the late notice, however, the meeting's organizers claimed that the agenda for the meeting's plenary sessions was fixed and could accommodate no time for a representative of these local neighbors of military installations and victims of military pollution to present their views to the group at large. Despite the repeated requests of these local activists and the fact that several plenary sessions were planned during the two-day conference, the meeting's planners held firm, allowing the activists no forum other than the meeting's smaller, interactive workshops.

The planners' initial lack of organization and later inflexibility led to an unexpected outcome, however. As *Defense Cleanup*, a private industry trade journal later reported, "military jaws around the room dropped" when Ted Smith, an activist from the Silicon Valley Toxics Coalition rose immediately after Cheney's opening speech to present a seven-point "citizen's agenda" endorsed by virtually all of the environmental groups in attendance at the meeting.

Smith and fellow activist Rose Marie Augustine from Tucson, who also rose unannounced to speak, were eventually gaveled down by master of ceremonies Thomas Baca. His efforts received the hearty applause of the predominantly military crowd. But Smith did manage to list the groups' demands in Cheney's presence, including full disclosure of the Pentagon's environmental contamination, recognition of citizens' right to know about pollutants and practices that threaten their health and environment, an end to military claims of exemption from environmental laws, and increased funding for cleaning up the Pentagon's mess.

Before she was cut off, Augustine had begun a hard-hitting account of the suspected health effects of the poisoned groundwater in her community in South Tucson, Arizona. At this locale, solvents and other contaminants dumped at Air Force Plant No. 44, operated by Hughes Aircraft, polluted groundwater over some thirty square miles. The breadth of the groundwater contamination earned the installation the dubious distinction of having one of the largest single Superfund sites in the nation. Some 47,000 people living within this poisoned zone unknowingly drank the water for years.

Adrienne Anderson, a member of the grass-roots National Toxics Campaign in Denver, stated later that she endorsed Jeremiah's concern for a strong national defense, but, citing her own involvement with the ponderous cleanup effort at the Army's Rocky Mountain Arsenal, she stressed that some people have suffered illness and birth defects because defense facilities have polluted their drinking-water supplies. These people "should not have to sacrifice their family health and property values for national defense," she said. "We should not have to fight chemical warfare at home."

The presence of local activists like Augustine and Anderson grounded the meeting with a poignant sense of pollution's harsh effects upon neighbors of military dumpsites. Meanwhile, though, the military's internal battle over its environmental future could be even more clearly discerned once the meeting's initial plenary session broke up into working groups. These working sessions, on a dozen specific topics ranging from environmental compliance to the military acquisition process, displayed the workings of a lumbering bureaucracy and the breadth and variety of the attending officers' assignments and responsibilities.

Many participants' level of frustration about the issue was palpable. Rear Admiral John Bitoff, a commanding officer at the Treasure Island Naval Station in San Francisco, decried the $100,000 he was forced to spend annually for environmental compliance out of his base's operating funds—just to "wade through the tangled regulatory requirements," as he put it. Mike Donnelly, then the Air Force's chief environmental legal counsel, urged a cautious approach toward environmental issues, worrying aloud that the Pentagon might be "wandering into environmental compliance naively, like they did into Vietnam."

Meanwhile, Lieutenant General Henry ("Hank") Hatch, Chief of the Army Corps of Engineers, complained of a lack of specific Pentagon policies to guide environmental cleanup efforts. "We're ready to execute," Hatch claimed, "but we lack the standards." In short, the workshops brought to light numerous obstacles to a successful program, from questionable levels of personal commitment to poorly understood and complex regulations, from lack of instructions and standards to poor communication on environmental matters within the military infrastructure. To everyone's credit, at least the discussions were taking place.

Overall, the meeting underscored the dramatically changed Pentagon rhetoric on environmental issues. The question that remains is whether the words can translate into tangible gains. For their part, environmentalists stand divided about the prognosis. The recently formed Military Toxics Network, a coalition of many of the groups attending the meeting, struck an optimistic note in an issue of their newsletter that appeared shortly after the Washington gathering. "The tide is finally turning," the group asserted. "The top leadership of the Defense Department has accepted—at least on paper—its environmental obligations. Congress, the states, and the Environmental Protection Agency are watching the military more closely."

At the meeting, many environmentalists expressed their surprise and satisfaction not only that Cheney came but also that the meeting was so well attended by high-ranking military officers. The turnout, they contended, was an important statement of widespread military interest in the issue. This conclusion would prove slightly erroneous; a press account later revealed that the Pentagon had virtually forced the officers from around the country to come to the meeting. Cheney's office had classified the officers' attendance "mission essential"— a designation normally reserved for occasions when the Pentagon needs to rush people or equipment to ongoing military missions that might otherwise fail without them.

In his Pentagon office much later, top-ranking Air Force environmental official Gary Vest explained that the military stands currently in the midst of a "culture change." Vest conceptually divides the Pentagon's environmental problems into three discrete parts—cleanup, compliance, and prevention—corresponding respectively to the department's past, present, and future. Of the three parts, Vest points with particular pride to changes in compliance, especially in his own service, the Air Force; his department is also beginning to tackle the issue of pollution prevention. Cleanup, he says, will be a problem for a long time to come.

At the meeting Secretary Cheney had made a similar assessment. "In recent years, this department has gained significant ground in environmental management," Cheney said. "But the problems of the past, problems generated years before current knowledge was gained, will take time and effort to solve. We need to start from that realistic base if we are to make any progress at all."

Without any question, the vast portion of the military's cleanup work still lies ahead. And if the Defense and the Environment Initiative meeting is any indication, the successful management of the military toxic waste problem will require greater public involvement and increased institutional oversight. Perhaps even more fundamentally, however, the issue demands a reexamination of the conventionally accepted military paradigm of national security—a view which sees protection of the nation only in terms of external military threats.

Senator John Glenn captured the problem in the twilight of the Cold War several years ago, in a comment about the nation's nuclear production facilities: "The costs of cleaning up these sites will be extraordinarily high, but the costs of doing nothing will be higher. After all, what good does it do to protect ourselves from the Soviets . . . if we poison ourselves in the process?"

CHAPTER THIRTEEN

Dead Guppies Make Waves

The federal judge who presided over the trial called it one of the worst cases of environmental violations ever brought to court. Army officials, on the other hand, contend that dedicated employees were scapegoated. Either way, "the Aberdeen Three"—as they have come to be known in military circles—may well have done more to improve environmental practices at U.S. military installations than a dozen years of congressional urgings and admonitions.

In the 1989 Aberdeen verdict, for the first time ever, employees of the U.S. military were found guilty on criminal charges and held personally liable for environmental violations committed in the course of routine duties. Not surprisingly, base commanders and military personnel across the country have viewed this dramatic precedent with alarm. Admiral John Bitoff, base commander of the Alameda Naval Station in California, captured the sentiment more than a year after the verdict, at the Defense and the Environment Initiative meeting in Washington, D.C. As Bitoff explained candidly in the quaint vernacular of the military, "I would be lying if I said the Aberdeen case didn't make me cover my six o'clock."

Maryland's Aberdeen Proving Ground, the Army's major base for chemical weapons research and development, had been home to environmental horrors for decades, as the recollections of former Army worker Dean Dickey show in detail (see Chapter 4). The particular legal case at hand, though, springs from a small specific source—an outdoor tank of sulfuric acid that developed a small leak in the fall of 1985. Records show that Army workers noticed the leak on September 17, but judged that a repair could wait until the following day. The workers placed a bucket under the tank to catch the acid and left for the day.

The fateful decision to postpone work on the leaky tank would, through several odd twists, eventually reverberate throughout the country. That night, as it turned out, the small leak grew. Roughly 200 gallons of acid overflowed the bucket, overwhelmed an inadequately maintained dike around the tank, and emptied into Canal Creek, a small stream that feeds the Gunpowder River, which flows into the Chesapeake Bay several miles away.

In the aftermath of the spill, David Parks, a newly hired Army inspector, wrote an internal memo about the accident. Parks's report included a scathing assessment of environmental conditions at Aberdeen's Pilot Plant, the aging chemical warfare research facility with jurisdiction over the leaky tank. Like the particulars of the acid spill itself, the tenor of Park's memo would have major ramifications. Without it, the case might never have reached the public. The Pilot Plant complex, the Army inspector wrote, represented "a Pandora's box of potential sources of contamination."

A whistleblower at Aberdeen (Army officials say a disgruntled worker) leaked Parks's potent critique to the *Baltimore Sun*, and the paper promptly brought the situation before the local public in glaring terms. The *Sun* accurately reported the Army memo's "Pandora's box" assessment, and noted that the acid spill had "killed some aquatic life" in a waterway that flowed to the Chesapeake.

Jim Allingham, a press officer at Aberdeen, recalls visiting the site the day the spill was discovered. "The stream in question is a matter of ankle-deep water," he says. "It is true that there were 200 or 300 fish killed, but most were the size of guppies. I saw one dead frog, and one turtle that was upside down—presumably dead. Even the state's immediate testing of the water downstream found no trace of pollutants." Allingham's next contention is more dubious, though, revealing his bitterness about the case: "I probably could have done more damage with a quart of motor oil."

Allingham maintains that the severity of the acid spill was inflated in its initial presentation to Aberdeen's frightened neighbors, but the same could not be said of the ensuing revelations. Further investigation into the operations of the Pilot Plant soon confirmed the worst nightmares of the local public: the spill reported in the newspaper paled beside the plant's routine practices.

Army inspector Parks, presumably chagrined that his internal memo had inflamed such intense outside scrutiny, said later that his Pandora's box image may have been too strong. But local, state, and federal officials begged to differ. To their eyes, Aberdeen's Pilot Plant presented an environmental disaster of rare proportion; no embellishment could outdo the grim reality it presented. As the public soon learned, the plant was home to military experiments with deadly chemical weapons and their components; workers there made routine use of numerous lethal chemicals. EPA officials called in later to investigate the case found evidence of more than 100 different toxic compounds in the sludge of the drainage pits behind the plant facility. Among the toxic chemicals in the ground at the plant were deadly chemical nerve agents and phosgene, an older chemical that had demonstrated its lethality to humans ever since its initial use in World War I.

Because the materials used were chosen precisely for their toxic and lethal effects on humans, activities at the plant should naturally have bound its workers to the highest occupational safety and environmental standards. But this was not so. "The Pilot Plant was an operating industrial facility and it looked like one. And yes, it was in a state of disrepair," Allingham admits tersely. Breckinridge Willcox, the former U.S. Attorney for Maryland who ultimately prosecuted the case, elaborates on Allingham's assessment: "It was a run-down, seedy facility." As an example, Willcox offers a particularly vivid portrayal of a chemical storage area adjacent to the Pilot Plant—the "paint shed."

"This so-called paint shed," Willcox says, "was an unheated, unventilated building which held hundreds of drums of unknown chemicals over the course of some twenty years. Many of the drums were rusted and leaky and many of these chemicals were incompatible with each other and could have caused an explosion." As Willcox remembers it, "The fumes in this facility were so caustic that they had eaten through a metal door at the entrance. You could see through to the barrels inside. When the cleanup was finally done, any worker going in had to wear a self-contained breathing apparatus."

But even aside from the lethality of many of the chemicals dumped and stored at the Pilot Plant was the issue of their instability and explosive potential. Picric acid stored at the "paint shed," for instance, probably accounted for the holes in the building's metal door. Aside from being highly toxic and explosive, the substance is known to corrode virtually all metals on contact. Stored alongside this corrosive acid was the suspected carcinogen hydrazine, an even more volatile chemical—the 1990 *Pocket Guide to Chemical Hazards* published by the U.S. National Institute for Occupational Safety and Health warns that hydrazine "can ignite SPON-TANEOUSLY on contact with oxidizers or porous materials such as earth, wood, and cloth."

The men who ran the Pilot Plant—the men who would become the Aberdeen Three—were all experienced scientists, senior managers of the munitions directorate of the Army's Chemical Research Development and Engineering Center at Aberdeen. All three were civilians, but each had worked for the military throughout his career. Bill Dee, the former head of the munitions directorate, is known as the father of the binary chemical weapon. The Pentagon's aging chemical stockpile of some 25,000 tons of chemical agents is made up of mostly older, so-called unitary weapons, whose lethal contents present a constant threat of environmental catastrophe during transportation and storage. The binary weapon concept offered a way for the United States to amass a modernized generation of chemical weapons while improving their safe handling at home. In the binary chemical weapon Dee developed, two toxic but non-lethal chemicals are stored in separate chambers; the weapons' deadly gas is formed only when the chemicals mix upon firing.

Co-worker Bob Lentz was a classmate from Dee's undergraduate days at Johns Hopkins University. An engineer by training, Lentz specialized in designing equipment and processes for the manufacture of the Army's chemical munitions. Like Dee, at the time of the acid spill in 1985 he had worked at Aberdeen for more than two decades. The third senior manager, Carl Gepp, was also a longtime employee of Aberdeen. Gepp, in his role as manager of the Pilot Plant itself, oversaw the facility's day-to-day operations.

In their lives outside the Pilot Plant, Dee, Lentz, and Gepp were by all accounts upstanding citizens. Allingham calls them "pillars of their communities." In his spare time, Dee collected rare books and seashells. Bob Lentz coached a local amateur baseball team. A week before Gepp was indicted for environmental violations, his family was selected as Maryland's "4-H Family of the Year."

Unfortunately, the Aberdeen Three, like most of their co-workers, were cavalier about environmental matters. As the criminal trial established clearly, the three presided over a seat-of-the-pants laboratory facility where workers paid little attention to housekeeping or safety protocol. A reporter for the *Washington Post* wrote, "A number of Aberdeen safety inspections found flammable and cancer-causing substances left in the open; chemicals that become lethal if mixed were kept in the same room; drums of toxic substances were leaking. There were chemicals everywhere—misplaced, unlabeled or poorly contained. When part of the roof collapsed, smashing several chemical drums stored below, no one cleaned up or moved the spilled substance and broken containers for weeks."

Aside from the existence of sloppy procedures at the Pilot Plant, however, was the fact that the plant's managers were aware of the dangers presented by the toxic mess but failed to address them. This aspect of the situation came out in some detail during the trial. In just one of the five criminal counts brought against the men, for instance, the government charged that Army safety inspectors issued notices of violations reporting the improper storage of excess chemicals, incompatible storage of chemicals, storage of unknown wastes, and the failure to turn in wastes generated at the Pilot Plant complex, but the men did nothing to correct these problems.

During the trial it came to light that Dee and the other managers were, in fact, notified on several occasions by Army inspectors of the severity of the environmental problem posed by their facility. A base safety officer said, for instance, that at one meeting he called Dee's attention to the fact that environmental violations of the type presented at the Pilot Plant's storage facility could threaten the facility's workers. The inspector said that Dee shrugged off the warning at the time. Later, however, workers addressed the situation by removing some of the barrels from the storage area and dumping their contents into open sump pits which drained into the ground behind the building.

What the trial did not illuminate is why Dee and his fellow managers failed to bring the Pilot Plant's severe environmental problems and disrepair to the attention of higher-ups in the military.

The Pilot Plant's problems throughout the early 1980s were undoubtedly augmented by the fact that the Army's actual production of chemical weapons was in a dormant phase. An aerial nerve gas test in Utah had gone awry in 1968, spewing VX—the military's most potent nerve agent—over a piece of the vast Utah desert, killing some 6,000 sheep. Public outrage at the incident and a resulting congressional investigation spurred President Richard Nixon to halt all production of chemical weapons—an edict that held for eighteen years.

Prosecutor Willcox and others speculate that because of the tenuous status of the Pilot Plant's research program during this period Dee was reluctant to alert his superiors of his facility's mounting environmental problems for fear that the Army might shut the program down altogether. By the time a new generation of binary chemical weapons production was slated to begin (after Vice President George Bush cast the deciding vote in the Senate in 1988), the Pilot Plant's decrepit condition may have seemed too costly and embarrassing to bring to light.

Even if Dee, Lentz, and Gepp didn't notify their superiors, the Army bureaucracy's blatant failure to follow up on its own inspections and properly oversee the facility is itself revealing. The widespread, systemic disregard for environmental matters within the military goes far toward explaining the situation, but, as Allingham explains, the size and complexity of Aberdeen's own bureaucratic structure also played an important role. The Aberdeen Proving Ground is home to approximately fifty different Army organizations that fall within six entirely separate Army commands. The Pilot Plant, for instance, was part of the Munitions Directorate of the Aberdeen Chemical Research Development and Engineering Center, which in turn reported to the Armament, Munitions, and Chemical Command within the Army Materiel Command. It doesn't change the severity of Aberdeen's environmental problems, but the base's elaborate bureaucratic hierarchy does help to explain how glaring problems might have been overlooked.

As the criminal case proceeded, it became increasingly clear that the Army was not the only body lacking in oversight. The state of Maryland had never done its job to enforce federal environmental laws at Aberdeen either. This lack of state regulation is representative of a continuing lack of enforcement at military facilities by states throughout the country. Historically, state authorities have been reluctant to inspect military installations within their borders. As Willcox explained, state agencies often "didn't feel comfortable trying to regulate the federal government."

Aside from the question of jurisdiction, however, the enormity of the environmental problem at the Pilot Plant overwhelmed the state's capacity to regulate it. State workers lacked training and equipment to test for some of the exotic contaminants found in the soil there; consequently the state never took charge of the case, but instead passed it on to the federal government, ultimately to the EPA. Only then, after the EPA's involvement, did Breckinridge Willcox's branch of the federal Department of Justice assume responsibility for prosecuting the case.

With the sensational revelations emerging about pollution at Aberdeen since 1985, and growing environmental concerns nationwide, it was clear to all involved that the public demanded a response. The question was, who should be prosecuted? Over the course of two years, with the help of agents from the Federal Bureau of Investigation, Willcox's office scoured base records intensively to determine who could be held accountable for the mess. After careful study, Willcox says, his branch of the Justice Department determined that it had a strong case against the two base commanders who had presided at Aberdeen during the early 1980s.

"We wanted to pin responsibility to the highest levels," Willcox says, and an established legal canon, the "responsible corporate officer doctrine," seemed applicable. This doctrine holds that people in positions of authority—like corporate officers—can be held liable for legal infractions even if they don't participate in the wrongdoing themselves; their position of authority, Willcox explains, is also a position of responsibility.

But this was a criminal trial. It was to be heard before a jury, and Willcox says that his office came to believe that they simply couldn't win a conviction against the base commanders. Each of the men had known little of the conditions at the Pilot Plant. One of them, for instance, General James Klugh, stated definitively that he had never set foot in the complex during his entire two-year tenure. Legal responsibility notwithstanding, Willcox's team decided it would be hard to convince a jury of these officers' culpability.

It was on these pragmatic grounds—in the hope of obtaining a conviction—that the Department of Justice decided to prosecute Dee, Lentz, and Gepp. The three represented the highest-level managers whose direct responsibility for the plant could clearly be established in court. All three were civilians, but the Department of Justice reasoned that the distinction mattered little; any legal precedent established would hold equally for any employees of the federal government, including the military's uniformed officers and enlisted personnel.

The men were each charged with five counts of environmental violations and were found guilty of many of them. Almost all of the counts charged violations of the Resource Conservation and Recovery Act (RCRA), which governs the storage and disposal of hazardous materials. The federal government held that the Aberdeen Three had unlawfully stored large quantities of hazardous materials and illegally dumped toxic substances into the sewer system over a three year period.

Many in the military contend, undoubtedly accurately, that Dee, Lentz, and Gepp were only doing their jobs and were guilty of nothing far different from the actions of many of their counterparts at Aberdeen and at military bases around the country. Allingham is particularly biting on this point, using the prevalence of environmental problems in the military and the private sector to argue that the Aberdeen Three were unfairly singled out. "There was a conscious effort on the part of the henchmen who went after them," he says, speaking of the federal prosecutors, "not to tackle the overall problem with environmental management."

"I have no doubt that Dee, Lentz, and Gepp were honorable men, but there was an arrogance among these men—a feeling that environmental laws didn't apply to them," Willcox counters. "Unfortunately, it is true that their mentality was common within the military," he continues, "but that does not excuse their actions." As Willcox portrays it, the Aberdeen Three knew the applicable environmental regulations; they were even reminded on several occasions of the severity of the situation they oversaw. And yet they still chose to ignore the law, endangering themselves, their co-workers and the neighboring community, not to mention causing possibly irrevocable environmental damage to the area's soil and groundwater. Ultimately Willcox's portrayal prevailed in court; all three men were found guilty of violating federal environmental laws. Appeals have since been denied; the verdicts stand.

"We brought the case to send a message," Willcox says, and by almost any measure the message has reverberated throughout the military. As an article in *International Defense Review* put it in January 1991, the outcome of the Aberdeen case finally caused the Pentagon to "feel the teeth" of environmental laws. There is hardly a base commander around the country who is not threatened with the possibility of criminal charges. Many have already sought private legal counsel.

In 1989 the *Air Force Law Review* devoted an entire special issue to environmental law. Its prominent article on the implications of the Aberdeen case captured the sentiments of many military personnel. The Aberdeen case, an Air Force lawyer wrote, has introduced "a host of new ways for the federal employee to get in trouble." As the article explains, military personnel and other government workers are not protected by their employment against prosecution for environmental or other crimes. "The general rule is straightforward: Federal employees have no immunity from federal criminal prosecution by virtue of their federal employment. The federal employee is fully liable under the specific law being violated, just as if the person were not a federal employee." Just as environmental laws have whittled away at the military's institutional claim to sovereign immunity, the Aberdeen case has finally established that employees of the military are bound by the same environmental laws as everyone else.

Moreover, as the article notes, the military (and other government agencies) are even prohibited from paying any part of the legal defense fees for employees charged with federal criminal violations. The rationale, according to the article, is that the Department of Justice, as a rule, "represents the interests of the United States. In a federal criminal case, the interests of the United States are in the prosecution of the case, and not in the defeat of that prosecution." In the case of the Aberdeen Three, the clear-cut determination on the issue meant that the men had to underwrite the cost of their own legal defense, which by one estimate amounted to roughly $65,000 apiece.

Interestingly, though, military and other federal employees are not the only ones shaken by the Aberdeen case. At the 1990 Defense and the Environment Initiative meeting, a consortium of industry representatives distributed a statement entitled "Environmental Issues of Concern for the U.S. Defense Industry," which cited "a growing trend to significantly stiffen the criminal provisions of the various environmental laws."

"While no one can argue with stiff penalties for deliberate acts which harm the environment and public health," the group writes, "we worry about provisions which would be enforced for minor infractions or omissions. This issue is particularly important to the defense industry because of debarment, namely the fact that a federal contractor may be prohibited from receiving government contracts if convicted of certain transgressions." The consequences of environmental violations committed while under contract to the Pentagon, in other words, were beginning to look frightening to industry. The power of the Aberdeen verdict had begun to sink in.

Today, for Dee, Lentz, and Gepp, the ordeal is largely over. The three men received suspended sentences. All have kept their security clearances and employment at Aberdeen. Bill Dee was even selected as one of two U.S. officials to inspect Iraqi chemical weapons facilities in the aftermath of the Persian Gulf War. The trial was undoubtedly humiliating to the men, and a significant blow to their reputations. Yet, in truth, the only tangible punishments suffered by the three are the large legal fees they incurred and the fact that they are now prohibited by the Army to sit in positions with direct responsibility over toxic wastes.

The men's guilt in the case is no longer contested. For years they operated a facility in a heinous violation of environmental law. But the three were singled out as an example for a longstanding and accepted type of environmental wrongdoing that to some degree still plagues the military. Interestingly, the verdict of the case paid an ironic tribute to both of these facts. The three were found guilty on most of the counts against them, but not of the alleged violation of the Clean Water Act that resulted from the highly publicized 1985 acid spill. Indirectly, that spill would ultimately lead military employees around the world to be held personally responsible for their environmental actions, but as it turned out, the charge pertaining to the incident that started the entire episode and drew the attention of the public and governmental regulators to the case in the first place was the only charge all three men were cleared of.

CHAPTER FOURTEEN

Nerve-Wracking Prototype

To hear the sirens blare at 8:04 on Saturday morning, December 8, 1990, an outsider would think Johnston Island was under attack. The impression would not be entirely inaccurate: Johnston Island's sirens are set off when sensors detect the presence of deadly chemical weapons agents in the air. But the island's alarm does not mark an enemy attack, merely a fact of everyday life on this tiny dot in the middle of the Pacific Ocean.

Here, at one of the most remote spots on the planet, some 800 miles from its nearest neighbors in Hawaii, the U.S. Army is conducting a challenging and dangerous experiment to prove that it can safely incinerate—and thereby dispose of—the Pentagon's arsenal of lethal and aging chemical weapons. The job is dangerous, complex, and costly. In all these respects it offers important lessons about the military's cleanup plans at home.

The Army program is known as JACADS—the Johnston Atoll Chemical Agent Disposal System. Roughly 1,000 workers staff the facility, sharing the formerly uninhabited desert island and wildlife preserve with the vast incinerator complex and some 4 million pounds of chemical weapons agents—including more than 170,000 chemical bombs in all. It would be logistically impossible to disseminate it all, but technically, as of this December day, Johnston Island's chemical stockpile contains enough lethal doses to kill nearly everyone on the planet. It is a fact that keeps the island's inhabitants vigilant and on edge.

Army chemists say that the incinerator should generate fewer toxic emissions than many trash-burning incinerators in the United States because of its state-of-the-art design and because of the fact that the chemical components of the nerve, mustard, and blister agents to be burned are known so precisely. Most everyone involved in the project, though, concedes the very real chance, however slim, that a deadly accident could occur. It adds little comfort that the prototype project has been fraught with technological difficulties, cost overruns, and personnel problems. The alarm on December 8 marks the island's only documented release of chemical agents into the atmosphere. But it is just one of dozens of similar nerve-wracking incidents the island's inhabitants have weathered since the project began.

To make matters worse, as Marilyn Tischbin, the Army's spokesperson for the project, acknowledges, the tiny island is "extremely crowded." JACADS' 1,100 workers live together in cramped barracks. ("It's like college," Tischbin says.) Each worker must be constantly on guard against a potentially lethal mishap; regular accidents, false alarms, and drills send the island's inhabitants reaching for their personal gas masks and dashing toward the island's one specially pressurized building for safety. "The first thing that happens when you arrive at Johnston Island is you get your protective mask fitted," Tischbin says.

The installation of JACADS is not the first time that Johnston Island has been punished by the modern world for its remote location. First Johnston atoll (of which Johnston is the largest island) was the target for the test explosions of two hydrogen bombs dropped by the United States Air Force in the atmospheric nuclear tests of the 1950s. Then, in 1971, Johnston Island was chosen as a storage facility for tens of thousands of chemical weapons that had been stationed in the Pacific during World War II. In 1990, 100,000 more were brought from Germany to be destroyed.

The large incinerator on the island was completed in 1988. In July 1990, in a testing phase, the first chemical weapons were burned—and thereby decontaminated. Full-scale operation on one particular type of munitions—M55 shells containing the nerve agent GB, a mainstay of the U.S. chemical stockpile—began shortly thereafter. The alarm on December 8 was caused by the release of a small amount of GB into the air outside; it is the first release outside the facility to date, but there have been almost daily mishaps and mechanical failures that have forced the facility to shut down for roughly half of its scheduled operating time.

The shutdowns stem, to a large degree, from the plant's complexity. A remote-control facility shears the weapons' metal shells and drains their liquid contents. The contaminated metal parts are cut into pieces and incinerated in one furnace complex, while the deadly GB liquid is sent to another specialized kiln which burns it at a temperature of 2,700 degrees Fahrenheit. The complex even includes an additional furnace to handle the weapons' explosives compounds and another one for other, less hazardous packing materials as well as the protective clothing worn by the workers.

As with any highly complex industrial plant, many things can go wrong. According to the project manager's logs from the first three months of operation, the JACADS plant was plagued by broken meters, clogged burners, faulty circuit breakers, and blocked pipes. Pieces of the contaminated metal casings from the weapons broke the heating coils in their designated furnace, causing delays and adjustments. More disturbingly, the hottest furnace—the liquid incinerator—burned a hole through the thick outer plate of its secondary containment chamber and had to be redesigned. In addition, throughout the entire period of operation of the JACADS facility, a component of the liquid incinerator continually failed to reach the temperature required to insure complete incineration of the chemicals. It was this last problem that is believed to have led to the air emissions of the deadly agent.

All told, incineration of GB was conducted at the facility for nearly seven months, until February 1991. The job took exactly twice as long as planned, and still the military did not incinerate nearly all the GB weapons it had initially scheduled. Since the completion of "the GB campaign" the incinerator has idled for close to a year while workers have repaired it and readied it to handle the agent VX—the Army's most potent nerve agent. The Army says it is unsure exactly when the incinerator will return to operation. Now years behind schedule, the facility is still slated to demonstrate the Army's capability to destroy other types of chemical munitions, such as mustard gas and other so-called blister agents, as well.

In the spring of 1990 the Americans and the Soviets were hailed worldwide for their landmark agreement to destroy the vast majority of their chemical stockpiles. Yet U.S. and Soviet officials have acknowledged repeatedly that destroying a chemical stockpile is a nasty and dangerous business. As important as the agreement is to the world's international security, it presents severe political obstacles because of the environmental threat it poses. As with so many aspects of the broader toxic cleanup job confronting the military, few people involved during the creation of these hazardous materials and wastes seemed to have considered the immense difficulties presented by their disposal and cleanup.

Ironically, the Pentagon does not even consider the unwanted, often corroding, chemical weapons to be waste products. In a recent decision, the Environmental Protection Agency agreed, ruling that unused ordnance of any type—even that which is buried in the ground—is not considered waste under the Resource Conservation and Recovery Act, the nation's major hazardous waste law. The indefinite storage or burial of these weapons, the EPA's ruling held, must be considered part of their normal life cycle.

The ruling is badly flawed in practice. The fact is, besides the clear danger of accidental explosion, aging ordnance—especially chemical weapons—poses the same kinds of long-term, chronic ecological damage as do other toxic wastes. As one correspondent explained clearly in the January 1991 issue of *International Defense Review*, ordnance left buried, submerged in water, or in inadequate storage areas "exudes liquid that solidifies and forms sensitive crystals that can initiate an accidental explosion. Moreover, this exudation forms toxic pollutants that contaminate soil, aquifers, groundwater, rivers, ponds and lakes."

But if the dangers presented by aging ordnance, like those of other toxic wastes, demand some kind of cleanup action, these cleanup efforts also engender their own varying ecological costs. The principle certainly holds true in the case of the chemical stockpile, because of the dangers posed by the incineration process. These dangers are most severely pronounced in the destruction of the chemical arsenal because of the ever-present threat of a catastrophic accident. While it is small comfort to Johnston Island's workers, the project *is* geographically remote. The threat to human health and safety will mount greatly in the future, though, because the Army plans to bring the sophisticated JACADS technology home, building incinerator facilities around the country to destroy the rest of its huge chemical weapons stockpile, as mandated by Congress and by the 1990 treaty signed with the Soviet Union to destroy the chemical weapons.

Unfortunately, even when the Johnston Island prototype project is complete, the vast bulk of the chemical demilitarization will lie ahead. The weapons to be destroyed on Johnston Island (including those from

Germany) total less than 7 percent of the U.S. chemical weapons currently slated for destruction. The current plan calls for the other 93 percent to be incinerated at eight locations in the continental United States—at military facilities in Alabama, Arkansas, Colorado, Indiana, Kentucky, Maryland, Oregon, and Utah. The Army's decision to build the eight U.S. facilities is based on the fact that unstable, corroding weapons are too dangerous to transport in large numbers. In truth, however, such large amounts of the chemical agents are currently stored at each of these locations that their quantities alone merit separate incinerators; the largest stockpile, at Tooele Army Depot, not far from Salt Lake City, Utah, harbors more than 10,000 tons' worth of chemical weapons.

Meanwhile, the Army's own worst-case estimates conclude that accidents at the planned incinerators "could have environmental consequences of major proportions . . . [including] human fatalities, chronic illnesses, destruction of wildlife and wildlife habitat, destruction of economic resources and adverse impacts on the quality of life." In a worst-case scenario, the Army says, as many as 45,000 people will be placed at some risk of dying in a catastrophic accident in the vicinity of the Aberdeen Proving Ground in Maryland, where one incinerator is planned. And in the northwest corner of Lexington, Kentucky (the most populous area slated for an incinerator), approximately 53,000 people live within a seven-mile radius of the proposed site. The Army estimates, meanwhile, that a worst-case accident could cause fatalities up to twelve miles away.

In an effort to make the domestic incinerators at least slightly more palatable to the local communities who will be saddled with them, Congress initially required that the Army be prohibited from using them for any purpose other than the destruction of the chemical arsenal; the Army was instructed to tear them down after the destruction of the weapons is completed. Now, however, given the cost and effort involved in the project, Congress has changed its mind. Consequently, the military is now studying the prospect of using the high-tech incinerators to burn other types of hazardous wastes that plague its installations around the country.

Since the beginning of its age-old use to burn municipal trash, incineration has always held the appeal of reducing the volume of unwanted refuse materials, but between the air pollution it creates and the need to dispose of hazardous ash and brines left over from the process, its outcome is increasingly seen as less than ideal. Nevertheless, the Army has already begun at least six incineration efforts (of a more mundane, low-tech nature than the JACADS facility) to rid the soil of contaminants at Army ammunition plants around the country; all of the armed services will undoubtedly attempt to use the technology more in the years to come.

Aside from the dangers posed by the wastes, the threat of an accident during the cleanup process, and the chronic hazards presented in the routine operation of the cleanup program itself, the sheer complexity of the JACADS program stands as a symbol of the difficulties inherent in the environmental mission before the military. Cleaning up after past practices that have left trace amounts of extremely hazardous materials in the soil and groundwater is a difficult and technologically challenging job.

Technologies are relatively new and still emerging, even for detecting and monitoring the movement of the infinitesimal quantities of the toxic chemicals that are now known to pose potential hazards. An Air Force program to develop a sophisticated computer modeling technique to predict the migration of contaminants in groundwater, for example, is one of only a handful of its kind anywhere.

Traditionally, over the past few decades soil cleanup has usually meant merely identifying the contaminated area, scooping up as much contaminated soil as was deemed necessary, and carting it off to dump it back in the ground in a certified (and, one hopes, lined) hazardous waste landfill. The job has often curtailed the contaminants' migration at the polluted site, but it has always been seen by most of those involved as an imperfect—even misguided—effort. Many of the nation's most serious hazardous waste problems emanate from leaching landfills, and it is widely agreed that even the most technologically advanced landfills will leak at some time in the future. William Ruckelshaus, the original director of the Environmental Protection Agency, underscored the point in 1989. "Of course landfills will leak," Ruckelshaus told a California audience. "Our instincts tell us that, whether it is 10 years, 100 years or 1000 years . . . every landfill will leak in the sense that some liquids will come down through [the ground] in periods of high rainfall or other occasions."

The disposal of contaminated materials in landfills is still the most common cleanup method. Incineration, one of the only other established methods, can be complex and dangerous, as JACADS shows in the extreme. Most of the other options available today are still emerging or have been used only to a limited extent. Methods under development include: bioremediation, which uses bacteria or other organisms to break down toxic materials; chemical treatment solutions, wherein chemicals are added to react with particular contaminants to degrade them to more benign constituents; so-called vitrification technologies, in which an area is heated to crystallize its contaminants into a glasslike form to keep them from migrating; and finally, vacuum extraction, in which contaminants are literally sucked out of the ground.

In pilot projects or preliminary efforts, all of these novel methods have been (or are being) tried by the military. At Eglin Air Force Base in Florida, military contractors have tested a full-scale bioremediation project on a jet fuel spill site. Fuel-eating bacteria were added to groundwater at the base, and after eighteen months the Pentagon says the area showed a significant reduction in groundwater contamination. The project failed, though, to reduce the quantity of fuel in the soil above the water table, a fact the Air Force says it will take into account in its future use of the technology.

In 1989 the Navy conducted a pilot project which used chemical treatment to remove contaminants from soil at its Public Works Center in Guam. In the initial project, the Navy cleaned up approximately 5,000 cubic yards of soil that had been contaminated with formidable concentrations of PCBs—polychlorinated biphenyls—extremely toxic chemicals formerly used in electrical transformers. PCBs are believed to cause cancer even in tiny doses and have been outlawed for most applications by Congress. Ultimately, the EPA says, even the most infinitesimal amounts of PCBs present a threat and should be removed. The soil at the Guam naval base, meanwhile, even eight feet below ground in some places, contained concentrations of PCBs as high as 5,000 parts per million—over a million times in excess of the EPA's permissible concentrations.

In batches of two tons each, Navy workers treated this poisonous soil with a chemical called potassium polyethylene glycol, designed to decontaminate a whole family of toxins like PCBs—called halogenated organic compounds. Navy workers poured the soil into a huge vat, mixed in the chemical additive, and stirred. Heartened by initial results indicating that the additive successfully neutralized the PCBs, the Navy is currently testing a larger facility to handle more PCB-laden soil at the base.

Even more experimentally, workers at Arnold Air Force Base in Tennessee have conducted a test of vitrification technology on soils at the base's firefighting training area, a site contaminated with high concentrations of a wide range of chemicals. The technique involves heating the waste-laden soil to a molten state and allowing it to cool into a crystalized, glasslike form. The vitrification process is designed to retain or immobilize contaminants like heavy metals and even radioactive isotopes. Based on the preliminary test, a full-scale project employing the technology is already underway at the base.

At the Twin Cities Army Ammunition Plant outside of Minneapolis–St. Paul, Minnesota, the Army has operated a pilot project in so-called vacuum extraction, or soil venting, since 1987. Like the Cornhusker Ammunition Plant in Nebraska, the Twin Cities' plant produced bombs for the military during the years since World War II. The plant's contamination problems came to light in 1981, and soil borings at the base soon thereafter detected volatile organic compounds like TCE at concentrations as much as 10,000–40,000 times allowable levels.

To address the formidable contamination levels, the Army used the soil venting procedure, which takes advantage of the fact that chemicals like TCE and other fuels and solvents turn readily into a gaseous form. Vacuum blowers pull large columns of air through contaminated soil. The air flow causes these soil contaminants to volatilize—or turn to gas—and thereby sucks them from the soil. At the Twin Cities' base, the Army has already sucked thousands of gallons of solvents from the soil.

To be sure, the military's interest in these exotic cleanup technologies has fostered growth in the private sector in these areas. But the scattered diversity and experimental nature of the technologies show how tenuous the inroads are. While most of the techniques listed above have been used to treat soil contamination, groundwater cleanups face similar constraints.

In an operation similar to the one at Twin Cities, a cleanup effort in Tucson, Arizona, at Air Force Plant No. 44, has removed some 750 gallons of TCE from local groundwater—a remarkable amount given the fact that the substance is dangerous in quantities that would fit on the head of a pin. But these 750 gallons had to be removed from literally billions of gallons of groundwater over the course of years of the treatment facility's operation. Air Force environmental official Gary Vest says that calculated on a gallon-by-gallon basis, his branch of the military spent some $48,000 for each gallon of the TCE retrieved.

Among its other similarities to the rest of the military's cleanup program, JACADS has the problem of skyrocketing cost overruns. The JACADS project's $560 million price tag is already $190 million over the amount budgeted in 1985 and will undoubtedly rise even further before the program is through. The overall chemical weapons destruction program, meanwhile, was initially projected in 1985 to cost the Army $1.7 billion. Now the Army anticipates an overall cost of roughly $6.5 billion for the same program.

This kind of wildly accelerating cost estimate has plagued the entire cleanup field. David J. Berteau, one of the Pentagon's top-ranking officials with financial oversight over the military's cleanup program, told Congress last year that the Pentagon's agreements with outside contractors can normally be expected to rise a full third in price over initial estimates. Largely because of this fact, the Pentagon requested $517 million in 1990 for its environmental cleanup program for fiscal year 1991 but had to come back to Congress before the year was over to ask for an additional $233 million. The huge figures themselves are overshadowed by the stunning inaccuracy of the Pentagon's initial budget. The military undertook no more environmental work than planned—it just cost almost 50 percent more than anticipated earlier in the same year.

The rising cost estimates are rivaled only by the extent and complexity of the Pentagon cleanup program's bureaucracy. Again, Johnston Island's JACADS program offers a prime example. JACADS is not even considered by the Pentagon to be part of its so-called environmental restoration program. Rather, the program is jointly managed by three separate Army organizations. The majority of the actual work on Johnston Island is done by a contractor, a subsidiary of the defense and electronics firm Raytheon. But the manager of the Program for Chemical Demilitarization, located at the Aberdeen Proving Ground in Maryland, exercises technical and managerial control over the JACADS program. Meanwhile, a branch called the U.S. Army Support Command/Hawaii provides a separate officer to oversee the JACADS "operations and maintenance contract." Finally, the U.S. Army Chemical Activity/Western Command, also based in Hawaii, maintains (and guards) the chemical weapons stored on Johnston Island.

The majority of the military's cleanup work, as is the case with JACADS, will likely be done by private firms—often the same defense contractors that sell the weapons and equipment to the Pentagon. But, as the military's three top environmental officials from the respective services explained to a bewildered congressional committee in 1990, the three services all handle their environmental contracts differently. Lewis Walker, top Army environmental representative, explained that the Army uses the Army Corps of Engineers to allot its environmental contracts but employs "a small cadre" called USATHAMA, the U.S. Army Toxic and

Hazardous Materials Agency, "that watches over" the Army's cleanup efforts.

The Navy manages its cleanup programs through something called the Naval Facilities Engineering Command, which has regional offices around the world managed by its engineering field divisions. These divisions have responsibility for Marine Corps cleanups as well.

Finally, the Air Force seems to use some vague kind of combination of these bureaucratic structures. As the Air Force's Gary Vest explained at the same hearing, "Mr. Chairman, in most all of the lower 48 states, the Air Force contracts either through the [Army] Corps [of Engineers] or the DOE [Department of Energy] National Laboratories. Some of it is done at the base level. Some of it is done at the major command. Some of it is done by other service centers. The exception to that is that we maintain a team of Air Force employed people in Alaska. Most of the Alaska cleanup work we do with Air Force employees."

The disparate and complicated systems, frequently using different methods and environmental cleanup standards, make clear-cut accountability all but impossible in the overall process. Partly because of this problem, Congress has asked the military repeatedly whether it is economical to contract out the lion's share of its environmental cleanup work. The obvious answer is that it is undoubtedly not the cheapest way to get the job done. But Gary Vest explained a position held by all the armed services. "The Air Force," Vest stated, does "not want to build up a self-sustaining professional infrastructure that we would have to dismantle at some time in the future."

To some extent, no matter who does the work, staffing the job will present problems because of its dangerous and disagreeable nature. At Johnston Island, the contractor staffing the JACADS plant for the Army says that they have simply been unable to find a full complement of people willing to do the job. Consequently, top management, control room operators, and maintenance personnel have consistently operated short-handed. During 1989, staff turnover was 29 percent. A 1991 Army report says turnover since JACADS opened has run as high as 45 percent. The reports state that employees have given reasons for leaving including crowded housing, poor food, lack of recreation, and a belief that contractor management "did not show enough concern for their welfare."

The revelations about personnel problems inspire little confidence in the project's safety or in its prospects for timely completion. They also raise discouraging questions about the caliber of the employees the military and its contractors are able to attract to handle this important and dangerous work. For close to two years, the General Accounting Office discovered, the complex and deadly incineration program on Johnston Island was run by an employee of the military contractor who had neither an engineering degree nor previous experience starting up an industrial plant.

The chemical demilitarization problem begun at Johnston Island epitomizes many of the exceedingly difficult problems that lie ahead for the military's broader environmental cleanup program. Like the rest of the military's toxic wastes, the aging chemical stockpile poses a serious health and environmental threat. Something needs to be done. In the case of the chemical weapons, incineration may in fact be the best option. But the military's track record to date—of inertia, baroque bureaucratic structures, gargantuan cost overruns, and lack of trained personnel—cries out for greater oversight and accountability. Unless and until some of these major problems are addressed, the military's environmental efforts remain fraught with danger and uncertainty and deserve public skepticism.

CHAPTER FIFTEEN

A Military Toxic Network

Many communities wake up to the shock of military pollution only when their local base publicly announces the problem. Other towns have found contamination during a routine inspection of municipal water, only later to trace its source to a nearby military installation. Residents of the four towns adjacent to the Massachusetts Military Reservation in western Cape Cod, though, were jolted into action in 1982, when a neighborhood boy brought a live, unexploded grenade into school for "show and tell."

Many portions of the vast military installation were without a fence; the child had simply found the grenade on the beach. Alerted by the highly publicized incident, other parents discovered that their children too played war games with stray munitions from the huge military reservation, which includes an Air Force Base, an Army National Guard installation, and other military facilities. No one in the neighboring communities had yet been killed or injured, but the dangers posed by the base's discarded ordnance brought harsh public attention to practices at the military reservation.

Many residents of the four surrounding towns of Sandwich, Bourne, Falmouth, and Mashpee were already upset at the nuisance posed by their local military installation. For them, the facility stood as a 22,000-acre blemish on an otherwise idyllic, sandy region a half hour south of Plymouth Rock. Cape Cod, much of which is protected as a National

Seashore, draws flocks of visitors to its scenic towns and beaches. The Massachusetts Military Reservation begins artillery practice at 8:00 A.M., and the volume is especially heavy in the summer and on weekends because of National Guard activities. As one resident complained, "With artillery going off, machine guns, planes, helicopters—all just three miles away—it often feels like a war zone around here."

In 1982, in the aftermath of the grenade incident, local residents Joel and Freda Feigenbaum joined neighboring Cape Cod residents to form a community group, Upper Cape Concerned Citizens, primarily to deal with the noise pollution and potential dangers from artillery presented by the base. Five years later, the group was the major force in determining that western Cape residents face the highest cancer rates in the state of Massachusetts. In the towns surrounding the base, the overall cancer rate is 12 percent higher than in the rest of the state. For certain subpopulations the numbers are even more striking. State figures show, for instance, that women living in the town of Falmouth, just south of the reservation, are 46 percent more likely to have cancer than their counterparts elsewhere in the state. In Bourne, just west of the reservation, women face a 37 percent elevation in cancer rates.

The citizens' group has also been instrumental in getting officials to study these elevated cancer rates in relation to air and groundwater pollution from the military base. A path-breaking epidemiological study funded by the state is currently underway to test the link empirically, by systematically examining other possible causes for the high disease rate.

The military's environmental studies estimate that personnel at the base have dropped as many as 6 million gallons of aviation fuel into the sand simply to test planes' automatic fuel release mechanisms. The military has also dumped and burned solvents like benzene and toluene, flammable wastes, lubrication fluid, diesel fluids, hydraulic fluids, transformer oils, and paint thinners. Many of these substances were poured on the sand and ignited, causing an increased hazard for nearby residents. Others were left to drain into the contiguous aquifer that serves all of Cape Cod. Many people, however, believe that elevated disease in the area may be due primarily to the high levels of TCE dumped by the military.

Upper Cape Concerned Citizens has tried many avenues in the fight to expose and curb practices at the base; almost all have met with resistance. When they first tried to raise their concerns with personnel from the military base at public meetings, they were told that only elected officials could speak. When they pressed for a health study, they were initially denied. When a preliminary health study was finally conducted, showing elevated cancer rates, state public health officials tried to explain these cancers away as owing to "lifestyle factors" such as smoking and diet.

"The cancer rates are horrendous and have been for as long as the state has been keeping records," says Joel Feigenbaum, who is a physics professor at the local community college. "Initially, the state department of health tried to explain away these higher rates as a factor of our lifestyles, but we demanded a close comparison between the lower Cape (to the east), where there is no proximity to a military base, and the four upper Cape towns that adjoin the military reservation."

When the group appealed to Michael Dukakis, then governor, they got no response. And when they held demonstrations, Joel Feigenbaum was singled out and sentenced to two months in jail for lying down in the road at the entrance of the facility to protest pollution at the base. The judge in the trial, sentencing Feigenbaum for "disorderly conduct," acknowledged that he was making an example of Feigenbaum to discourage future actions.

After learning in the summer of 1984 of a multi-million-dollar Army plan to expand the base, residents, in conjunction with the Conservation Law Foundation (CLF), sued the National Guard, one of the main users of the base, in an effort to require an environmental impact statement. Since that time, after further evidence of health problems linked to military practices, citizens groups have joined with the CLF to sue for violation of EPA regulations at the base. Feigenbaum describes his local struggle as arduous and says that many of the obstacles to changing the military's environmental practices are "deeply woven into the fabric of our political culture." Still, he says, "we wouldn't have even gotten the awareness of the problem, and the health studies—we would never have gotten this far if we hadn't kept at them."

Two thousand miles away, in the early 1980s residents of a section of Tucson, Arizona, called Southside began to notice what they believed were unusually high levels of cancer and other diseases in their neighborhood. About the same time, workers at Air Force Plant No. 44, located nearby, acknowledged that the plant had found levels of TCE thousands of times in excess of permissible standards. Hughes Aircraft, which runs the plant for the Air Force, admitted to having dumped TCE and other toxic chemicals into the desert soil for decades.

In 1981, after finding levels of TCE as high as 400 parts per billion, eighty times higher than the maximum permitted by federal and Arizona law, the state closed municipal wells in the area. Southside residents learned that at least 47,000 people in their part of the city had been drinking polluted groundwater, possibly for decades. Using groundwater monitoring wells at the plant itself, environmental officials found TCE levels as high as 16,000 parts per billion.

In 1986, Southside residents filed a class-action lawsuit, charging that Hughes Aircraft at the Air Force's Plant No. 44 in Tucson had contaminated their groundwater drinking supplies with TCE and caused a high incidence of disease. A full epidemiological study has still not been done, but a 1987 study by researchers at the University of Arizona confirmed that Southside residents' children show an abnormally high level of birth defects.

In 1991, 1,600 Southside residents involved in the suit agreed to a settlement with Hughes of nearly $85 million, one of the largest of its kind ever allotted. Now, ten years since the contamination was first uncovered, the state health department is finally holding hearings and trying to get government money to set up health monitoring and screening. Many of the local activists are still concerned and angry despite winning their case, but the settlement's gag order stipulates that they cannot publicly discuss their concerns. The records of the case have been sealed.

Over the course of the decade that Southside residents have fought the military toxic contamination in their community, they have had scattered glimpses of problems elsewhere around the country. But for the most part, the people in Tucson, Arizona, did not know about their counterparts in Cape Cod, Massachusetts. They did not know, for instance, that Cape Cod residents were fighting a similar battle over similar military practices involving the same primary pollutant—TCE.

Some military officials, however, did have a sense of the national picture as they watched lawsuits and other citizen actions spring up across the country. One high-ranking Air Force general complained to a military reporter in 1989 that communities were coming at the military from all sides. As he put it, "The whole environmental issue has now become so volatile that people are almost ready to march on our bases."

In 1990, after the Cape Cod and Southside actions, a group of activists at an environmental organization called the National Toxics Campaign Fund noticed that disparate communities around the country were facing the same kinds of military-made environmental problems. Fledgling local groups, they realized, were not benefiting from each others' experiences.

The activists decided to form a coalition, dubbed the Military Toxics Network, to aid small groups fighting military pollution and to encourage them to work together to bring changes on the national level that would help them all.

The Military Toxics Network is a scattered collection of activists from California to Maine. Dyan Oldenburg, a Seattle-based Network founder and its director until 1991, emphasizes particularly the benefits that the coalition provides to local activists in remote and rural areas by "showing them that they are not alone and encouraging them to fight for their rights." Lenny Siegel, a Network member and longtime environmental activist in Mountain View, California, stresses the national picture, saying that the Military Toxics Network has helped bring increased attention to the issue of military pollution by uniting scattered local groups and identifying the similar problems they share.

In the spring of 1991, the Network flew several activists from around the country to Washington, D.C., to make their demands directly to top-ranking Pentagon environmental officials. For instance, as Siegel recounts, Bennie Muniz, from a local group called People Against Arsenal Toxic Hazards, told Pentagon officials that her community needed an alternative water supply so that they would not have to wash and bathe in water contaminated by nerve gas byproducts and other contaminants from the Rocky Mountain Arsenal. Another Network member, Grace Bukowski, from the Nevada-based Citizen Alert, told Pentagon officials to halt the open burning of solid rocket fuel at the Sierra Army Depot just across the border in California.

The Military Toxics Network's overall agenda, endorsed by many of the nation's largest and most respected environmental groups, includes several broad, well-considered recommendations. The group calls upon the Pentagon to recognize citizens' right to know about toxic chemicals used in their communities and citizens' right to participate in local environmental cleanup efforts. Along these lines, the group rightfully demands that every military installation should immediately disclose its toxic chemical releases into the air, water, and land as private firms are required to do.

The Network has called upon the Pentagon to fully disclose base contamination at all military facilities, foreign and domestic, and to end the military's longstanding claim of exemption from state and EPA oversight. In particular, it has encouraged the Pentagon to stop trying to block currently pending legislation—the Federal Facilities Compliance Act—which would allow states and local governments to enforce environmental laws and back up the enforcement with fines and other penalties if necessary.

Finally, the Network has proposed that the Pentagon establish a "high level, comprehensive environmental protection program with an emphasis on pollution prevention." The program, the activists say, should immediately review all military specifications requiring the use of toxic or dangerous chemicals, changing or eliminating the toxic requirements on a set timetable. In addition, Network members call for the removal of the Pentagon's Defense Reutilization and Marketing Service (responsible for the toxic contents of the Collinsville barn) from all responsibility for managing the Defense Department's hazardous waste.

These recommendations are all vital if the military is to successfully address its environmental problems. Drawing upon the experience of activists and local officials from around the country, many more specific lessons can also be gleaned. Foremost among them is the following advice: *if you are confronted with a potential military pollution problem in your community, demand your right to know exactly what poisons have been released into your neighborhood, in what quantities, and over what time period.* The military, and even local, state, and federal officials, may contest your right to this information, but the tide of legislation, court precedents, and public opinion continues to strengthen the public's right to full disclosure and accountability.

Whatever its faults, the military hierarchy has repeatedly shown itself to be susceptible to public pressure—at least to some degree. In light of this, the lack of outside oversight of military practices over the past few decades can be seen as a significant contributor to the current environmental debacle. In truth, the military's longstanding penchant for secrecy has undoubtedly been driven to a dysfunctional outcome by the fact that base officials are normally uncomfortable standing at odds with the local community. After all, they know full well that ultimately the armed forces are accountable to Congress, and indirectly to the taxpaying public, for their operating funds.

Military officials also know that on environmental matters the armed services are vulnerable to the considerable power of the Freedom of Information Act. A request that even vaguely threatens to invoke this law can open many doors because of the access it unequivocally affords the public to a wide array of internal government information.

Many who have fought local battles against military polluters say also that former (and sometimes current) base employees can be of invaluable help for their internal knowledge of base rules and hierarchy. Similarly, many outside government agencies can be enlisted. Local, state, and federal representatives, state health and environmental agencies, the regional office of the Environmental Protection Agency, and even the local public library can be of service.

To aid its cleanup efforts, the military often establishes advisory panels or so-called technical review committees to oversee cleanup. The record shows how vital it is for local environmental activists and other concerned residents to fight to be included on these committees.

Citizens must stand firm so as not to be cowed by the national security arguments often used by the military to defend current environmentally destructive practices or to suppress the release of environmental information. It is never unpatriotic to fight for sound military practices and a clean environment.

Nationally, the issue stands at a momentous turning point. The Pentagon now says it wants to change its environmental ways, but it has yet to produce much evidence of this change. Even Cheney's 1990 Defense and the Environment Initiative seems to have been unable to build upon its initial meeting to take high-profile action. Representative Richard Ray, a Democrat from Georgia who oversees the congressional subcommittee that allots the Pentagon its cleanup funds, notes the inconsistency between word and deed. As Ray puts it, Congress is witnessing "beyond compliance rhetoric" coupled with "barely compliance funding levels." The bottom line, he says, is that the military continues to fail to "live up to the rising expectations of the environmental community."

Ray attributes the problem to a lag within the Pentagon between the recommendations made by the military's "environmental leaders" and the actions of the rank and file. Gatherings like the Defense and the Environment Initiative forum bear out his contention. As Ray has noted, the fact that "environmental leaders [inside and outside the Pentagon] agree on various recommendations is not going to mean much in the [Defense] Department if the comptrollers, the programmers, the operators, logisticians, and research and development and acquisition communities are not involved and on board."

The armed forces have promised to cut their output of waste in half in coming years. But the pledge needs to be scrutinized in light of Ray's warning. The minimization of hazardous waste is a tricky business and can easily be undercut. One tactic is to concentrate pollutants, thereby reducing their volume but not actually reducing the hazards they present. To truly reduce the use of toxic materials, the Pentagon would do well to take up the recommendation of the Military Toxics Network, streamlining the Pentagon's environmental bureaucracy and publicly accounting for all hazardous materials used and wastes produced.

Finally, an important piece of the coming cleanup picture will be the way the Pentagon ranks its polluted installations for initial cleanup funds. Without more vigorous public input, many communities with formerly used or closing bases or installations contaminated with unexploded ordnance will be shunted to the bottom of the list. It may not be possible to clean up all of the military's pockets of pollution at once, but decisions about which ones to address first should be based upon public, not military, criteria. Accordingly, for instance, buried ordnance should be counted for the hazard it is and included in any ranking system.

If any theme emerges throughout—from Rocky Mountain Arsenal to the Massachusetts Military Reservation, from California's McClellan Air Force Base to New Jersey's Lakehurst Naval Air Engineering Center—it is the importance of public accountability and local oversight of the military's environmental cleanup and environmental practices. *Without exception, things have worked better, cleanups have progressed faster, and public health has been more adequately safeguarded at those locations where the military has pursued an open and accountable policy with respect to the local community.*

Meanwhile, many troubling issues still lie ahead. The Pentagon is expected now, and for many years to come, to spend at least a billion dollars per year on environmental cleanups. With the additional costs of chemical weapons demilitarization, cleanup at closing and overseas bases, and the monumental Energy Department cleanup of the nuclear weapons production facilities, the annual environmental costs of the military infrastructure will be several times higher. Because the Pentagon pays outside contractors to handle most of its cleanup work, many insiders fear the kind of corruption and malfeasance that has plagued other defense contracting arrangements in the past, milking taxpayers of millions of dollars in misallocated funds.

Oversight and accountability are watchwords here as well. Many of the Pentagon's environmental cleanup dollars are currently being paid to the same large defense contractors that helped spawn the toxics problems in the first place. As mentioned earlier, in some cases the Pentagon is even awarding cleanup contracts that will allow the same firms that caused specific military toxic pollution to handle the cleanup efforts.

Tucson's Air Force Plant No. 44 offers a striking example. At the Tucson installation, Hughes Aircraft improperly dumped TCE and other toxic wastes into the desert over the course of decades, and the pollutants eventually leached into the area's groundwater. Rather than fault the company, the Air Force agreed to pay for the cleanup and awarded the lucrative water treatment contract to Hughes itself. As Oklahoma representative Mike Synar exclaimed, "This is crazy. Here we have a company that improperly disposed of hazardous waste. Rather than hold the company liable for its pollution, we're going to pay them, plus a profit, to clean it up."

Incidents like the Hughes cleanup contract make many environmental activists wary of allotting the Pentagon increasing cleanup funds. The issue carves the environmentalist community into two camps: those who favor more funds to get the job done quicker and those who hesitate to allot increasing cleanup dollars to the same agencies that caused the problem in the first place. The Pentagon and the Department of Energy, this latter faction says, must earn the right to this money through completely revamped, open, and accountable procedures—procedures that they maintain have yet to materialize.

Division on this issue reached a dramatic climax in the spring of 1990, when on the heels of the twentieth anniversary of Earth Day an influential group of senators led by conservative Georgia Democrat Sam Nunn suggested the idea of a "Strategic Environmental Initiative." The idea, which was ultimately funded by Congress that same year, opens the door to a dramatic new environmental mission for the U.S. military. As Nunn stated on the floor of the Senate, "As our defense requirements change, we have an opportunity to redirect this tremendous national resource toward the environmental challenges we face in the 1990s."

At roughly the same time, others were monitoring the globe's worsening environmental state. Lester Brown, the planet's well-known environmental pulse taker—president of Worldwatch Institute and editor of its annual *State of the World Report*—captured the feeling of the moment that spring in an article comparing Earth Day's twentieth birthday with the original event. As Brown put it, "On April 22nd [1990] the sun will rise on a planet far more crowded, degraded, and polluted than it was on Earth Day 1970." Brown cited increasing population, deforestation, erosion of topsoil, global warming, ozone depletion, worsening air pollution, loss of species, and toxic dumping. As Brown noted darkly, "No comparable two-decade period in human history has witnessed such a wholesale destruction of the natural systems and resources on which civilization depends."

To combat such ills, as Nunn envisions in his Strategic Environmental Initiative plan, Navy submarines might measure the temperature of the polar ice caps to monitor greenhouse effects. Military satellites could monitor deforestation or collect atmospheric data. The military infrastructure could help foster new cleanup technologies and energy research. By all accounts the new initiative to "paint the Pentagon green," as a *New York Times* editorial dubbed it, marks a watershed in the mainstream importance attached to environmental matters. But the impulse also proves worrisome to many.

Skeptics wonder how much of Nunn's plan is motivated by his long-standing desire to retain high levels of military spending at a time when such governmental expense has become harder to justify. To be sure, the program perfectly melds the forces of two strong currents: the sudden lessening of international tension and the dramatically increasing concern about the environment. Given the Pentagon's environmental record to date, however, it seems all but incredible to many people that the nation would entrust a vastly expanded environmental mandate to the military. In a hard-nosed response to the initiative, a statement from the Military Toxics Network registered these concerns: "Before the DOD unleashes its exotic technological capability to fight the war on pollution, as Senator Nunn has suggested, it should clean up its own backyard without endangering surrounding communities."

Watertown and Local Strategies

While planning a visit to a military site in a western state in 1989, I was caught off guard by an official from USATHAMA. "Why travel all the way out there?" she asked, trying lightly to deflect attention from the site I hoped to investigate. "You've got a similar situation right in your own town." I stuck to my travel plans, but her remark left me shaken.

Ironic but true, in my effort to understand the problems at the military's toxic trouble spots around the country, I had ignored the obvious—a base I drove by almost every day. Despite the evidence I was collecting, I had continued to view the military's environmental situation as a problem that occurred "out there," one confronted only by communities less fortunate than my own. Granted, my local facility, the Watertown Arsenal (now known as the Army Material Technology Laboratory) in Watertown, Massachusetts, does not compare in scope to Jefferson Proving Ground or the Rocky Mountain Arsenal. But sure enough, as my colleague Dan Grossman and I would ultimately discover, my local base—one of the eighty-six initially ordered shut by Congress in 1989—is badly polluted. Some nineteen separate suspected toxic sites are scattered less than a mile from my home—my backyard's portion of the nation's 20,000.

Founded in 1816 for the manufacture, storage, and repair of arms, ammunition, and other military supplies, the Watertown Arsenal has an illustrious history of contribution to nearly every military venture this country has known. The facility's endeavors include everything from the production of a path-breaking Civil War cannon to the design of bullet-proof materials for President Bush's latest limousine. Sequestered from outside oversight since it opened a century and a half ago, the Watertown Arsenal has also been home to practices involving some of the most potent contaminants known, many with hazardous consequences for neighboring residents and the local environment.

Army documents acknowledge that the facility is so old and its environmental accounting so poor that many toxic spills, leaks, and waste piles have long since been forgotten. "Toxic, radioactive, and/or explosive materials may have been used as backfill around construction areas," says an Army report from March 1988. The extensive operations at the facility, the report continues, have "almost certainly" resulted in "hazardous materials being deposited in the soil and groundwater." But the Army report maintains that "the details of those releases and the exact amount of material that still exists in the environment is unknown." Even with the uncertainty, though, the base's director, Edward Wright, has stated that some of the arsenal's buildings are so contaminated they will have to be demolished "brick by brick—wrapped" before the site can be put to new uses.

Grossman and I learned that the Army dumped toxic and low-level radioactive wastes on the outskirts of my neighborhood; that the facility failed to notify the town about a 1969 spill of radioactive wastewater from an accident at its small nuclear reactor; that a plume of fuel oil at the base, steadily migrating toward the nearby Charles River, was brought to the Army's attention by one of its contractors years ago, but no cleanup has even been planned to date.

Meanwhile, the facility continues periodically to burn pieces of "depleted" (but nonetheless radioactive) uranium. The installation, immediately adjacent to an elderly housing complex, vents the airborne radioactive particles through a smokestack I can almost see from my kitchen window. Cleaning up this small local facility alone is expected to cost U.S. taxpayers as much as $100 million. Compared to many sites, though, we are lucky: some $50 million has already been pledged to the effort.

Two blocks away from the current arsenal grounds, across a busy intersection, another parcel of land sits fenced-off and forgotten. In the ten years I've lived in the area, it has always looked the same: buried in weeds, wrapped in a tall chainlink fence with a rusting padlock at the gate, overlooking the handsome Charles River. Small, aging signs warn of radioactivity; a larger billboard explains that this several-acre plot is the property of the General Services Administration (GSA)—a major land-holder for the federal government.

The GSA acquired the property from the Army in 1967, when the Watertown Arsenal sold nearly half its land and downscaled operations. What the GSA didn't know at the time was that the Army had used this area for storing radioactive waste and for burning scraps of uranium discarded from arsenal activities. A team from the Department of Energy surveying this site found radioactive contamination on a concrete slab in the center of the site and in surrounding soil and groundwater. The team concluded that the site suffered "significant contamination" and estimated that as many as twenty tons of soil might need to be removed.

Today this formerly used Army site remains contaminated. It is purported to be in the midst of a cleanup, but to date the effort only shows how difficult and expensive such undertakings can be. GSA contractors began decontamination work on a small piece of the property in 1988 at a cost of a million dollars. They planned to complete the job quickly. But in addition to the radioactive contamination in the site's soil and groundwater, the cleanup team found additional toxic contamination—delaying the project and promising considerable additional cost. Not only was more uranium discovered, but petroleum products and chunks of metal were also unearthed, suggesting that barrels of toxic materials may have been buried there. Frank Camacho, the GSA representative who is overseeing the project, says that the cleanup is now on hold until the GSA determines what further steps are necessary.

Across the road from the GSA site, a path follows the banks of the Charles River as it meanders gracefully inland. A short walk along the thin sylvan strip beside the river, a craggy pink granite stone rises from the bank. A bronze plaque from the local historical society, imbedded in the stone, marks a spot where a small band of settlers called Roger Clap and the Dorchester Men came ashore in the year 1630 and traded biscuits for fish offered by the local Indians. The hopeful prospects this riverbank once offered newcomers etch a sharp contrast beside the abandoned GSA site's gloomy present status.

The fear in my neighborhood, of course, is that with the Army arsenal closing, it could become another GSA site—lost in a seemingly endless bureaucratic tangle. Raymond Hinxman, a chemist at the Watertown Arsenal and head of the local branch of the American Federation of Government Employees, is a forceful inside critic of the base-closing process so far. "The Army's record of dealing with environmental matters is horrible," he says bluntly. And Hinxman speaks for many in the community when he expresses his worst fear about the facility's current status. "Most of all," he says, "I don't want to see them locking the gate and leaving this mess behind."

If my toxic travels helped me to understand many aspects of the nation's military toxic waste problem, the contamination at my local facility has proven, with some sort of poetic justice, at least as instructive. Sparked in part by the investigation Grossman and I conducted and by the commitment of our local environmental group, Watertown Citizens for Environmental Safety, our town officials have increasingly risen to the challenge presented by our closing, contaminated facility. Sentiment is now strong to make sure that the arsenal does not become yet another forgotten dumpsite. The town council fought a precedent-setting battle to make the Army pay for an independent technical consultant to advise town officials as the cleanup process inches forward. We lost the fight, but earned new allies in the process.

Our local elected representatives are now so wary of the way the bungled cleanup assessment has proceeded so far that they have decided to spend tens of thousands of dollars in unallocated town funds to hire an independent technical expert anyway, even if the Army is unwilling to foot the bill. Due partially to our heightened attention to the issue, we learned that the contractor conducting the Army's studies at our installation had been indicted for falsifying data in environmental studies at other federal facilities. Embarrassed, the Army agreed to throw out all of the now-questionable environmental test results it had gathered to date and start over.

At every point in our efforts to investigate the environmental situation at the arsenal for a local magazine article, Grossman and I were denied access. Initially the Army would not allow us to visit the facility and would not provide us with copies of its environmental studies of the base. Getting any information at all was at first so difficult that under different circumstances I might well have given up. After all, I knew at the time that nothing extraordinary would be likely to emerge from the Watertown Arsenal that I hadn't already seen at other facilities. I certainly bore this local facility no particular malice; in truth, I had never intended to become so involved with the military's environmental problems in the first place.

But my journalistic interest in the material shrank beside my growing concern as a neighbor. It was time-consuming and often painstaking, but in our work we adopted the attitude that we had the *right* to find out what was being done to the environment behind the Army's barbed wire fence in our town. And, keeping each other from getting too discouraged, we persisted. After appeals that ascended through many levels of military bureaucracy, we finally received permission to tour the facility. The permission came from none other than the nation's deputy assistant secretary of defense for public affairs. But even this access was granted only with one enormous and preposterous caveat. We were told that we would be allowed permission to tour the base only if we agreed not to ask any questions about environmental contamination.

In a country that prides itself publicly on its free and unfettered press, one would think that the issue of the government's perpetration of environmental contamination at thousands of locations around the country and the world would be a mainstay of hard-hitting journalists. But this is clearly not the case. Lofty philosophical considerations aside, true freedom of the press depends largely upon the quality of information to which reporters can get access and upon the determination of reporters to probe and investigate. Of course, gaining public disclosure of the military's toxic waste problems is merely a tiny first step toward redressing them, and a thankless task at that. But the stakes are undeniably high.

All in all, in an immediate sense, our article was met with hostility from most quarters. Army officials had been largely uncooperative throughout, but after the article appeared they held a press conference at the base to discredit what we had written and then sent a delegation of twelve military experts to the Watertown town council specifically to debunk our claims. Under questioning, Mary Allingham, the head of the delegation, was forced to admit that she could not find a single factual error in our story. But the admission lent us little satisfaction in the face of much louder claims that we had "needlessly inflamed public concern."

Meanwhile, the owner of a mall who had purchased his property from the Army years before tried unsuccessfully to suppress publication of our magazine article in which we detailed that the mall's parking lot sat atop radioactive residue left from still-secret nuclear weapons research at the Watertown Arsenal decades ago. Even more disheartening, many of our neighbors sought to downplay and dismiss the issue because of fears that confronting it might hurt the town's image and lower their property values.

Such a view was trumpeted prominently even by one of the town's newspapers, which had for decades scrupulously avoided the topic of environmental problems at the base. Rather than deal prominently with the findings we presented in our article, the *Watertown Sun* began its front page story about our investigation by saying that our article would give the town a bad name. As the newspaper's lead paragraph put it, "*Toxic Secrets*, in the current issue of *Boston* magazine is, to put it mildly, unlikely to improve property values in east Watertown."

Perhaps most disturbing of all, in the course of our investigation we discovered that virtually no local, state, or federal officials had known anything about the arsenal's environmental status. The town's health inspector, for instance, had ignored the facility throughout his tenure, even though the facility was technically required to report certain on-going activities to his office. Even the regional office of the EPA was uninformed of Army activities at the base. The agency's euphemistically titled 1983 "Perimeter Survey" of the arsenal facility epitomized the problem. The one-page report consisted only of the banal remarks of a hapless investigator who had walked around the outskirts of the facility, noting that the site "appeared to encompass several blocks" and "appeared to be old"; according to this sad excuse for an environmental report, nothing more could be determined about the facility "since it was completely enclosed by gates and secured by Department of Defense security police."

The success of our local investigation owes most, perhaps, to our stubbornness. We pursued almost every avenue open to us and simply would not quit. We made use of the public library and the powerful Freedom of Information Act. We continued to appeal to the Army even when they consistently delayed and tried to stonewall our efforts. We enlisted the support of our local, state, and federal officials when we could, and contacted local environmental activists, union leaders, and university scientists.

Finally our efforts paid off when we stumbled upon a former arsenal employee who knew the information we sought. Outraged at an Army environmental report that she knew ignored countless problems at the base, Rose Toscano, the former environmental manager at the arsenal, gave us the background information we needed in order to know which specific questions to ask the Army. "The Watertown Arsenal is and was and probably always will be a closed facility," Toscano said. But she believed that the upcoming base closure would ultimately bring the arsenal's environmental problems to light. Environmental problems at the facility, she said, were simply "too obvious to hide from the general public."

In the aftermath of our investigation, the Arsenal Task Force, a branch of our local environmental group, drafted a set of principles that have helped guide citizen involvement since. They are reprinted here in the hopes that they can be of use to other local citizens groups:

1. The first priority of the Arsenal cleanup should be to protect the health and safety of the residents and workers of Watertown.
2. While closure of the Arsenal was initiated as a cost-cutting measure, financial considerations should not dictate the scope of the cleanup plan.
3. The public should have access to all pertinent environmental information regarding the cleanup and should be informed and integrally involved in the decision-making process for investigating and assessing the toxic contamination at the site.
4. The remedial action at the Arsenal should be conducted in a timely manner and be consistent with state and federal environmental standards and regulations.
5. The public has the right to know what hazardous materials are currently being used at the site and the methods of storage, disposal, and removal for these materials and past materials used at the plant.
6. The Army should be liable for any remediation of hazardous wastes found and proven to be generated by the military after the remedial action has been done.
7. As the Army continues its work at the site until closure, it should reduce the amount of hazardous materials it uses in its industrial process.

Despite some measure of success in our current efforts, we all know that the GSA site across the street from the current arsenal property bodes ill for the facility's near-term prospects. Hundreds of mammoth environmental tragedies around the world certainly continue to torment the Pentagon, but the full military toxic debacle encompasses many thousands of small, often forgotten parcels of land such as the GSA site, poisoned by past—and sometimes by continuing—military practices.

Sadly, the chances are good that you, like me, live somewhere near a military base. Your community's air and drinking water may be threatened. Like me, you may justifiably feel anger and outrage about the military's sorry stewardship of your neck of the woods. My outrage remains, but my struggle against military contamination in my neighborhood has taught me an important lesson. There is some real consolation in the fact that each of our communities is not alone in this mess—that with increased public scrutiny and a shrinking military infrastructure, we may be able to insure a careful and thorough cleanup.

With some luck and hard work, my community may someday be able to reclaim its currently poisoned military land. I am convinced that with increased public attention and, where necessary, public outcry, with vigilant community oversight and a concerted, determined effort to enforce the military's compliance with state and federal environmental laws, my nation can do the same.

Strategies for Action

It is more than likely that there is a military facility of some kind near you. To find out more about a local base and whether its environmental practices pose a threat to your community's land and public health, your best first stop is the local public library. The military sometimes files copies of its environmental reports at nearby libraries. Even in the absence of such information, local press accounts may be helpful.

Don't hesitate to call your local, state, and federal representatives for more information. If environmental problems at your local base have been recognized in the past, these officials should know. If not, a problem could still exist. Ask these officials to find out more for you.

Next, try the public affairs representative at the base in question. These officials can be very helpful, although it is common for them to try to allay fears and downplay any environmental concerns at the facility. Ask for copies of relevant environmental studies and other records. Request a tour of the facility and a meeting with the environmental managers at the installation. Information may not be immediately forthcoming, but the public's right to know is gaining ground. Much of the information about environmental practices at a local base can ultimately be yours by invoking the Freedom of Information Act (FOIA), if necessary (see Appendix C). FOIA requests should be addressed to the base FOIA officer and should contain language along the following lines: "Pursuant to 5 USC 552, the Freedom of Information Act, I am requesting a copy of the latest environmental survey of your base. . . ."

All of the military's cleanup efforts go through a specified process, beginning with a preliminary assessment/site inspection (PA/SI), followed by a remedial investigation/feasibility study (RI/FS), and finally a remedial design/remedial action (RD/RA). If you know the current progress of the base in question along this specified series of steps, it is a good idea to request the most recent document by name, i.e., the "preliminary assessment" or the "remedial investigation report."

Be sure to be clear about whether you want a copy of the document mailed to you or just made available for your inspection. There may be copying fees; you can ask to be notified of any charges before material is sent. It is also helpful to include, in closing your request, the following reminder: "I look forward to hearing from you within ten days as the law stipulates." Requests are often not fulfilled in that time, but the base is under a legal obligation to at least respond to let you know the status of such a request.

Also potentially useful to an investigation of a local military installation are the offices of the state department of environmental protection and the regional offices of the federal Environmental Protection Agency. Historically, these agencies have had limited authority over environmental contamination at military facilities, but they may well have in their files relevant military environmental studies or other helpful information. If you are unsure of the location of the regional EPA office nearest you, call the headquarters in Washington, D.C. (see listing below).

National agencies and environmental organizations can also be of service. If you are frustrated by local military officials, don't hesitate to try to get information from public affairs officers higher up in the military hierarchy. Try the Department of Defense's public affairs office or the corresponding office of the relevant branch of the armed forces in Washington (addresses and phone numbers are listed below). Questions about formerly used facilities can be directed to the public affairs office at the Army Corps of Engineers. Finally, for a nationwide overview of the problem, try the Defense Environmental Restoration Program.

The following addresses and phone numbers offer starting points:

Defense Environmental Restoration Program
206 N. Washington Street, Suite 100
Alexandria, VA 22304
703/325-2211

Chief, Army Environmental Office
Attn: ENVR
The Pentagon
Washington, DC 20310–2600
703/693-4635

Office of the Chief of Naval Operations
Environmental Protection, Safety, and Occupational Health Division
OP-45
Crystal Plaza 5, Room 678
Arlington, VA 22202
703/602-2570

Air Force Environmental Division
Directorate of Engineering and Services
HQUSAF/LEEV
Building 516, Bolling AFB
Washington, DC 20332–5000
202/767-4178

Defense Logistics Agency
Staff Director, Office of Installation Services and Environmental
    Protection
(DLA-W)
Cameron Station
Alexandria, VA 22304–6100
703/274-6967

Army Corps of Engineers
Pulaski Building
20 Massachusetts Avenue, NW
Washington, DC 20314–1000
202/272-0010

U.S. Department of Energy
Office of the Secretary, Environment, Safety, and Health
1000 Independence Avenue, SW
Washington, DC 20585
202/586-5000

U.S. Environmental Protection Agency
401 M Street, SW
Washington, DC 20460
202/382-2090

The EPA has regional offices around the country:

EPA Region I
[serving Connecticut, Massachusetts, Maine, New Hampshire,
    Vermont, Rhode Island]
JFK Federal Building
Boston, MA 02203
617/565-3420

EPA Region II
[serving New Jersey, New York, Puerto Rico, Virgin Islands]
26 Federal Plaza
New York, NY 10278
212/264-2657

EPA Region III
[serving Delaware, Maryland, Pennsylvania, Virginia, West Virginia,
District of Columbia]
841 Chestnut Building
Philadelphia, PA 19107
215/597-9800

EPA Region IV
[serving Alabama, Florida, Georgia, North Carolina, South Carolina,
Kentucky, Mississippi, Tennessee]
345 Courtland Street, NE
Atlanta, GA 30365
404/347-4727

EPA Region V
[serving Illinois, Indiana, Michigan, Minnesota, Ohio, Wisconsin]
230 South Dearborn Street
Chicago, IL 60604
312/353-2000

EPA Region VI
[serving Arkansas, Louisiana, New Mexico, Texas, Oklahoma]
1445 Ross Avenue
Dallas, TX 75202
214/655-6444

EPA Region VII
[serving Iowa, Kansas, Missouri, Nebraska]
726 Minnesota Avenue
Kansas City, KS 66101
913/551-7000

EPA Region VIII
[serving Colorado, Montana, North Dakota, South Dakota, Utah,
Wyoming]
One Denver Place
999 18th Street, Suite 500
Denver, CO 80202
303/293-1603

EPA Region IX
[serving Arizona, California, Hawaii, Nevada, American Samoa, Guam,
  Trust Territories of the Pacific]
75 Hawthorne Street
San Francisco, CA 94105
415/744-1305

EPA Region X
[serving Alaska, Idaho, Oregon, Washington]
1200 Sixth Avenue
Seattle, WA 98101
206/442-1200

In addition to the government agencies cited above, the following national organizations are among those that have contributed to the debate over the military's environmental legacy:

The National Toxic Campaign Fund
1168 Commonwealth Avenue
Boston, MA 02134
617/232-0327

The Military Toxics Network
RR1 Box 220
Litchfield, ME 04350
207/268-4071

Friends of the Earth
218 D Street, SE
Washington, DC 20003
202/544-2600

Sierra Club
408 C Street, NE
Washington, DC 20002
202/547-1141

Citizen's Clearinghouse for Hazardous Wastes
PO Box 926
Arlington, VA 22216
703/276-7070

Center for Defense Information
1500 Massachusetts Avenue, NW
Washington, DC 20005
202/862-0700

Greenpeace
1611 Connecticut Avenue, NW
Washington, DC 20009
202/462-1177

Natural Resources Defense Council
1350 New York Avenue, NW
Washington, DC 20005
202/783-7800

Suspected Sites of Contamination by Type

The following lists reflect the military's own assessment of its toxic legacy and its cleanup status. The information is drawn primarily from the *Defense Environmental Restoration Program Annual Report to Congress for Fiscal Year 1990* (February 1991). Designations of closing bases are based on a list compiled by the National Toxics Campaign Fund.

In an effort to provide a rough overview of the kinds of contamination problems faced by the military today, the installations are grouped below by *type*. Many facilities have multiple missions—which have left diverse kinds of toxic contamination; consequently, these groupings are meant only as a rough guide to the size and variety of the problems faced nationally, not as an authoritative statement about the precise pollution problems faced by any given installation.

Similarly, the number of sites of suspected contamination listed beside each installation should be considered as only a starting point for investigation. These are the Pentagon's official numbers, but as military officials readily acknowledge, some individual sites can be enormous in size and consequences, others relatively benign. Helpful for an overall picture of the problem, these numbers nonetheless give only the most superficial assessment of the degree of contamination present at any given installation.

Arsenals and Ammunition Plants

As illustrated by the Cornhusker Army Ammunition plant in Grand Island, Nebraska (see Chapter 8), the production of conventional bombs and shells is harmful to the environment. At virtually all of the military's arsenals and ammunition plants, a residue of toxic explosive compounds

ARMY

AK	Fort Wainwright	
AL	Alabama Army Ammunition Plant	
	Anniston Army Depot	
AZ	Yuma Proving Ground	
CA	Fort Ord	
	Riverbank Army Ammunition Plant	
	Sacramento Army Depot	
	Sharpe Army Depot	
CO	Rocky Mountain Arsenal	
HI	Schofield Barracks	
IA	Iowa Army Ammunition Plant	
IL	Joliet Army Ammunition Plant	

IL	Savanna Army Depot Activity
IN	Jefferson Proving Ground
KS	Fort Riley
KY	Fort Knox
LA	Louisiana Army Ammunition Plant
MA	Fort Devens
	Fort Devens Sudbury Training Annex
MD	Aberdeen Proving Ground
MN	Twin Cities Army Ammunition Plant
MO	Lake City Army Ammunition Plant
NB	Cornhusker Army Ammunition Plant
NJ	Fort Dix
	Picatinny Arsenal
NY	Seneca Army Depot

OK	McAlester Army Ammunition Plant
OR	Umatilla Army Depot
PA	Letterkenny Army Depot
	Tobyhanna Army Depot
TN	Milan Army Ammunition Plant
TX	Lone Star Army Ammunition Plant
	Longhorn Army Ammunition Plant
UT	Tooele Army Depot
WA	Fort Lewis

NAVY

CA	Concord Naval Air Weap
	Station
	Moffet Naval Air Station
	Treasure Island Naval St
	Hunter's Point Annex
FL	Cecil Field Naval Air Stat
	Jacksonville Naval Air S
	Pensacola Naval Air Sta
ME	Brunswick Naval Air Sta
MN	Fridley Naval Industrial
	Reserve Ordnance Plant
NC	Camp Lejeune Military F

Military Hot Spots

A selection of some of the nation's most contaminated military sites

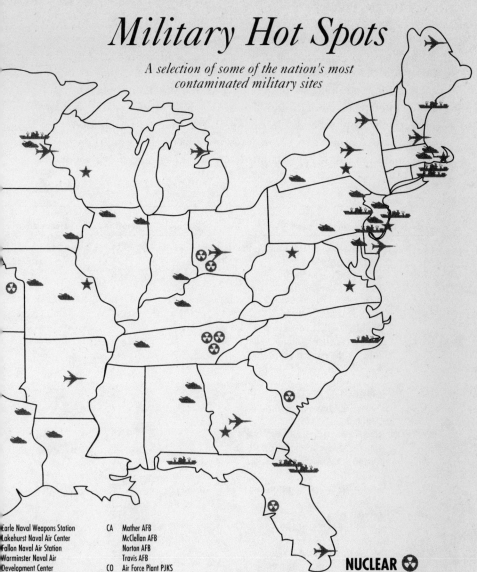

Earle Naval Weapons Station
Lakehurst Naval Air Center
Fallon Naval Air Station
Warminster Naval Air
Development Center
Davisville Naval Construction
Battalion Center
Newport Naval Education and
Training Center
Bangor Naval Submarine Base
Whidbey Island Naval Air Station
Keyport Naval Undersea
Warfare Station

R FORCE ✈

Eielson Air Force Base (AFB)
Elmendorf AFB
Little Rock AFB
Luke AFB
Williams AFB
Castle AFB
Edwards AFB
George AFB
March AFB

CA	Mather AFB
	McClellan AFB
	Norton AFB
	Travis AFB
CO	Air Force Plant PJKS
DE	Dover AFB
FL	Homestead AFB
GA	Robins AFB
ID	Mountain Home AFB
MA	Otis Air National Guard Base/
	Camp Edwards
ME	Loring AFB
MI	Wurtsmith AFB
MN	Twin Cities A.F. Reserve Base
NH	Pease AFB
NY	Griffiss AFB
	Plattsburgh AFB
OH	Wright-Patterson AFB
OK	Tinker AFB
SD	Ellsworth AFB
TX	Air Force Plant Four
UT	Hill AFB
WA	Fairchild AFB
	McChord AFB
WY	F.E. Warren AFB

OTHER MILITARY ★
(includes formerly owned sites)

AZ	Yuma Marine Corps (MC) Air Station
	Litchfield Park Naval Air Station
CA	Barstow MC Logistics Base
	Camp Pendleton MC Base
	El Toro MC Air Station
	Tracy Defense Depot
GA	Albany MC Logistics Base
MO	Weldon Spring
NB	Hastings East Industrial Park
NJ	Federal Aviation Administration
	Technical Center
NY	Marathon Battery
UT	Ogden Defense Depot
VA	Defense General Supply Center
	Engineering Station
WI	Eau Claire Ordnance Plant
WV	Morgantown Ordnance Works

NUCLEAR ☢

CA	Lawrence Livermore National
	Laboratory
	Sandia National Laboratory
	(Livermore)
CO	Rocky Flats Plant
FL	Pinellas Plant
ID	Idaho National Engineering
	Laboratory
KS	Kansas City Plant
NM	Los Alamos National Laboratory
NM	Sandia National Laboratory
	(Albuquerque)
NV	Nevada Test Site
OH	Fernald Plant
	Mound Plant
SC	Savannah River Plant
TN	Oak Ridge Gaseous Plant
	Oak Ridge National Laboratory
	Oak Ridge Y-12 Plant
TX	Pantex Plant
WA	Hanford Nuclear Reservation

has been left in the soil and groundwater. Compared to other toxic chemicals, these explosive compounds, including trinitrotoluene (TNT) and hexahydro-1,3,5-trinitro-1,3,5-triazine (RDX), are not particularly water soluble and tend to linger for long periods in the soil, however, their ability to migrate in groundwater has been amply demonstrated at Cornhusker and many other facilities around the country. In addition, some arsenals and ammunition plants have manufactured weapons with even more toxic and exotic components like mustard gas and nerve agents.

State	Military installation	Status	Sites identified	Sites cleaned
AL	Alabama Army Ammunition Plant	S*	36	12
AL	Redstone Arsenal		71	
AR	Pine Bluff Arsenal		66	23
CA	Riverbank Army Ammunition Plant	S	11	
CO	Rocky Mountain Arsenal	S	155	1
CT	Naval Weapons Industrial Reserve Plant, Bloomfield		6	
IL	Joliet Army Ammunition Plant	S	42	3
IL	Rock Island Arsenal		31	
IN	Crane Army Ammunition Activity		76	
IN	Indiana Army Ammunition Plant		25	
IN	Newport Army Ammunition Plant		12	
IA	Iowa Army Ammunition Plant		43	2
KS	Kansas Army Ammunition Plant		38	
KS	Sunflower Army Ammunition Plant		31	
LA	Louisiana Army Ammunition Plant	S	7	1
MI	Detroit Arsenal		15	
MN	Naval Industrial Reserve Ordnance Plant, Fridley	S	5	
MN	Naval Industrial Reserve Ordnance Plant, St. Paul	S	2	
MN	Twin Cities Army Ammunition Plant	S	19	2
MS	Mississippi Army Ammunition Plant		46	
MO	Gateway Army Ammunition Plant		10	
MO	Lake City Army Ammunition Plant	S	35	7
MO	Weldon Springs Chemical Plant	S	28	
NE	Cornhusker Army Ammunition Plant	S	64	58

Table continued

State	Military installation	Status	Sites identified	Sites cleaned
NV	Hawthorne Army Ammunition Plant		78	
NJ	Picatinny Arsenal	S	57	
NY	Naval Weapons Industrial Reserve Plant, Calverton		10	
NC	Tarheel Army Missile Plant		19	
OH	Ravenna Army Ammunition Plant		31	
OK	McAlester Army Ammunition Plant		50	
PA	Hays Army Ammunition Plant		1	
PA	Scranton Army Ammunition Plant		10	*
TN	Holston Army Ammunition Plant	S	24	
TN	Milan Army Ammunition Plant		19	
TN	Naval Weapons Industrial Reserve Plant, Bristol		9	
TN	Volunteer Army Ammunition Plant		28	
TX	Lone Star Army Ammunition Plant	S	38	
TX	Longhorn Army Ammunition Plant	S	59	1
TX	Naval Weapons Industrial Reserve Plant, Dallas		11	
TX	Naval Weapons Industrial Reserve Plant, McGregor		16	
WV	West Virginia Ordnance Works	S	6	3
WI	Badger Army Ammunition Plant		32	

S = *site listed on EPA Superfund National Priorities List.*
* = *facility slated for closure.*

Industrial Manufacturing and Maintenance

Industrial processes like electroplating are conducted at many different kinds of facilities. The following bases, however, are involved in the production of aircraft or other heavy machinery. Some of these facilities also build missiles (like the ammunition plants above), but usually only in conjunction with other kinds of industrial processes. Waste materials at these installations will be diverse, but will often include heavy metals, waste oils, acids, and cyanide.

State	Military installation	Status	Sites identified	Sites cleaned
AZ	Air Force Plant No. 44, Tucson		14	
CA	Air Force Plant No. 19, San Diego		6	
CA	Air Force Plant No. 42, Palmdale		27	
CA	Air Force Plant No. 70, Folsom		12	1
CA	Construction Battalion Center, Port Hueneme		22	1
CO	Air Force Plant PJKS	S	33	
CT	Stratford Army Engine Plant		9	
GA	Air Force Plant No. 6, Marietta		15	
MA	Air Force Plant No. 28, Everett		4	
MA	Air Force Plant No. 29, Lynn		3	
NM	Air Force Plant No. 83, Albuquerque		6	
NY	Air Force Plant No. 38, Lewiston		10	6
NY	Air Force Plant No. 59, Johnson City		8	
OH	Air Force Plant No. 36, Evandale		4	
OH	Air Force Plant No. 85, Columbus		8	
OH	U.S. Air Force Plant 85, Columbus (Navy)		1	
OK	Air Force Plant No. 3, Tulsa		12	
RI	Construction Battalion Center, Davisville	S*	14	
TX	Air Force Plant No. 4, Ft. Worth		29	
TX	Saginaw Army Aircraft Plant		1	
UT	Air Force Plant No. 78, Corinne		19	
UT	Naval Industrial Reserve Operating Plant, Magna		6	

S = site listed on EPA Superfund National Priorities List.
* = facility slated for closure.*

Depots

As military officials explain, depots "overhaul, repair, modify, and reno-vate" military equipment to keep the armed forces in a state of readiness. To accomplish this mission, these installations stockpile large amounts of toxic chemicals and potentially dangerous equipment. In fiscal year 1989, for example, the military's depots in the United States repaired more than 64,000 aircraft components and more than 180,000 "combat vehicle com-ponents." Historically, the careless disposal of waste oils and solvents has left contamination problems at most of these installations. Documented cases of improper storage, including leaking drums and improper mark-ings, and other violations of safeguards have been widespread.

SUSPECTED SITES OF CONTAMINATION

State	Military installation	Status	Sites identified	Sites cleaned
AL	Anniston Army Depot	S	45	1
AZ	Navajo Army Depot	*	47	
CA	Sacramento Army Depot	S*	15	
CA	Sharpe Army Depot	S	38	
CA	Sierra Army Depot		35	
CO	Pueblo Depot Activity		35	
GA	Marine Corps Logistic Base, Albany	S	13	
HI	Kipapa Army Ammunition Storage		2	
HI	Naval Magazine, Lualualei		7	
IL	Savannah Army Depot Activity	S	72	
KY	Blue Grass Activity-Lead		53	
KY	Lexington Activity/Blue Grass Army Depot	*	45	
MD	Naval Ordnance Center, Indian Head		29	
MD	Naval Surface Weapons Center, White Oak		14	
MI	Lima Army Tank Center		16	
MI	Pontiac Storage Activity	*	7	
MI	Tank-Automotive Command Activity		10	
NY	Seneca Army Depot	S	32	
OR	Umatilla Army Depot Activity	S	116	
PA	Letterkenny Army Depot	S	63	2
PA	New Cumberland Army Depot		20	
PA	Tobyhanna Army Depot	S	21	
SC	Marine Corps Recruit Depot, Parris Island		19	
TX	Corpus Christi Army Depot		17	
TX	Red River Army Depot		32	
VA	Naval Surface Weapons Center, Dahlgren		37	
UT	Toole Army Depot, North Area	S	44	
UT	Toole Army Depot, South Area		27	

S = site on EPA Superfund National Priorities List.
* = facility slated for closure.

Air Force Bases, Air Fields, and Naval Air Stations

The Air Force has acknowledged that virtually all of its air fields are contaminated with solvents like trichloroethylene (TCE), which were used to de-ice and spray down planes. Historically, these chemicals—many of which are now known to be toxic in minute quantities—were allowed to drain directly into the ground. Similarly, aviation fuel containing lead and other toxic additives has routinely leaked or been dumped at Air Force bases and Navy air stations around the world. Fuels and solvents like TCE are known as volatile organic compounds (VOCs) because they turn readily into a gaseous form. They can also migrate quickly in groundwater and have, at numerous locations, tainted the water supplies of large urban areas.

State	Military installation	Status	Sites identified	Sites cleaned
AL	Gunter Air Force Base		1	
AL	Maxwell Air Force Base		23	1
AK	Alaskan Dewline		51	
AK	Cape Lisburne Air Force Station		6	
AK	Cape Newenham Air Force Station		6	6
AK	Cape Romanzof Air Force Station		17	
AK	Champion Air Force Station		8	
AK	Clear Air Force Base		15	
AK	Cold Bay Air Force Station		4	
AK	Eielson Air Force Base	S	64	
AK	Elmendorf Air Force Base	S	56	
AK	Fort Yukon Air Force Station		5	
AK	King Salmon Air Force Station		19	
AK	Murphy Dome Air Force Station		8	
AK	Naval Air Station, Adak		32	
AK	Shemya Air Force Base		52	23
AK	Sparrevohn Air Force Station		9	
AK	Tatalina Air Force Station		13	12
AK	Tin City Air Force Station		11	
AZ	Davis Monthan Air Force Base		51	
AZ	Luke Air Force Base	S	31	3
AZ	Williams Air Force Base	S*	14	
AR	Eaker Air Force Base	*	13	
AR	Little Rock Air Force Base		52	
CA	Beale Air Force Base		32	
CA	Castle Air Force Base	S*	39	
CA	Edwards Air Force Base	S	70	
CA	George Air Force Base	S*	69	1
CA	Hamilton Army Air Field	*	17	
CA	Los Angeles Air Force Station		37	
CA	March Air Force Base	S	41	
CA	Mather Air Force Base	S*	44	6
CA	McClellan Air Force Base	S	179	1
CA	Naval Air Field, El Centro		17	
CA	Naval Air Station, Alameda		20	
CA	Naval Air Station, Lemoore		17	
CA	Naval Air Station, Miramar		13	1
CA	Naval Air Station, Moffett Field	S*	21	
CA	Naval Air Station, North Island		12	
CA	Naval Auxiliary Landing Field, Crows Landing		5	
CA	Naval Auxiliary Landing Field, San Clemente Island		15	

Table continued

State	Military installation	Status	Sites identified	Sites cleaned
CA	Norton Air Force Base	S*	38	
CA	Onizuka Air Force Station		5	
CA	Outlying Field Imperial Beach		5	
CA	Travis Air Force Base	S	49	
CA	Vandenberg Air Force Base		49	
CO	Lowry Air Force Base	*	12	
CO	Peterson		10	
DE	Dover Air Force Base	S	112	
DC	Bolling Air Force Base		4	
FL	Cape Canaveral		2	
FL	Eglin Air Force Base		40	1
FL	Homestead Air Force Base	S	20	
FL	Hulbert Air Force Base		11	
FL	MacDill Air Force Base	*	56	
FL	Naval Air Station, Cecil Field	S	19	
FL	Naval Air Station, Jacksonville	S	47	1
FL	Naval Air Station, Key West		16	
FL	Naval Air Station, Pensacola	S	38	
FL	Naval Air Station, Richmond		1	
FL	Naval Air Station, Whiting Field		24	
FL	Patrick Air Force Base		35	
FL	Tyndall Air Force Base		28	
GA	Dobbins Air Force Base		7	
GA	Hunter Army Airfield		10	
GA	Moody Air Force Base		20	
GA	Robins Air Force Base	S	23	
HI	Bellows Air Force Base		3	
HI	Hickam Air Force Base		17	
HI	Kaala Air Force Station		8	
HI	Kanea Point Station		3	
HI	Kokee Air Force Station		2	
HI	Maui Air Force Station		13	
HI	Marine Corps Air Station, Keneohe Bay		20	
HI	Naval Air Station, Barbers Point		10	
HI	Punamano Air Force Station		1	
HI	Wheeler Air Force Base		8	
ID	Mountain Home Air Force Base	S	22	
IL	Chanute Air Force Base	*	22	2
IL	Naval Air Station, Glenview		9	
IL	Scott Air Force Base		9	
IN	Grissom Air Force Base	*	11	
KS	Forbes Field		11	
KS	McConnell Air Force Base		29	
LA	Barksdale Air Force Base		32	
LA	England Air Force Base	*	43	
LA	Naval Air Station, New Orleans		12	

Table continued

State	Military installation	Status	Sites identified	Sites cleaned
ME	Loring Air Force Base	S*	42	
ME	Naval Air Station, Brunswick	S	12	
MD	Andrews Air Force Base		31	1
MD	Naval Air Station, Patuxent River		31	1
MA	Cape Cod Air Force Station		1	
MA	Hanscomb Air Force Base		20	
MA	Naval Air Station, South Weymouth		8	
MA	Westover Air Force Base		16	
MI	K. I. Sawyer		17	
MI	Wurtsmith Air Force Base	*	20	3
MN	Duluth Airport		26	
MN	Minneapolis-St. Paul Airport	S	12	
MS	Columbus Air Force Base		29	10
MS	Keesler Air Force Base		15	4
MS	Naval Air Station, Meridian		4	
MO	Whiteman Air Force Base		18	
MT	Harve Air Force Station		1	
MT	Mallstrom		22	
NE	Offutt Air Force Base		32	
NV	Naval Air Station, Fallon		27	
NV	Nellis		59	
NH	New Boston Air Force Station		14	1
NH	Pease Air Force Base	S*	36	
NJ	McGuire Air Force Base		39	
NJ	Naval Air Engineering Center, Lakehurst	S	45	
NM	Cannon Air Force Base		22	
NM	Holloman Air Force Base		51	
NM	Kirtland Air Force Base		42	1
NY	Griffiss Air Force Base	S	49	
NY	Hancock Field		15	
NY	Niagara Falls Airport		14	
NY	Plattsburgh Air Force Base	S	30	
NC	Marine Corps Air Station, Cherry Point		34	2
NC	Pope Air Force Base		13	
NC	Seymour-Johnson Air Force Base		22	
ND	Grand Forks Air Force Base		7	
ND	Minot Air Force Base		4	
OH	Newark Air Force Station		10	
OH	Wright-Patterson Air Force Base	S	112	
OK	Altus Air Force Base		10	
OK	Tinker Air Force Base	S	34	
OK	Vance Air Force Base		22	8
OR	Kingsley Field		12	
PA	Greater Pittsburgh Airport		12	
PA	Naval Air Development Center, Warminster	S	9	
PA	Naval Air Station, Willow Grove		17	

Table continued

State	Military installation	Status	Sites identified	Sites cleaned
RI	Naval Air Station, Charlestown		1	
RI	Naval Air Station, Quonset Point		1	
SC	Charleston Air Force Base		31	
SC	Marine Corps Air Station, Beaufort		23	
SC	Myrtle Beach Air Force Base	*	27	
SC	Shaw Air Force Base		19	
SD	Ellsworth Air Force Base	S	25	
TN	Arnold Air Force Base		25	
TN	Naval Air Station, Memphis		13	
TX	Bergstrom Air Force Base	*	31	
TX	Brooks Air Force Base		13	1
TX	Carswell Air Force Base		18	
TX	Dyess Air Force Base		10	
TX	Goodfellow Air Force Base		6	1
TX	Kelly Air Force Base		72	
TX	Lackland		24	10
TX	Laughlin		13	5
TX	Naval Air Station, Chase Field	*	4	
TX	Naval Air Station, Corpus Christi		15	
TX	Naval Air Station, Dallas		12	
TX	Naval Air Station, Kingsville		13	
TX	Randolph Air Force Base		32	6
TX	Reese Air Force Base		13	3
TX	Sheppard Air Force Base		18	4
UT	Hill Air Force Base	S	39	
VA	Langley Air Force Base		36	
VA	Naval Air Station, Oceana		21	
WA	Fairchild Air Force Base	S	44	
WA	Makah Air Force Station		1	
WA	McChord Air Force Base	S	77	
WA	Naval Air Station, Whidbey Island	S	50	
WV	Yeager		4	
WY	F. E. Warren Air Force Base	S	30	

S = site listed on EPA Superfund National Priorities List.
* = facility slated for closure.

Proving Grounds and Test Sites

Jefferson Proving Ground (see Chapter 1) and Aberdeen Proving Ground (see Chapters 4 and 13) illustrate the scale and breadth of contamination found at the nation's proving grounds and test sites. Most frequently, as at JPG, these facilities have been used by the United States to test its weapons, leaving a dangerous scattering of unexploded munitions buried in the soil. These munitions threaten to explode at any time, leaving the land unusable for other purposes and making cleanup dangerous and difficult. In addition, if left for long periods these munitions threaten to leach their contents into the soil and groundwater. The military's proving grounds have also been home to the testing of some of the military's most dangerous and exotic weapons, such as chemical and biological agents.

State	Military installation	Status	Sites identified	Sites cleaned
AK	Gerstle River Test Site		5	
AZ	Yuma Proving Ground		43	
CA	Pacific Missile Test Center, Point Mugu		18	
IN	Jefferson Proving Ground	*	37	
MD	Aberdeen Proving Ground	S	58	
MD	Aberdeen Proving Ground, Edgewood Area	S	8	
MD	Blossom Point Field Test Activity		26	
NM	White Sands Missile Range		73	
NY	Youngstown Test (RADC)		10	
UT	Dugway Proving Ground		127	
UT	Green River Test Site		12	
VT	Ethan Allen Firing Range		6	
WA	Yakima Firing Center		37	

S = site listed on EPA Superfund National Priorities List.
* = facility slated for closure.

Naval Bases, Shipyards, and Stations

In the routine repair and maintenance of the Navy's fleet of ships and submarines, the military has contaminated soil, groundwater, and coastal waters with the toxic residue from paints and paint strippers, as well as fuels, solvents, waste oils, grease, and polychlorinated biphenyls (PCBs). Some of the facilities below are also involved in the production and storage of ammunition for the Navy.

State	Military installation	Status	Sites identified	Sites cleaned
CA	Naval Amphibious Base, Corona		5	
CA	Naval Shipyard, Long Beach		6	1
CA	Naval Shipyard, Mare Island		26	
CA	Naval Station, Long Beach	*	6	
CA	Naval Station, San Diego		8	

Table continued

State	Military installation	Status	Sites identified	Sites cleaned
CA	Naval Station, Treasure Island		26	
CA	Naval Station, Treasure Island-Hunter's Point Annex	S	22	1
CA	Naval Submarine Base, San Diego		4	
CA	Naval Weapon Command, China Lake		45	
CA	Naval Weapon Station, Concord		30	
CA	Naval Weapon Station, Seal Beach		42	
CA	Naval Weapon Station, Seal Beach Fallbrook Annex		10	
CT	Naval Submarine Base, New London	S	13	
DC	Naval Station, Anacostia		3	
FL	Naval Command Support Center, Panama City		9	
FL	Naval Station, Mayport		16	
GA	Naval Submarine Base, Kings Bay		16	
HI	Naval Shipyard, Pearl Harbor		15	1
HI	Naval Station, Pearl Harbor		5	
IN	Naval Weapon Station, Command Crane		30	
ME	Naval Shipyard, Portsmouth		14	
NJ	Military Ocean Terminal, Bayonne		33	
NJ	Naval Weapons Station Earle, Colts Neck	S	29	
NY	Naval Station, New York		1	
NY	Naval Station, New York/Stapleton		1	
NY	Naval Station, New York/Staten Island		3	
NC	Military Ocean Terminal, Sunny Point		14	
PA	Naval Shipyard, Philadelphia	*	16	
PA	Ship's Part Control Center, Mechanicsburg		11	1
SC	Naval Base, Charleston		12	4
SC	Naval Weapons Station, Charleston		18	
VA	Commander Naval Base, Norfolk		20	
VA	Naval Amphibious Base, Little Creek		17	
VA	Naval Fuel Depot/Naval Safety Center, Craney Island		13	
VA	Naval Safety Center Yorktown Fuels Division		20	
VA	Naval Shipyard (Norfolk), Portsmouth		19	
VA	Naval Weapons Station, Yorktown		20	
WA	Naval Submarine Base, Bangor	S	41	1
WA	Naval Undersea Warfare Engineering Station, Indian Island		10	2
WA	Naval Undersea Warfare Engineering Station, Keyport	S	9	
WA	Puget Sound	*	18	

S = site listed on EPA Superfund National Priorities List.
* = facility slated for closure.

Forts and Camps

Forts and camps are often large multipurpose facilities, and frequently military training is conducted at these locations. Such facilities often also contain equipment and supplies similar to those found at military depots. In some cases, entire divisions of military troops will be stationed at a given fort or camp. Toxic contamination at these facilities is prevalent, but often less extreme than that found at other types of facilities. Training in firefighting, during which oils and many other chemicals are repeatedly burned in pits on the ground, has left serious environmental problems, as has the routine dumping of petroleum products, pesticides and herbicides, solvents, and polychlorinated biphenyls (PCBs).

State	Military installation	Status	Sites identified	Sites cleaned
AL	Fort McClellan		60	
AL	Fort Rucker		106	
AK	Fort Greely		21	
AK	Fort Richardson		39	
AK	Fort Wainwright	S	50	3
AZ	Fort Huachuca		62	
AR	Fort Chaffee	*	34	
CA	Camp Roberts		38	
CA	Fort Cronkite		1	
CA	East Fort Baker		1	
CA	Fort Hunter Ligett		21	
CA	Fort Irwin		36	
CA	Fort MacArthur		18	
CA	Fort Ord	S*	166	
CA	Oakland Army Base		7	
CA	Presidio of Monterey		14	
CA	Presidio of San Francisco	*	35	
CO	Fort Carson		48	
CO	U.S. Air Force Academy		11	
DC	Fort McNair		7	
FL	Naval Training Center, Orlando		10	
GA	Fort Benning		87	
GA	Fort Gillem		5	
GA	Fort Gordon		78	
GA	Fort McPherson		9	
GA	Fort Stewart		85	
HI	Camp H. M. Smith, Oahu		2	
HI	Fort Kamehameha		1	
HI	Fort Shafter		5	
HI	Kapalma Military Reservation		4	

SUSPECTED SITES OF CONTAMINATION

Table continued

State	Military installation	Status	Sites identified	Sites cleaned
HI	Kilauea Military Reservation		5	
HI	Makua Military Reservation		4	
HI	Pohakuloa Training Area		7	
HI	Schofield Barracks	S	19	
IL	Fort Sheridan	*	10	1
IL	Naval Training Center, Great Lakes		14	
IL	St. Louis Area Support Center		40	
IN	Fort Benjamin Harrison	*	15	
IA	Fort Des Moines		9	
KS	Fort Leavenworth		56	
KS	Fort Riley	S	31	4
KY	Fort Campbell		35	
KY	Fort Knox		199	
LA	Fort Polk		22	
MD	Fort Detrick		45	
MD	Fort George G. Meade		72	
MD	Fort Ritchie		5	
MD	Phoenix Military Reservation		4	2
MA	Fort Devens	S*	56	
MA	Fort Devens/Sudbury Annex	S	12	1
MO	Camp Clark		1	
MO	Fort Leonard Wood		51	
MT	Fort Missoula		2	
NJ	Fort Dix	S	19	
NJ	Fort Monmouth		9	
NM	Fort Wingate	*	18	
NY	Fort Drum		70	
NY	Fort Hamilton		5	
NY	Fort Tilden		3	
NY	Fort Totten		1	
NY	West Point Military Academy		4	
NC	Camp Mackall		4	
NC	Fort Bragg		26	
NC	Marine Corps Base Camp LeJeune	S	82	3
OK	Camp Gruber		1	
OK	Fort Sill		47	
RI	Naval Education and Training Center, Newport		15	
SC	Fort Jackson		21	
TX	Camp Bullis		16	
TX	Fort Bliss		29	
TX	Fort Hood		52	
TX	Fort Sam Houston		28	
UT	Fort Douglas	*	23	
VA	Fort A. P. Hill		245	
VA	Fort Belvoir		59	

Table continued

State	Military installation	Status	Sites identified	Sites cleaned
VA	Fort Eustis		26	
VA	Fort Lee		23	1
VA	Fort Monroe		3	
VA	Fort Myer		5	
VA	Fort Story		3	
VA	Marine Corps, Quantico		19	1
WA	Fort Lewis	S	68	1
WI	Camp Williams		1	
WI	Camp Wismer		1	
WI	Fort McCoy		26	

S = site listed on EPA Superfund National Priorities List.
* = facility slated for closure.

Research Facilities

Military research—using relatively small quantities of exotic and often highly toxic chemicals and other materials—is conducted at numerous locations around the United States. The selected sites listed below are devoted exclusively to specific research and development missions and have left a diverse toxic legacy, including heavy metals, exotic toxics, and sometimes even radioactive contamination.

State	Military installation	Status	Sites identified	Sites cleaned
AK	Indian Mountain Research Site		20	
AK	Naval Arctic Laboratory, Barrow		13	
MA	U.S. Army Materials Technology Laboratory	*	19	
MD	Harry Diamond Laboratory (Adelphi)		39	
MD	Naval Explosive Ordnance Disposal Technology Center, Indian Head		9	
VA	Woodbridge Research Facility	*	13	1
WV	Automated Biological Laboratory, Mineral County		10	

* = facility slated for closure.

Nuclear Production Facilities

The United States' nuclear production facilities, run by the Department of Energy, are an integral piece of the nation's legacy of environmental contamination. Here the military's nuclear weapons have been built, leaving some of the most serious radioactive and mixed toxic and radioactive contamination known on the planet. The number of individual sites of contamination is not included, but virtually all of the facilities below are listed on the Superfund National Priorities List and no sites at any of these locations have yet been cleaned up.

State	Military installation
CA	Lawrence Livermore National Laboratory
CA	Sandia National Laboratory (Livermore)
CO	Rocky Flats Plant
FL	Pinellas Plant
ID	Idaho National Engineering Laboratory
KS	Kansas City Plant
NM	Los Alamos National Laboratory
NM	Sandia National Laboratory (Albuquerque)
NV	Nevada Test Site
OH	Fernald Feed Materials Production Center
OH	Mound Plant
SC	Savannah River Plant
TN	Oak Ridge Gaseous Plant
TN	Oak Ridge National Laboratory
TN	Oak Ridge Y-12 Plant
TX	Pantex Plant
WA	Hanford Nuclear Reservation

Miscellaneous

The above listing omits many participants in the overall military toxic picture—defense contractors, for instance, whose production of military weapons and equipment has frequently left a dangerous legacy of contamination. Also omitted for the sake of simplicity are hundreds of smaller polluted sites (such as many military reserve and national guard sites), roughly 7,000 formerly used lands suspected or known to be polluted, and the United States' more than 300 overseas bases. The military's (often contaminated) radar relay facilities have been largely omitted, as have facilities run by the Defense Logistics Agency and some of the potentially contaminated sites that the military has deemed—at least for the moment—to merit no further cleanup measures. Below are some facilities that fit none of the above categories.

State	Military installation	Sites identified	Sites cleaned
CA	Naval Cryptologic School, Stockton	7	
CO	Fitzsimmons Army Medical Center	25	
DC	Walter Reed Army Medical Center	3	
HI	Naval Communications Area Master Station, Eastern Pacific	14	
HI	Tripler Army Medical Center	4	
VA	CONUS Radar Sites	37	1
WA	Naval Radio Station, Jim Creek	8	

Pertinent Laws

The following section draws heavily upon (often simply paraphrases) a government document entitled *Federal Facilities Compliance Strategy*, published in November 1988 by the Office of Federal Activities of the U.S. Environmental Protection Agency. Some additional material derives from an excellent resource entitled *The Poisoned Well: New Strategies for Groundwater Protection*, edited by Eric P. Jorgensen, Sierra Club Legal Defense Fund (Island Press, Washington, D.C., 1989). Excerpts are taken, of course, from the texts of the laws themselves.

Clean Air Act

First enacted in 1955, the Clean Air Act (CAA) broke new ground in environmental legislation. Today this act calls upon the EPA to establish national ambient air standards. These standards, called the National Ambient Air Quality Standards (NAAQS), are expressed as concentrations of designated pollutants.

To meet these standards, states are required to file state implementation plans (SIPs). An SIP provides emission limitations and timetables for compliance for stationary sources as well as "transportation control plans" for mobile sources. In addition, the EPA also sets the following national air emission standards: New Source Performance Standards, National Emission Standards for Hazardous Pollutants, and standards governing mobile sources of air pollution (including those covering motor vehicle fuels). Special programs have also been developed to prevent significant deterioration in "clean air areas" and for stringent controls in "non-attainment areas."

The CAA focuses primarily upon "major" stationary sources of air pollution, which are defined as sources which generally emit more than 100 tons per year of a designated pollutant. Section 118 (42 USC 7418) governs "Control of Pollution from Federal Facilities" and holds these facilities subject to the legislation with a broad waiver of "sovereign immunity," both substantively and procedurally. Simply put, federal facilities (including military installations) are technically bound by the same air pollution laws as anyone else:

> Each department, agency, and instrumentality of the executive, legislative, and judicial branches of the Federal Government (1) having jurisdiction over any property or facility, or (2) engaged in any activity resulting, or which may result, in the discharge of air pollutants, and each officer, agent, or employee thereof, shall be subject to, and comply with, all Federal, State, interstate, and local requirements, administrative authority, and process and sanctions respecting the control and abatement of air pollution in the same manner, and to the same extent as any nongovernmental entity. The preceding sentence shall apply (A) to any requirement whether substantive or procedural (including any record keeping or reporting requirement, any requirement respecting permits and any other requirement whatsoever), (B) to the exercise of any Federal, State, or local administrative authority and (C) to any process and sanction, whether enforced in Federal, State, or local courts or in any other manner.

Section 118 (b) provides two kinds of exemption for federal facilities. The president may exempt a particular federal facility from compliance and/or issue regulations exempting specific military weaponry, equipment, etc. Each exemption is subject to the president's determination that it is "in the paramount interest of the United States to do so." The first exemption is for one year, renewable annually; the second is subject to presidential reconsideration at three-year intervals.

(Now codified at 42 USC 7401–7642; first enacted July, 1955 at 69 Stat. 485; first major amendments were PL 91-604, December 1970; completely revised August 1977; amended 1978, 1980, 1981, 1983.)

Clean Water Act

During the 1950s and 1960s, it fell to the states to set ambient water quality standards and develop plans to achieve these standards. In 1972, however, the existing Federal Water Pollution Control Act was significantly amended. These changes emphasized a new approach, combining water quality standards and effluent limitations. In 1977, the act was further amended to address toxic water pollutants and since then has been commonly referred to as the Clean Water Act (CWA).

The CWA authorizes states to establish ambient water quality standards and makes it illegal for any person (or organization, including federal facilities) to discharge pollutants from a "point source" into waters of the United States without a permit. Permits must be obtained (from either the EPA or the state) under the National Pollution Discharge Elimination Standards (NPDES) program of the CWA; permits allow only a specified and limited discharge of effluents.

The permitting authority (either the EPA or the state) is authorized to require dischargers to use "best management practices" (BMPs) to control the discharge of toxic and hazardous pollutants into waters of the United States. BMPs do not have numerical limits but are described in narrative form. Dischargers must also file "discharge monitoring reports," "noncompliance reports," and "emergency reports" regarding any discharge of toxic pollutants.

With language almost identical to the Clean Air Act (see above), section 313 (a) of the CWA also subjects federal agencies to federal, state, and local water pollution controls both substantively and procedurally:

Each department, agency, or instrumentality of the executive, legislative and judicial branches of the Federal Government (1) having jurisdiction over any property or facility, or (2) engaged in any activity resulting, or which may result, in the discharge or runoff of pollutants, and each officer, agent, or employee thereof, in the performance of his official duties, shall be subject to, and comply with, all Federal, State, interstate, and local requirements, administrative authority, and process and sanctions respecting the control and abatement of water pollution in the same manner, and to the same extent as any nongovernmental entity including the payment of reasonable service charges. The preceding sentence shall apply (A) to any requirement whether substantive or procedural (including any record keeping or reporting requirement, any requirement respecting permits and any other requirement whatsoever), (B) to the exercise of any Federal, State, or local administrative authority and (C) to any process and sanction, whether enforced in Federal, State, or local courts or in any other manner.

The CWA, in sections 505 (a) (1) and (f), provides for citizen lawsuits against federal facilities for failing to obtain the necessary permits, violations of the terms of a permit, or violation of effluent standards or limi-

191

tations. However, section 313 (a) limits federal facility liability to "civil penalties arising under federal law or imposed by a State or local court to enforce an order or the process of such a court." Like the CAA, the CWA also provides for presidential exemptions for executive branch agencies.

(Enacted October 18, 1972, as PL 92-500, a comprehensive revision of the Federal Water Pollution Control Act; now codified at 33 USC 1251–1376 amended every year between 1973 and 1983; most recently amended February 1987 by the Water Quality Control Act of 1987.)

Resource Conservation and Recovery Act

The Resource Conservation and Recovery Act (RCRA) was signed in 1976 and subsequently amended in 1978, 1980, 1984, and 1986. The 1984 amendments to RCRA brought about dramatic changes in the scope of the act. The Act deals primarily with current and future waste handling activities; section 7003, however, addresses problems which may have arisen prior to 1976.

According to section 7003, the EPA may take action against persons conducting past or present activities that present "an imminent or substantial endangerment to health or to the environment." The 1984 amendments also provide for corrective actions against contamination resulting from past releases of hazardous waste even without an imminent hazard.

All nonhazardous wastes (if they are disposed of on land) are regulated through state programs under subtitle D of RCRA. Hazardous solid wastes are subject to regulation in their generation, transport, treatment, storage, and disposal under subtitle C.

RCRA section 6001 (42 USC 6961) states that all branches of the federal government must comply with solid waste and hazardous waste requirements. The president may exempt any solid waste management facility from these regulations for one year if it is "in the paramount interest of the United States to do so."

Each department, agency, and instrumentality of the executive, legislative and judicial branches of the Federal Government (1) having jurisdiction over any solid waste management facility, or disposal site or (2) engaged in any activity resulting, or which may result, in the disposal or management of solid waste or hazardous waste shall be subject to, and comply with, all Federal, State, interstate, and local requirements, substantive or procedural (including requirement for permits or reporting or any provisions for injunctive relief and such sanctions as may be imposed by a court to enforce such relief), respecting control and abatement of solid waste or hazardous waste disposal in the same manner, and to the same extent, as any person is subject to such requirements, including payment of reasonable service charges. Neither the United States, nor any agent, employee, or officer thereof, shall be immune or exempt from any process or sanction of any State or Federal Court with respect to the enforcement of any such injunctive relief.

(Now codified at 42 USC 6901 et seq.; see also PL 94-580; enacted October 1976; amended 1978, 1980, 1984.)

Toxic Substances Control Act

The EPA regulates new and existing chemical substances and mixtures under the Toxic Substances Control Act (TSCA). Persons who "manufacture or import, process, distribute in commerce, use, or dispose of chemicals" can be required to submit information and to conduct tests; their activities may be limited in other ways as well.

Under section 8 (b) of TSCA, the EPA publishes and maintains an inventory of chemical substances in commerce. Any substance that is not included in that inventory is a "new chemical substance," and persons must notify the EPA at least ninety days in advance of manufacturing such a chemical. In that time the EPA may act to prohibit manufacture of that chemical.

Under section 4 of TSCA, the EPA can issue rules requiring manufacturers and processors of chemicals to test those chemicals for health and environmental effects. Manufacturers and distributors of chemicals must keep records and make reports concerning their actions regarding those chemicals. They must also maintain records of significant adverse effects on human health or the environment alleged to have been caused by the chemicals and must submit copies of those records to the EPA upon request.

TSCA also includes a "National Defense Waiver," codified at 15 USC 2621:

The Administrator shall waive compliance with any provision of this chapter upon request and determination by the President that the requested waiver is necessary in the interest of national defense. The Administrator shall maintain a written record of the basis upon which such a waiver was granted and make such a record available for camera examination when relevant in judicial proceeding under this chapter. Upon the issuance of such a waiver, the Administrator shall publish in the Federal Register a notice that the waiver was granted for national defense purposes, unless, upon the request of the President, the Administrator determines to omit such publication because the publication itself would be contrary to the interests of national defense, in which event the Administrator shall submit notice thereof to the Armed Services Committees of the Senate and the House of Representatives.

(15 USC 2601, et seq.; enacted September, 1976; amended 1981 [reauthorization only].)

Comprehensive Environmental Response, Compensation, and Liability Act (CERCLA, or the Superfund Act)

In December 1980, the Superfund Act authorized the federal government to clean up toxic or hazardous contaminants at closed and abandoned hazardous waste dumps. The law permits the government to recover the cost of this cleanup and associated damages by suing the responsible parties involved. Under the act, additional cleanup funds can be drawn from a "superfund" created by taxes on chemicals and hazardous wastes.

The act provides that when there is a release of a hazardous substance, either real or threatened, the parties who operate the vessel or facility which created the release are liable for the costs of containment, removal, remedial action and response, and for injury damages to natural resources under section 107 (a). The act also establishes limits on liability.

Regulatory provisions under sections 102 and 103 of the act require that the release of hazardous substances into the environment be reported unless the release is in accordance with an established permit or in an amount that is not a "reportable quantity."

Under the original act, all owners or operators of any facility handling and disposing of hazardous substances or that had handled hazardous substances in the past were required to inform the EPA by June 1981 of their facility activities unless they had a permit or had been accorded "interim status." Under the law, failure of notification is a crime, and if the party knowingly fails to provide this data they are not entitled to the prescribed limits and defenses of liability.

Federal agencies are specifically required to comply with CERCLA as stated at 42 USC 9607 (g):

Each department agency, or instrumentality of the executive, legislative, and judicial branches of the Federal Government shall be subject to, and comply with, this chapter in the same manner and to the same extent, both procedurally and substantively, as any non-governmental entity, including liability under this section.

CERCLA also established the Agency for Toxic Substances and Disease Registry (ATSDR) within the Public Health Service, to provide, in cooperation with other agencies, background toxicological and other information about hazardous chemicals:

> The ATSDR is to cooperate with the States to establish and maintain a national registry of serious diseases and illnesses; a national registry of persons exposed to toxic substances; an inventory of literature, research, and studies on the health effects of toxic substances; a listing of areas closed to the public or otherwise restricted in use because of toxic substance contamination; in cases of public health emergencies caused or believed to be caused by exposure to toxic substances, provide medical care and testing to exposed individuals; and either independently or as part of other health status survey, conduct periodic survey and screening programs to determine relationships between exposure to toxic substances and illness.

(42 USC 9601–9657; enacted December 1980; amended 1982, 1986.)

Superfund Amendments and Reauthorization Act

In October 1986, the Superfund Act was amended under the Superfund Amendments and Reauthorization Act (SARA). These amendments provide mandatory schedules for the completion of various phases of remedial response activities, establish detailed cleanup standards, and generally strengthen existing authority to effect the cleanup of superfund sites.

SARA section 120 restated and elaborated upon the requirement that federal facilities must comply with CERCLA and added that they must comply with state environmental laws as well. This section, codified at 42 USC 9620, is very clear:

> (a) (2) All guidelines, rules, regulations, and criteria which are applicable to preliminary assessments carried out under this chapter for facilities at which hazardous substances are located, applicable to evaluations of such facilities under the National Contingency Plan, applicable to inclusion on the National Priorities List, or applicable to remedial actions at such facilities shall also be applicable to facilities which are owned or operated by a department, agency, or instrumentality of the United States in the same manner and to the extent as such guidelines, rules, regulations, and criteria are applicable to other facilities. No department, agency, or instrumentality of the United States may adopt or utilize any such guidelines,

rules, regulations, or criteria which are inconsistent with the guidelines, rules, regulations, and criteria established by the Administrator under this chapter. . . .

(a) (4) State laws concerning removal and remedial action, including State laws regarding enforcement, shall apply to removal and remedial action at facilities owned or operated by a department, agency, or instrumentality of the United States when such facilities are not included on the National Priorities List.

Section 211 of SARA set forth a number of requirements and guidelines directed specifically at the Defense Department's environmental restoration activities. In particular, SARA called for the establishment of three programs: the Defense Environmental Restoration Program (DERP), an environmental research and development program, and a program for commonly found unregulated hazardous substances. In accordance with section 211, a special fund—the Defense Environmental Restoration Account (DERA)—was established.

Although technically not an amendment to the Superfund Act, an integral part of SARA is the Emergency Planning and Community Right-to-Know Act (see below).

Emergency Planning and Community Right-to-Know Act

Also known as SARA Title III, this act is intended to encourage and support emergency planning efforts at the state and local level and to provide local residents with information concerning potential chemical hazards in their communities.

Section 313 of the act requires manufacturers to report to the EPA and to the states the amounts of over 300 toxic chemicals that they release to the air, water, or land, or that they transfer to off-site facilities that treat or dispose of wastes. The law also requires the EPA to compile these reports into an annual assessment called the Toxics Release Inventory—also available to the public in a computerized database.

Federal facilities are not legally obligated to comply with the requirements of Title III because federal facilities are technically not included in the Title III definition of "person" in section 329 (7). (Contractor operators of "government-owned/contractor-operated" (GOCO) facilities, however, are subject to Title III to the same extent as any other operator.) The exclusion of federal facilities based on this narrow definition runs counter to the intent of the act to include any possible sources of chemical hazards in a community, as stated in 42 USC 11002:

(b) (1) Except as provided for in section 11004 of this title, a facility is subject to the requirements of this subchapter, if a substance on the list referred to in subsection (a) of this section is present at the facility in an amount in excess of the threshold planning quantity established for such substance.

(2) For purpose of emergency planning, a Governor or a State emergency response commission may designate additional facilities which shall be subject to the requirements of this subchapter, if such designation is made after public notice and opportunity for comment.

(42 USC 11001–11005; see also PL 99-499; enacted October 1986.)

Safe Drinking Water Act

The Safe Drinking Water Act (SDWA) of 1974 was established to ensure safe drinking water to the public. Both primary and secondary standards have been set by EPA regulations which apply to public water systems. National interim primary regulations were adopted in 1975, regulations concerning radionuclides in 1976 and for trihalomethanes in 1979. Secondary regulations were established in 1979 as guidelines to the states to protect non-health-related qualities of drinking water.

In 1986, amendments to the SDWA established a mandatory schedule requiring the establishment of primary drinking water regulations for eighty-three contaminants. In addition, the amendments prohibit the use of lead in public water systems, provide civil and criminal penalties for persons who tamper with public water systems, and allow closer scrutiny of state programs, including direct enforcement of drinking water standards, if necessary.

The 1986 amendments in SDWA section 1428 require all states to develop programs to protect wellhead areas. Section 1428 (h) requires all federal agencies having jurisdiction over any potential source of contaminants identified by a state wellhead protection program to be subject to and comply with all the requirements of the state program "as any other person, including payment of reasonable charges and fees." Presidential waivers are provided if such a waiver would protect the national interest.

Each Federal agency (1) having jurisdiction over any federally owned or maintained public water system or (2) engaged in any activity resulting, or which may result in, underground injection which endangers drinking water (within the meaning of section 300h(d) (2) of this title) shall be subject to and comply with, all Federal, State and local requirements, administrative authorities, and process and sanctions respecting the provision of safe drinking water and respecting any underground injection program in the same manner and to the same extent, as any nongovernmental entity.

(42 USC 300f, et seq.; enacted December, 1974; amended 1976, 1977, 1986, 1988.)

Freedom of Information Act

The Freedom of Information Act (FOIA) is not an environmental law, but for investigative purposes it is a vital piece of legislation. FOIA requires each federal agency to promulgate requirements and procedures enabling the public to request information from that agency. Each agency is required to publish their requirements and a description of their procedures in the Federal Register.

The types of documents which must be made available to the public are described in the following sections of the law:

(2) Each agency, in accordance with published rules, shall make available for public inspection and copying—

(A) final opinions, including concurring and dissenting opinions, as well as orders made in adjudication of cases;

(B) those statements of policy and interpretations which have been adopted by the agency and are not published in the Federal Register; and

(C) administrative staff manuals and instructions to staff that affect a member of the public;

unless the materials are promptly published and offered for sale. To the extent required to prevent clearly unwarranted invasion of personal privacy, an agency may delete identifying details when it makes available or publishes an opinion, statement of policy interpretation, or staff manual or instruction. However, in each case the justification for the deletion shall be explained fully in writing. Each agency shall also maintain and make available for public inspection and copying current indexes providing identifying information for the public as to any matter issued, adopted, or promulgated after July 4, 1967 and required by this paragraph to be made available or published. . . .

(3) Except with respect to the records made available under paragraphs (1) and (2) of this subsection, each agency, upon any request for records which (A) reasonably describes such records and (B) is made in accordance with published rules stating the time, place, fees (if any), and procedures to be followed, shall make records promptly available to any person.

(Now codified at 5 USC 552; see also PL 89-554, Sept. 6, 1966; amended 1967, 1974, 1976.)

Text of Executive Order 12088

October 13, 1978

Federal Compliance with Pollution Control Standards

By the authority vested in me as President by the Constitution and statutes of the United States of America, including Section 22 of the Toxic Substances Control Act (15 USC 2621), Section 313 of the Federal Water Pollution Control Act, as amended (33 USC 1323), Section 1447 of the Public Health Service Act, as amended by the Safe Drinking Water Act (42 USC 300j-6), Section 118 of the Clean Air Act, as amended (42 USC 7418(b)), Section 4 of the Noise Control Act of 1972 (42 USC 4903), Section 6001 of the Solid Waste Disposal Act, as amended (42 USC 6961), and Section 301 of Title 3 of the United States Code, and to ensure Federal compliance with applicable pollution control standards, it is hereby ordered as follows:

1-1. APPLICABILITY OF POLLUTION CONTROL STANDARDS

1-101. The head of each Executive agency is responsible for ensuring that all necessary actions are taken for the prevention, control, and abatement of environmental pollution with respect to Federal Facilities and activities under the control of the agency.

1-102. The head of each Executive agency is responsible for compliance with applicable pollution control standards, including those established pursuant to, but not limited to, the following:

(a) Toxic Substances Control Act (15 USC 2601 et seq.).

(b) Federal Water Pollution Control Act, as amended (33 USC 1251 et seq.).

(c) Public Health Service Act, as amended by the Safe Drinking Water Act (42 USC 300f et seq.).

(d) Clean Air Act, as amended (42 USC 7401 et seq.).

(e) Noise Control Act of 1972 (42 USC 4901 et seq.).

(f) Solid Waste Disposal Act, as amended (42 USC 6901 et seq.).

(g) Radiation guidance pursuant to Section 274(h) of the Atomic Energy Act of 1954, as amended (42 USC 2021(h); see also, the Radiation Protection Guidance to Federal Agencies for Diagnostic X rays approved by the President on January 26, 1978 and published at page 4377 of the Federal Register on February 1, 1978).

(h) Marine Protection, Research, and Sanctuaries Act of 1972, as amended (33 USC 1401, 1402, 1411–1421, 1441–1444 and 16 USC 1431–1434).

(i) Federal Insecticide, Fungicide, and Rodenticide Act, as amended (7 USC 136 et seq.).

1-103. " Applicable pollution control standards" means the same substantive, procedural, and other requirements that would apply to a private person.

1-2. AGENCY COORDINATION

1-201. Each Executive agency shall cooperate with the Administrator of the Environmental Protection Agency, hereinafter referred to as the Administrator, and State, interstate, and local agencies in the prevention, control, and abatement of environmental pollution.

1-202. Each Executive agency shall consult with the Administrator and with State, interstate, and local agencies concerning the best techniques and methods available for the prevention, control, and abatement of environmental pollution.

1-3. TECHNICAL ADVICE AND OVERSIGHT

1-301. The Administrator shall provide technical advice and assistance to Executive agencies in order to ensure their cost effective and timely compliance with applicable pollution control standards.

1-302. The Administrator shall conduct such reviews and inspections as may be necessary to monitor compliance with applicable pollution control standards by Federal facilities and activities.

1-4. POLLUTION CONTROL PLAN

1-401. Each Executive agency shall submit to the Director of the Office of Management and Budget, through the Administrator, an annual plan for the control of environmental pollution. The plan shall provide for any necessary improvement in the design, construction, management, operation, and maintenance of Federal facilities and activities, and shall include annual cost estimates. The Administrator shall establish guidelines for developing such plans.

1-402. In preparing its plan, each Executive agency shall ensure that the plan provides for compliance with all applicable pollution control standards.

1-403. The plan shall be submitted in accordance with any other instructions that the Director of the Office of Management and Budget may issue.

1-5. FUNDING

1-501. The head of each Executive agency shall ensure that sufficient funds for compliance with applicable pollution control standards are requested in the agency budget.

1-502. The head of each Executive agency shall ensure that funds appropriated and apportioned for the prevention, control, and abatement of environmental pollution are not used for any other purpose unless permitted by law and specifically approved by the Office of Management and Budget.

1-6. COMPLIANCE WITH POLLUTION CONTROLS

1-601. Whenever the Administrator or the appropriate State, interstate, or local agency notifies an Executive agency that it is in violation of an applicable pollution control standard (see Section 1-102 of this Order), the Executive agency shall promptly consult with the notifying agency and provide for its approval a plan to achieve and maintain compliance with the applicable pollution control standard. This plan shall include an implementation schedule for coming into compliance as soon as practicable.

1-602. The Administrator shall make every effort to resolve conflicts regarding such violation between Executive agencies and, on request of any party, such conflicts between an Executive agency and a State, interstate, or a local agency. If the Administrator cannot resolve a conflict, the Administrator shall request the Director of the Office of Management and Budget to resolve the conflict.

1-603. The Director of the Office of Management and Budget shall consider unresolved conflicts at the request of the Administrator. The Director shall seek the Administrator's technological judgements and determination with regard to the applicability of statutes and regulations.

1-604. These conflict resolution procedures are in addition to, not in lieu of, other procedures, including sanctions, for the enforcement of applicable pollution control standards.

1-605. Except as expressly provided by a Presidential exemption under this Order, nothing in this Order, nor any action or inaction under this Order, shall be construed to revise or modify any applicable pollution control standard.

1-7. LIMITATION ON EXEMPTIONS

1-701. Exemptions from applicable pollution standards may only be granted under statutes cited in Section 1-102(a) through 1-102(f) if the President makes the required appropriate statutory determination: that such exemption is necessary (a) in the interest of national security, or (b) in the paramount interest of the United States.

1-702. The head of an Executive agency may, from time to time, recommend to the President through the Director of the Office of Management and Budget, that an activity or facility, or uses thereof, be exempt from an applicable pollution control standard.

1-703. The Administrator shall advise the President, through the Director of the Office of Management and Budget, whether he agrees or disagrees with a recommendation for exemption and his reasons therefor.

1-704. The Director of the Office of Management and Budget must advise the President within sixty days of receipt of the Administrator's views.

1-8. GENERAL PROVISIONS

1-801. The head of each Executive agency that is responsible for the construction or operation of Federal facilities outside the United States shall ensure that such construction or operation complies with the environmental pollution control standards of general applicability in the host country or jurisdiction.

1-802. Executive Order No. 11752 of December 17, 1973, is revoked.

[Jimmy Carter]
The White House
October 13, 1978

Executive Order 12146

Among other things, Executive Order 12146 (signed on July 18, 1979), establishes the Federal Legal Council, which consists of the attorney general and representatives of fifteen federal agencies. The council is responsible for resolving problems that are beyond the capacity or authority of individual agencies. The Federal Legal Council is also responsible for resolving interagency disputes, including those concerning jurisdiction over problems and legal disputes between head agency officials. Under this executive order, legal disputes between federal agencies are to be referred to the attorney general for resolution.

Executive Order 12580

Executive Order 12580 (January 23, 1987, revoking E.O. 12316 and amending E.O. 12088) addresses the delegation of duties and powers assigned to the president in CERCLA as amended by SARA. It requires the National Contingency Plan (NCP) to provide for national and regional response teams composed of representatives from various federal agencies to plan and coordinate preparedness and response actions. Normally chaired by the EPA, agencies represented on the response teams include virtually all Cabinet offices as well as the EPA and the Nuclear Regulatory Commission, among others, and may include representatives from state and local governments.

Importantly, section 10 of E.O. 12580, entitled "Federal Facilities," provides for the use of E.O. 12580 "dispute resolution procedures" prior to the selection of a remedial action by the EPA administrator. This provision effectively shifted enforcement power into the hands of the Department of Justice. In the case of conflicts, this section states that "the Director of the Office of Management and Budget shall facilitate resolution of any issues."

Glossary

Aquifer Formation of porous rock through which groundwater flows and which is capable of holding water in usable quantities. The depth of such a formation varies; sometimes it is directly below the earth's surface. Beneath this porous rock, a layer of clay or other less permeable substance forms the base of the aquifer, usually sloped in a manner that determines the direction, and to some extent the speed, of the groundwater flow.

Army Armament, Munitions, and Chemical Command Major subordinate command of the Army Materiel Command, headquartered in Rock Island, Illinois. (This agency is responsible for procuring and managing DS2 for all the military services.)

Army Corps of Engineers Major Army command for technical matters. The Army Corps of Engineers is responsible for the Formerly Used Defense Sites Program, the remedial design/remedial action phase of all Army installation restoration programs.

Army Toxic and Hazardous Materials Agency Also known as USATHAMA, this agency is responsible for handling the initial study phases of the Army's installation restoration programs.

Carcinogen A substance known to cause or help the growth of cancerous cells. There is debate over what substances should be considered carcinogens. Some agencies require a greater weight of evidence than others; for example, a list of carcinogens developed by the U.S. Occupational Safety and Health Administration (OSHA) does not include trichloroethylene (TCE), but TCE is treated as a carcinogen under other regulatory programs.

CERCLA See Superfund.

Clean Air Act First enacted in 1955. The act's purpose is to "protect and enhance the quality of the Nation's air resources." Its primary application is through the National Emission Standards for Hazardous Air Pollutants and through "Prevention of Significant Deterioration" permits to regulate new potentially polluting facilities. For more information on the Clean Air Act's specific application to federal facilities, see Appendix C.

Clean Water Act Amended the Federal Water Pollution Control Act, which was first passed in 1956. The Clean Water Act's objective is to "restore and maintain the chemical, physical, and biological integrity of the Nation's waters." The act's major enforcement tool is the "National Pollutant Discharge Elimination Systems" permit. For more information on its specific application to federal facilities, see Appendix C.

Comprehensive Environmental Response, Compensation and Liability Act (CERCLA) See Superfund.

Curie A measure of radioactive decay of a substance. A curie is equivalent to the radioactivity of one gram of radium, or 37 billion disintegrations per second.

Cyanide Cyanide is a toxic chemical that attacks the central nervous and cardiovascular systems, liver, kidneys, and skin; it is fatal in high doses. Solutions containing cyanide are used in electroplating. The hazardous liquid wastes generated by this process are a common contaminant in military industrial activities. See Electroplating.

DCE See Dichloroethylene.

Decommissioning The process of removing a facility from operation, followed by decontamination, dismantlement, or conversion to another use.

Decontaminant Solution 2 See DS2.

Defense and the Environment Initiative A program developed by the Secretary of Defense to coordinate cooperative efforts between environmentalists, the military, and the defense industries to identify, and develop strategies to deal with, environmental issues that affect the military facilities and operations. The first forum on the initiative was held September 6–7, 1990, in Washington, D.C.

Defense Environmental Restoration Account (DERA) Account established by section 211 of the Superfund Amendments and Reauthorization Act of 1986 (SARA). DERP projects are funded out of this account.

Defense Environmental Restoration Program (DERP) The Department of Defense's overall program to clean up its military installations. Congress centralized and expanded the various installation restoration plans in 1984. The program consists of three major elements: the Installation Restoration Program (IRP), Other Hazardous Waste Operations (OHW), and Building Demolition and Debris Removal (BDDR).

Defense Logistics Agency The major agency that procures and manages materials for the Department of Defense. It has its own installation restoration program, which includes sites at defense depots and fuel support stations, and the Defense Reutilization and Marketing Service, which sells excess military property.

Defense Priority Model The Department of Defense's method of ranking sites in need of cleanup on a "worst first basis."

Defense Reutilization and Marketing Service (DRMS) A service of the Defense Logistics Agency, in charge of the military's surplus sales program. The DRMS has marketing offices around the country (DRMOs). In 1980, the secretary of defense tasked the Defense Logistics Agency with disposing of some hazardous materials through the surplus program.

Department of Energy (DOE) Formed in 1977, the Department of Energy absorbed its predecessor agencies, the Atomic Energy Commission (AEC) and the Energy Research and Development Administration (ERDA). The DOE is responsible for nuclear research and development and management of the nation's nuclear production facilities, including nuclear waste management.

DERA See Defense Environmental Restoration Account.

DERP See Defense Environmental Restoration Program.

Dichloroethylene (DCE) DCE is a volatile organic compound which is used as an industrial extraction solvent. It can cause damage to the central nervous and circulatory systems, lungs, liver, and kidneys.

Dinitrotoluene (DNT) 2,4 DNT and 2,6 DNT are the forms of dinitrotoluene most commonly found at hazardous waste sites. DNT breaks down relatively quickly in the presence of sunlight and bacteria, but it can linger persistently in soil or groundwater. DNT can be safely ingested in minute quantities in groundwater, but has long posed a significant danger to ammunition plant workers exposed via inhalation or ingestion. The chemical is believed to cause cancer and nervous system damage (and many other ailments).

DNT See Dinitrotoluene.

DS2 DS2, a combination of diethylenetriamine and ethylene glycol monomethyl ether, is a substance procured exclusively by the Department of Defense to decontaminate machinery after a chemical weapons attack. DS2 is incompatible with most metals and is not authorized for training due to the hazards it presents to humans who are exposed to it. DS2 can cause severe burns, stricture of the esophagus, and damage to the central nervous system, liver, and reproductive systems.

Electroplating An electrochemical process for coating a metal object with a thin layer of a different metal, usually for protective purposes. The object is placed in a conductive solution containing dissolved metals, and which often contains cyanide. Through electrolysis the dissolved metals are made to adhere to electrons on the submerged object. Strong solvents are used to prepare the metals for this process.

Environmental Protection Agency (EPA) Established in 1970, the EPA is charged with protecting and enhancing the environment today and for future generations to the fullest extent possible under the laws enacted by Congress. The EPA controls and abates pollution by establishing regulations in the areas of air, water, solid waste, noise, radiation, and toxic substances. For a listing of the EPA's regional offices, see Appendix A.

Fire training areas Areas of land where waste oils and other hazardous materials are poured directly on the ground and set ablaze to train firefighters.

Formerly Used Defense Sites Program (FUDS) The FUDS Program oversees the cleanup of contaminated properties used by any branch of the Defense Department. Sites are included in this program after a determination has been made as to the source of contamination at the site, land transfer, and current ownership of property. A survey of formerly used sites has been conducted to determine which sites should be investigated for possible contamination.

FUDS See Formerly Used Defense Sites Program.

General Accounting Office (GAO) The investigative arm of Congress which inspects the operations of governmental agencies.

Groundwater Precipitation that has percolated down into the soil and filled the spaces in the rock below in the same way that water fills a sponge. At this level, called the unsaturated zone, both air and water fill the space between the soil and rock. Water at this level may evaporate or be used by plants in a process called transpiration. (If neither of these occur, the water drains deeper into the ground, to the so-called saturated zone, where only water fills the spaces.) Nearly half of the population in the United States and a much higher percentage of rural residents depend on groundwater as their primary water source.

Hazardous Ranking System (HRS) In accordance with CERCLA, section 105, the EPA developed this system to evaluate the relative risks posed by a site to human health or the environment. The HRS is the principal mechanism for placing sites on the National Priorities List. It takes into account not only the toxicity of the contaminants present at a site but also the number of pathways present for the contaminants to reach the population or the environment.

Heavy metals These metals, such as arsenic, cadmium, lead, and mercury, are toxic at very low levels and can accumulate in living organisms over time; their specific health effects vary, ranging from nervous system damage to carcinogenesis.

Injection wells Used for the disposal of hazardous waste by injecting wastes directly into the ground. Injection wells were first used in the oil fields of the 1930s; as those operations diversified, so did the wastes that were injected into the ground. Some injection wells are shallow and unsealed, with the intention of letting the contaminants undergo percolation, while others are sealed or placed deep into rock formations in an effort to prevent the migration of contaminants.

Installation restoration program The military's program to address environmental contamination at its facilities. Before the military's environmental cleanup program was centralized under DERP, each branch had its own installation restoration program, beginning in the 1970s.

Interagency agreement The Superfund Amendments and Reauthorization Act of 1986 requires that an interagency agreement between the military and the Environmental Protection Agency be reached within 180 days of a record of decision. An interagency agreement is a formal document in which the two agencies (and often the appropriate state agency) agree to cooperate. It provides a detailed management plan for the cleanup of an installation, particularly the oversight roles each agency will play.

Interim action Action taken by an installation to control or abate a pollution source before the final installation restoration studies have been completed. A decision is made to execute an interim action if a source of pollution is readily identifiable and easily removed or if the source of pollution poses an immediate health risk. The studies then determine whether any additional action is needed.

Iodine-131 A radioactive material with a half-life of eight days. Iodine-131 collects in the thyroid gland if its receptors are not full of normal iodine. Iodine-131 was released in large quantities from Hanford Nuclear Reservation when fuel from the reactors was dissolved in acids to extract plutonium.

Landfill An in-ground disposal site for wastes. Landfills were designed to reduce air pollution and unsightly trash that resulted from open dumping and burning, however, landfills leak contaminants into the soil and groundwater. Today many are built with elaborate leak prevention systems, but most, especially the older ones, are simply large holes in the ground eventually covered with dirt.

Leaching pit Unlined lagoon, trench, or pit where liquid wastes are poured. Historically, it was thought the contaminants would undergo percolation and evaporation in the same manner as domestic waste in septic tank systems. Most types of hazardous wastes, however, do not biodegrade in the same manner as domestic waste does, and these pits are often the source of groundwater contamination.

Migration For our purposes, the movement of contaminants through the environment. The speed and extent of contaminant migration through the soil or groundwater depends on the geology of the site as well as the contaminant involved.

Mustard gas Also known as sulfur mustard. Exposure to mustard gas by breathing or skin contact can result in death accompanied by painful coughing, vomiting, burning eyes, and shock. Mustard gas was produced for chemical warfare, but it has not been manufactured in the United States since World War II. It is stored as a liquid and does not turn into a gas until it has been released into the atmosphere. The gas breaks down into other compounds quickly after dissolving in water.

Napalm A jellied gasoline substance widely used as an incendiary weapon during the Vietnam War.

National Priorities List The Comprehensive Environmental Response, Compensation, and Liability Act (CERCLA) of 1980 required the EPA to identify at least 400 sites for inclusion in the Superfund program. The EPA's Hazardous Ranking System is the principle mechanism for placing sites on the National Priorities List. CERCLA also allows states or territories to identify one top priority site, regardless of its score, to be included in the program and allows a site to be placed on the list if the Agency for Toxic Substances and Disease Registry of the U.S. Centers for Disease Control issues a health advisory recommending that people be removed from the site.

Nuclear Regulatory Commission (NRC) Established in 1974 as an independent regulatory agency to develop and enforce regulations for all commercial nuclear activities. It licenses and regulates commercial nuclear power plants, industries, individuals, and organizations that possess and use radioactive materials.

Parts per billion (ppb) A unit of measurement in which one part of a contaminant is diluted in a billion equal parts of water, soil, or air.

Parts per million (ppm) A unit of measurement in which one part of a contaminant is diluted in a million equal parts of water, soil, or air. Sometimes contamination is expressed in terms of ppm, but usually it is in parts per billion.

PCBs See Polychlorinated biphenyls.

Pentagon Headquarters for the Department of Defense, located in Washington, D.C. Built by the War Department in 1943 to consolidate its various office buildings, it is still considered the largest single office building in the world. In this book, the term also refers by extension to the Department of Defense itself.

Pentagon Inspector General Department within the Office of the Secretary of Defense responsible for investigating and reviewing military operations.

Plume Underground area of contamination. With the highest concentrations usually nearest to the pollution source, a plume spreads by moving along with the groundwater and becomes dispersed more evenly throughout the soil and groundwater at greater distances.

Plutonium Radioactive material used in nuclear weapons. Plutonium is obtained by irradiating enriched uranium, dissolving the irradiated fuel in acid, and separating out the plutonium.

Polychlorinated biphenyls (PCBs) A family of chemicals that are probable carcinogens, once widely used in electrical insulation. Even though their use was banned in the United States in 1979, PCB contamination has occurred on U.S. bases where abandoned electrical transformers have leaked into the environment.

Ppb See Parts per billion.

Preliminary Assessment/Site Inspection (PA/SI) The first step in the military's cleanup process. An installation-wide study to determine if sites are present that may pose a threat to public health or the environment. The site inspection consists of sampling and analysis to confirm the existence of actual contamination.

Rad (radiation absorbed dose) Expresses the amount of energy deposited by radiation into a substance, such as human tissue.

Radioactive isotope An unstable isotope of an element that will eventually undergo radioactive decay by spontaneous emission of charged particles, photons, or both.

RCRA See Resource Conservation and Recovery Act.

RDX An acronym for "Research and Development Explosive," chemical name, hexahydro-1,3,5-trinitro-1,3,5-triazine. RDX is the primary contaminant at the Cornhusker Army Ammunition Plant in Nebraska and at numerous other ammunition plants around the country. The Army noted toxic effects among soldiers in Vietnam who were exposed to RDX, either through accidental ingestion or prolonged exposure to RDX fumes. The chemical was sometimes used to heat the soldiers' rations. Its longterm effects are not well known but, U.S. soldiers were documented to have experienced seizures, vomiting, amnesia, and even coma from exposure to the chemical.

Rem Rem effective dose equivalent is a method of describing the amount of radiation a person has been exposed to in terms of the potential health risk of the exposure. It takes into account both the amount and type of radiation a person has been exposed to. This method is used to place different types of radiation exposure on an equivalent basis for comparison.

Remedial Design/Remedial Action (RD/RA) The final phase of the military's cleanup process, during which detailed plans for cleanup are prepared and implemented. The plans utilize information gained from a Remedial Investigation/Feasibility Study and incorporate any requirements included in the interagency agreement with the appropriate EPA or state regulatory authorities for the cleanup.

Remedial Investigation/Feasibility Study (RI/FS) The second phase of the military's cleanup process, providing more information on the nature, extent and significance of contamination and determining the risk posed to the general population by the contamination. Concurrent with a remedial investigation, a feasibility study is conducted to examine the alternatives for cleanup actions at the site.

Resource Conservation and Recovery Act (RCRA) First enacted in 1976 to regulate solid and hazardous wastes. Facilities that treat, store or dispose of hazardous waste on-site, in surface impoundments, underground tanks, injection wells, or other means and facilities who ship hazardous waste off-site are subject to close regulation under the act. For more on the specific application of RCRA to federal facilities, see Appendix C.

SARA See Superfund Amendments and Reauthorization Act.

Site For our purposes, a specific locus of contamination. Sites vary in size and may contain contamination from several different sources, so the number of sites at a facility does not necessarily indicate the extent of contamination present.

Solvents Volatile organic compounds, such as trichloroethylene, used as powerful cleaners, degreasers, and paint strippers, among other things. Solvents were widely used in the military's industrial production and maintenance operations and routinely dumped untreated into the ground.

Source reduction The Department of Defense has set the goal of reducing hazardous waste generation at its sources by 50 percent by 1992. This reduction is to be achieved through product substitution, recycling, and inventory control, and by developing new industrial processes that use less hazardous materials, such as bead-blasting rather than solvents to remove paint.

Sovereign immunity A longstanding U.S. legal doctrine with origins in medieval British law, which holds that the federal government cannot be sued by states or other parties except under special circumstances. Most recent environmental legislation has included specific waivers of sovereign immunity, and yet even these directives have so far proven difficult to enforce in the courts.

Spent fuel Uranium fuel that has been "burned" (irradiated) in a nuclear power plant's reactor to the point where it no longer contributes efficiently to the nuclear chain reaction. Spent fuel is thermally hot and highly radioactive—more so than when it is first inserted into the reactor.

Strontium-90 A highly radioactive byproduct of nuclear reactors. It has a half-life of twenty-eight years and is a particularly hazardous constituent of fallout because it is metabolized like calcium and included in bone.

Sump pit Primitive drainage pit, often lined with concrete or concrete blocks, designed primarily to receive run-off water.

Superfund Shorthand name for the Comprehensive Environmental Response, Compensation, and Liability Act (CERCLA), enacted in 1980 and reauthorized in 1986 by the Superfund Amendments and Reauthorization Act of 1986 (SARA). It provides the statutory authority for cleanup of hazardous substances that could endanger public health or welfare, or the environment. For more information on its specific application to federal facilities, see Appendix C.

Superfund Amendments and Reauthorization Act (SARA) Enacted in 1986 to clarify and expand CERCLA. Significant sections are SARA Title III, The Emergency Planning and Community Right-to-Know Act, section 120, reporting requirements regarding the progress of environmental cleanup at all federal facilities, and section 211, which establishes the Defense Environmental Restoration Account. For more information, see Appendix C.

TCE See Trichloroethylene.

Technical review committee A cleanup advisory committee which includes members of the community, local, state or federal regulatory agencies and base personnel. Also called by other names such as task force or steering panel.

TNT See Trinitrotoluene.

Toxic Poisonous. A chemical's toxic effects depend not only upon the intrinsic properties of the chemical, but also upon the conditions in which people or the environment are exposed to it. Chemicals vary greatly in their physical make-up, in the ways they travel through and react to the environment, in the potential routes and amounts of exposure, and in their fate in the environment or in biological systems. Furthermore, the issue of what effects, ranging from drowsiness to irreversible biological damage, are considered toxic is also the subject of debate. Thus, neither the EPA, nor Congress, nor the scientific community has ever created a universally accepted list of toxic chemicals. The EPA has generated many different toxicity lists (or toxicity indexes) under various environmental laws, including the Resource Conservation and Recovery Act (RCRA), the Safe Water Drinking Act, and the Emergency Planning and Community Right-to-Know Act. Each law requires the EPA to consider toxic effects of chemicals in different parts of the environment (air, land, or water); what level of a certain chemical is considered toxic would depend on where it was found. Other federal agencies, as well as state governments, have compiled their own lists of toxic chemicals, often using slightly different standards. In this book, unless otherwise noted, information about a chemical's toxicity is taken from the National Institute for Occupational Safety and Health (NIOSH) publication, *NIOSH Pocket Guide to Chemical Hazards* (Washington, D.C.: U.S. Government Printing Office, 1990).

Toxic Release Inventory (TRI) TRI is an annually updated, publicly available compilation of information collected by the EPA on the release of toxic chemicals by manufacturing facilities in the United States. This information is collected pursuant to the Emergency Planning and Community Right-to-Know Act of 1986 and is available on-line through the National Library of Medicine in Washington, D.C., or in printed form from the U.S. Government Printing Office in Washington, D.C. To date, the U.S. military is not required to submit information about its toxic releases.

Toxic Substances Control Act Enacted in 1976, the act authorizes the EPA to regulate the manufacture of chemical substances. Under the act, the EPA may require manufacturers to test chemicals to determine their toxicity and chemical properties and may take regulatory action to control the manufacture, distribution, use, or disposal of chemicals where such activities present an unreasonable risk of injury to health or the environment. For more information, see U.S. Environmental Protection Agency, *Federal Facilities Compliance Strategy* (Washington, D.C.: U.S. Government Printing Office, 1988) and Appendix C.

Trichloroethylene (TCE) A powerful degreasing solvent, once widely used. TCE sometimes degrades into even more toxic chemicals such as vinyl chloride, a known carcinogen.

Trinitrotoluene (TNT) A high explosive used in the manufacture of bombs and other munitions. It is primarily absorbed by humans through the skin or through inhalation or ingestion of its fumes and dust. Some of its effects are liver and kidney damage, anemia, leukocytosis, and peripheral neuropathy.

Unexploded ordnance (UXO) Munitions left over from test firings which may still have explosive potential. The question of whether or not unexploded ordnance is considered hazardous waste is a subject of much debate. The Department of Defense's Priority Model and the EPA's Hazardous Ranking System currently do not consider it so.

Unified command Composed of forces from two or more military services, a unified command has a broad and continuing mission and is normally organized on a geographical basis.

Unitary theory of the executive As enunciated by the Department of Justice, this theory requires that conflicts between executive branch agencies be resolved internally through administrative dispute resolution mechanisms and not in the courts. According to this theory, the EPA is barred from taking judicial actions against other federal agencies.

USATHAMA See Army Toxic and Hazardous Materials Agency.

UXO See Unexploded ordnance.

Vinyl chloride An easily liquified gas used in the production of certain kinds of plastics. Known to cause kidney, lung, and liver cancer when inhaled. It may also be a daughter compound of trichloroethylene.

VOCs See Volatile organic compounds.

Volatile organic compounds (VOCs) Substances which readily convert into gaseous forms, including many types of fuels and solvents. These substances migrate more easily through the soil and groundwater.

White phosphorus Used in incendiary weapons and as a marker in emergencies and night maneuvers (through the emission of white smoke). White phosphorus presents a particularly difficult cleanup problem because it ignites spontaneously in moist air. It can cause severe burns upon skin or eye contact; if inhaled, it is an irritant to the respiratory tract and may cause anemia and other toxic effects.

Notes

Preface

xi   *most toxic square mile.* Rocky Mountain installation commander, cited in *Rocky Mountain News*, February 1, 1984, p. 6.

xi   *well-known magazine.* See Stephanie Pollack and Seth Shulman, "The Environment: Toxic Responsibility," *The Atlantic*, vol. 263, no. 3, March 1989, pp. 26–31.

xi   *booklet about the arsenal contamination.* U.S. Army Materiel Command, "Meeting the Challenge: Contamination Cleanup at Rocky Mountain Arsenal," distributed by U.S. Army program manager's office for Rocky Mountain Arsenal Cleanup, Commerce City, Colo.

xii   *millions of gallons of wastes.* See Attorney General of Colorado, "Rocky Mountain Arsenal (RMA) Facts and Issues," prepared for *State of Colorado v. United States Department of the Army*, July 22, 1986, Denver, Colo.

xiii   *plume of highly toxic chemicals.* Karen B. Wiley and Steven L. Rhodes, "The Case of Rocky Mountain Arsenal," *Environment*, vol. 29, no. 3, April 1987, pp. 18–20, citing HRS Water Consultants, Inc., for South Adams County Water and Sanitation District, February 1985.

xiii   *greater than that of the top five.* Testimony by Carl Schafer, Jr., Deputy Assistant Secretary of Defense for Environment, U.S. House of Representatives, Hearing before the Subcommittee on Environment, Energy, and Natural Resources of the Committee on Government Operations, *Hazardous Waste Problems at Department of Defense Facilities*, November 5, 1987 (Washington D.C.: U.S. Government Printing Office, 1988), p. 78. See also "Toxic Waste: Pentagon # 1," *Recon*, vol. 9, no. 4, January 1987.

xiii   *Billions of gallons of toxic wastes.* Personal estimate based on Defense Department assessment that it generates more than 400,000 tons of hazardous waste annually and their acknowledgement that past practices included "discharge on the ground into unlined pits . . . or local creeks," "pouring and spraying on the ground," "drainage to industrial sewers," and "storage in leaking underground tanks." See U.S. Department of Defense, *Defense Environmental Restoration Program Annual Report to Congress for Fiscal Year 1988*, March 1989, for specific site descriptions.

xiv   *"At one early meeting.* author interview with Beth Gallegos, April 1989.

xiv   *Army officials admitted.* Citizens Against Contamination, "Summary of Water Problem, Events and Solution," unpublished fact sheet.

xiv   *the description of Basin F.* U.S. District Court for the District of Colorado, *State of Colorado, v. United States Department of the Army*, Civil Action No. 86-C-2524, request for preliminary injunction delivered November 30, 1987.

xv   *the Army's latest brochure.* U.S. Army Materiel Command, "Basin F: A Success Story," distributed by Public Affairs Office, Rocky Mountain Arsenal, Commerce City, Colo.

xv   *432 million cubic feet.* Cost projection from U.S. General Accounting Office, *Hazardous Waste: Selected Aspects of Cleanup Plan for Rocky Mountain Arsenal*, August 1986 (Washington, D.C.: U.S. Government Printing Office), p. 9.

One. Minefield in the Heartland

This chapter is based on author interviews with Morris Wooden, mayor of Madison, Ind.; Colonel Dennis O'Brien, commander of Jefferson Proving Ground (JPG); Gary Stegner, public affairs officer, JPG; Mike Moore, operations research analyst at JPG; and other JPG officials, Madison Ind., June 1990.

3   *fiscal belt-tightening measure.* The Commission on Base Closure and Realignment, Secretary of Defense, *Report to Congress*, December 1988.

3   *Jefferson Proving Ground.* For a history of JPG, see Sue Baker, *For Defense of Our Country: Echoes of Jefferson Proving Ground* (Indianapolis: Guild Literary Services, 1990).

3   *there aren't any funds.* "With the understanding the money will not be available, the Secretary of Defense has now informed Mr. Hamilton [U.S. Representative from Indiana] that portions of JPG will not be cleaned up at all." Letter to U.S. Attorney Deborah Daniels, no date given, Concerned Citizens of Jefferson County.

4   *the Army wants simply to abandon the site.* Letter from Assistant Secretary of Defense (Production and Logistics) Jack Katzen to the Honorable Lee Hamilton (U.S. Representative from the 9th District, Indiana), August 23, 1989. In response to a letter from Hamilton, Katzen writes, "I regret to inform you that it is unlikely that Jefferson Proving Ground will be completely cleaned up for unrestricted use." The letter goes on to explain the department's responsibility for cleanup, stating that "[c]leanup under DERP is executed on a worst first basis and it is not anticipated that the Jefferson Proving Ground sections will have a high priority. It is therefore

likely that some sections of Jefferson Proving Ground will remain under government control for a significant period of time."

4 *"largest contiguous contaminated area."* Letter from Senator Dan Coats to Secretary of Defense Richard Cheney, November 29, 1989.

4 *23 million rounds of ordnance.* Indiana Department of Environmental Management, *Report to the Governor: U.S. Army, Jefferson Proving Ground Evaluation*, Madison, Ind., April 20, 1989, pp. iv-v.

5 *another 6.9 million bombs and shells.* Ibid, p. vi.

5 *only 2,000 of the installation's 55,000 acres.* See Sue Baker, *For Defense of Our Country: Echoes of Jefferson Proving Ground* (Indianapolis: Guild Literary Services, 1990), p. xv, and *Report to the Governor,* cited above.

6 *"throw a fence around it."* Statement of Hayden Bryan as quoted by Lee Hamilton, U.S. House of Representatives, Hearings before the Environmental Restoration Panel of the Committee on Armed Services, *Overview of DOD Environmental Activities*, March 15, April 5, 11, 25, 26, May 2, 17, 1989 (Washington, D.C.: U.S. Government Printing Office, 1990), p. 425.

6 *as much as $5 billion.* From an internal JPG study cited by Mayor Wooden and others during interviews, June 1990.

6 *two children were killed.* See *Los Angeles Times*, San Diego County edition, February 4, 1985, p. 1; see also the comments of Representative Vic Fazio, U.S. House of Representatives, Hearings on H.R. 1872 before the House Subcommittee on Armed Services, *Defense Department Authorization and Oversight* (Washington D.C.: U.S. Government Printing Office, 1985), p. 986.

7 *more than 20,000 sites.* U.S. Department of Defense, *Defense Environmental Restoration Program Annual Report to Congress for Fiscal Year 1990*, February 1991, pp. 6–9.

7 *"Virtually every state."* "From Crisis to Commitment: Environmental Cleanup and Compliance at Federal Facilities," Report of National Governor's Association/National Association of Attorneys General Task Force on Federal Facilities, January 1990.

8 *only 404 have actually been cleaned up.* Thomas Wash, director of the Formerly Used Defense Sites (FUDS) Program, estimated that 108 FUDS sites had been cleaned up in August 1991, and 296 active sites have been cleaned up according to U.S. Department of Defense, *Defense Environmental Restoration Program Annual Report to Congress for Fiscal Year 1990*, February 1991, p. 7.

8 *hundreds of billions.* See James Broder, "Complex, Costly Cleanups May Snarl Base Closings," *Los Angeles Times*, June 19, 1990; Michael Satchell, "Uncle Sam's Toxic Folly," *U.S. News and World Report*, March 27, 1989; and Pat Towell, "Recruiting Defense Dollars for Environmental Duty," *Congressional Quarterly*, July 7, 1990.

8 *"among the most intractable."* Barry Breen, editor in chief, *Environmental Law Reporter*, Environmental Law Institute, U.S. House of Representatives, Hearings before the Subcommittee on Transportation, Tourism, and Haz-

ardous Materials of the Committee on Energy and Commerce, *Cleanup at Federal Facilities*, March 3, 10, 1988 (Washington, D.C.: U.S. Government Printing Office 1989), p. 156.

8 *complete at less than 2 percent.* U.S. Department of Defense, *Defense Environmental Restoration Program Annual Report to Congress for Fiscal Year 1990*, February 1991, p. 7.

9 *Some 2,000 residents of this land.* Sue Baker, *For Defense of Our Country: Echoes of Jefferson Proving Ground* (Indianapolis: Guild Literary Services, 1990), p. 67.

9 *more wildlife today.* Indiana Department of Environmental Management, *Report to the Governor: U.S. Army, Jefferson Proving Ground Evaluation*, Madison, Ind., April 20, 1989, pp. 4–5. The report reviews the diverse wildlife sightings and notes that "paradoxically, the wildlife at JPG has adapted well to the constant exposure."

Two. Teaching a Camel to Fly

This chapter contains extensive quotations from the proceedings of the U.S. House of Representatives, Hearing before the Subcommittee on Environment, Energy and Natural Resources of the Committee on Government Operations, *Hazardous Waste Problems at Department of Defense Facilities*, November 5, 1987 (Washington, D.C.: U.S. Government Printing Office, 1988). See also: "Poisons in the Pentagon," *Frontline*, Public Broadcasting Service, originally broadcast April 5, 1988.

11 *Cast Synar back in time.* Biographical fact sheet, "Congressman Mike Synar, Second District, Oklahoma, 102nd Congress, 1991–1992," furnished courtesy of Synar's office.

12 *seventy-two separate environmental violations.* U.S. General Accounting Office, *Hazardous Waste: DOD's Efforts to Improve Management of Generation, Storage, and Disposal*, May 1986 (Washington, D.C.: U.S. Government Printing Office, 1986), p. 19.

12 *Lakehurst Naval Air Engineering Center.* See chapter 7 and *Navy Assessment and Control of Installation Pollutants: Initial Assessment Study of Naval Air Engineering Center Lakehurst, New Jersey*, October 1983.

12 *Cornhusker Ammunition Plant.* See Chapter 8, and Environmental Protection Agency (EPA), Nebraska Department of Environmental Control (NDEC), and Cornhusker Army Ammunition Plant (CAAP), *Federal Facility Agreement (FFA)/Interagency Agreement (IAG)*, Docket No. VII-90-F-004, January 25, 1990. Section VI "Findings of Fact," section K.

12 *"overly anxious."* Tom Harris, "Ammo Plant Packs a Toxic Punch," *Sacramento Bee*, October 3, 1984, p. 37.

13 *"protecting the nation, not the environment."* Comment attributed to Colonel Norris, Harry Diamond Laboratory installation commander, by the Citizen's Clearinghouse for Hazardous Wastes, Inc., a national group based in

Arlington, Va. The comment was made at a community meeting held by the group and is documented in the group's report "Dealing with Military Toxics," March 1987.

14 *Pentagon issues a printed volume.* See U.S. Department of Defense, *Defense Environmental Restoration Program Annual Report to Congress for Fiscal Year 1988*, March 1989; U.S. Department of Defense, *Defense Environmental Restoration Program Annual Report to Congress for Fiscal Year 1989*, February 1990; U.S. Department of Defense, *Defense Environmental Restoration Program Annual Report to Congress for Fiscal Year 1990*, February 1991.

15 *Andersen Air Force Base.* U.S. House of Representatives, Hearing before the Subcommittee on Environment, Energy, and Natural Resources of the Committee on Government Operations, *Hazardous Waste Problems at Department of Defense Facilities*, November 5, 1987 (Washington D.C.: U.S. Government Printing Office, 1988), pp. 81–82.

18 *the Defense Department's own watchdog.* U.S. Department of Defense, Office of the Inspector General, *Final Report: Review of Hazardous Material/Hazardous Waste Management within the Department of Defense*, October 15, 1985–February 21, 1986 (Washington, D.C.: U.S. Department of Defense, Office of the Inspector General, 1986), p. 4.

Three. "Toxic Time Bomb"

20 *As Keith Tadewald remembers it.* Account based on interviews with Keith Tadewald, Rio Vista firefighter, and Mark S. Pollack, Deputy District Attorney, environmental crimes unit, County of Solano Criminal Division, Fairfield, Calif., June 1991.

21 *40,000 gallons of assorted chemicals.* Statement of Representative Vic Fazio, U.S. House of Representatives, Hearing before the Subcommittee on Environment, Energy, and Natural Resources of the Committee on Government Operations, House of Representatives, *Management and Disposal of Hazardous Materials by Government Agencies*, February 13, 1990, draft copy.

21 *fifteen drums of methyl di-isocyanate.* Ibid.

21 *Armor had purchased the massive stockpile.* Interview with Mark S. Pollack, June 1991.

21 *"we would throw in."* Interview with Kevin Doxey, director of the Pentagon's environmental restoration program, April 1991.

21 *an unusual congressional hearing.* U.S. House of Representatives, Hearing before the Subcommittee on Environment, Energy, and Natural Resources of the Committee on Government Operations, House of Representatives, *Management and Disposal of Hazardous Materials by Government Agencies*, February 13, 1990, draft copy.

22 *families who were evacuated.* Interview with Mark S. Pollack, June 1991.

23 *By its own estimate.* Comment of Carl Schafer, Deputy Assistant Secretary of Defense for Environment, U.S. House of Representatives, Hearing before

the Subcommittee on Environment, Energy, and Natural Resources of the Committee on Government Operations, *Hazardous Waste Problems at Department of Defense Facilities*, November 5, 1987 (Washington D.C.: U.S. Government Printing Office, 1988), p. 78.

23   *nearly 200 million barrels.* Defense Logistics Agency, "Defense Fuel Supply Center Fact Book, Fiscal Year 1990."

23   *The huge quantity of fuel.* See *The Defense Monitor,* Center for Defense Information newsletter, vol.18, no.6, 1989, p. 6.

23   *Officials at Exxon.* Interview with Exxon USA Regulatory Compliance Officer William Matney, July 1991 (conducted by Shawna Moos).

23   *40,000 underground storage tanks.* Congressional Budget Office, "Federal Liabilities under Hazardous Waste Laws," May 1990, table 7, draft copy.

23   *lithium sulfur batteries.* U.S. Department of Defense, Office of the Inspector General, *Final Report: Review of Hazardous Material/Hazardous Waste Management within the Department of Defense,* October 15, 1985–February 21, 1986 (Washington, D.C.: U.S. Department of Defense, Office of the Inspector General, 1986), p. 4.

24   *ozone-depleting chlorofluorocarbons.* See Michael Renner, "Tarnished Armories," *Environmental Action,* May/June 1991, p. 25.

24   *Air Force officials freely concede.* Interview with Gary Vest, Deputy Assistant Secretary of the Air Force (Environment, Safety, and Occupational Health), September 1991. See also John M. Broder, "U.S. Military Leaves Toxic Trail Overseas," *Los Angeles Times,* June 18, 1990; and Travis Brown, "Program Ignores Bases Abroad," *Sacramento Bee,* September 30, 1984.

24   *National Priority List.* U.S. Environmental Protection Agency, "National Priorities List, Supplementary Lists and Supporting Materials," February 1991, federal facilities section.

25   *Hansen has explained.* General Alfred G. Hansen, "Going to the Source," *Government Executive,* November 1989, p. 35.

25   *forced to evacuate.* Sixty military homes have stood vacant at the base since 1990 due to methane migration from a nearby landfill. Environmental officials have said the homes will remain vacant indefinitely while remediation plans are studied. "Wright-Pat Homes Stay Empty," *Defense Cleanup,* June 21, 1991.

25   *Dayton's wellfield.* Interview with Mark Allen, group leader, Division of Emergency and Remedial Response, Ohio EPA, Southwest District, July 1991 (conducted by Shawna Moos).

26   *half a million gallons of solvents.* David C. Morrison, "Managing Military Waste," *Government Executive,* November 1989, p. 37.

26   *more exotic compounds.* James Kitfield, "The Military Environmental Quagmire," *Military Forum,* April 1989, pp. 37–38.

27   *National Priority List.* U.S. Environmental Protection Agency, "National

Priorities List, Supplementary Lists and Supporting Materials," February 1991, federal section.

27 *Milan Army Ammunition Plant.* "Poisons in the Pentagon," *Frontline*, Public Broadcasting Service, originally broadcast April 5, 1988. See also U.S. Department of Defense, *Defense Environmental Restoration Program Annual Report to Congress for Fiscal Year 1988*, March 1989, p. A33.

27 *workers exposed to DNT.* U.S. Agency for Toxic Substances and Disease Registry, U.S. Public Health Service, *Toxicological Profile for 2,4-Dinitrotoluene, 2,6-Dinitrotoluene* (Springfield, Va.: U.S. Department of Commerce, 1989).

28 *"nasty stuff."* Tony Capaccio, "Army Still Buying Toxic Liquid Despite 'Acute' Storage Problems," *Defense Week*, February 12, 1990, p. 1

28 *DS2.* The military normally refers to this mixture by its abbreviation or full name (Decontamination Solution No. 2) rather than by its chemical composition. For information regarding the hazards it presents see U.S. Army Chemical Research, Development, and Engineering Center, "Material Safety Data Sheet," April 4, 1990; and N. Irving Sax, *Dangerous Properties of Industrial Materials* (New York: Van Nostrand Rheinhold Company, 1990), listings for constituent chemicals.

28 *DS2 is stockpiled.* Dan Charles, "American Army Ignores Toxic Warning," *Newscientist*, July 28, 1990, p. 25.

28 *DRMS officials say.* For figures given in text, see National Toxics Campaign Fund, *The U.S. Military's Toxic Legacy*, January 1991, p. 32.

29 *"but you might never see your fingers again."* Interview with Nancy Dunn, Pentagon spokesperson, June 1991. See also Seth Shulman, "Pentagon Pollution," *Technology Review*, July 1991, p. 14.

29 *four other cases involving the sale of DS2.* U.S. General Accounting Office, *Hazardous Materials: DOD Should Eliminate DS2 From Its Inventory of Decontaminants*," April 1990 (Washington, D.C.: U.S. Government Printing Office, 1990), p. 22.

29 *discarded alongside a highway.* U.S. General Accounting Office, *Hazardous Materials: Inadequate Safeguards Over Sales Pose Health and Environmental Dangers*, February 1990 (Washington, D.C.: U.S. Government Printing Office, 1990), p. 12.

29 *it will not sell DS2 to any bidders.* Statement by Brigadier General David A. Nydam, commanding general, U.S.A. Chemical Research, Development, and Engineering Center, before the U.S. House of Representatives Subcommittee on Environment, Energy, and Natural Resources of the Committee on Government Operations, June 28, 1990, draft copy.

29 *Nydam stated unequivocally.* Ibid.

29 *Army tests from as early as 1984.* U.S. General Accounting Office, *Hazardous Materials: DOD Should Eliminate DS2 From Its Inventory of Decontaminants*," April 1990 (Washington, D.C.: U.S. Government Printing Office, 1990), pp. 2–4.

30   *Thomas Ward.* Quoted in Dan Charles, "American Army Ignores Toxic Warning," *Newscientist*, July 28, 1990.

30   *internal Army report.* See Tony Carpaccio," Army Still Buying Toxic Liquid Despite 'Acute' Storage Problems," *Defense Week*, February 12, 1990, p. 1.

30   *"we learned to take our markings off."* Statement of Kevin Doxey, director of the Pentagon's environmental restoration program, during interview, April 1991.

31   *"most pervasive and protected polluter."* Bill Turque and John McCormick, "The Military's Toxic Legacy," *Newsweek*, August 6, 1990, p. 20.

31   *Vice Admiral Stanley Arthur.* Quoted in James Kitfield, "The Military Environmental Quagmire," *Military Forum*, April 1989, pp. 37–38.

Four. A Roadside Attraction

32   *U.S. Army Ordnance Museum.* Interviews with museum director William Atwater in May and June of 1991, Aberdeen Proving Ground, Md. Some historical detail comes from a fact sheet provided by the museum, entitled "Welcome to the U.S. Army Ordnance Museum."

33   *more than forty dangerous chemicals.* U.S. House of Representatives, Hearing before the Subcommittee on Environment, Energy, and Natural Resources of the Committee on Government Operations, *Hazardous Waste Problems at Department of Defense Facilities*, November 5, 1987, (Washington D.C.: U.S. Government Printing Office, 1988), p. 107.

34   *An Army study from 1976.* Ibid.

34   *"nothing available to deal with the mess."* Interview with Aberdeen environmental official Cindy Couch, May 1991 (conducted by Shawna Moos).

34   *Dean M. Dickey.* The reminiscences of Dean M. Dickey, a former employee of the Aberdeen Proving Ground in Maryland, were reprinted from the 1976 report in their entirety in U.S. House of Representatives, Hearing before the Subcommittee on Environment, Energy, and Natural Resources of the Committee on Government Operations, *Hazardous Waste Problems at Department of Defense Facilities*, November 5, 1987 (Washington D.C.: U.S. Government Printing Office, 1988), pp. 98–106.

35   *prevent the migration of contaminants.* For more on leaching pits and groundwater contamination see Eric Jorgensen, ed., *The Poisoned Well: New Strategies for Groundwater Protection* (Washington, D.C.: Island Press, 1989); and Tom Harris, "Toxic Wastes Won't Stay Buried," *Sacramento Bee*, September 30, 1984.

38   *Mustard gas.* U.S. Agency for Toxic Substances and Disease Registry, U.S. Public Health Service, *Toxicological Profile for Mustard "Gas" (Sulfur Mustard)* (Springfield, Va.: U.S. Department of Commerce, 1990), draft copy.

40   *Watertown Arsenal.* Interviews with personnel, visit to the facility (see the Epilogue for more details), and fact sheet "A History of the Watertown Arsenal and MTL," Watertown Arsenal, Watertown, Mass. See also Dan

NOTES

Grossman and Seth Shulman, "Toxic Secrets: Closing Watertown's Army Arsenal," *Boston Magazine,* November 1989.

41 *military facilities "took very few notes."* Statement of Robert Hayton, EPA project manager for Picatinny Arsenal, reported by Liv Osby, "Far Too Much, Far Too Long: Picatinny Contamination Severe," [Northwest New Jersey] *Daily Record,* April 10, 1988.

Five. The Latest Model

This chapter draws heavily upon the proceedings of the first meeting of the Panel on Remedial Action Priorities for Hazardous Waste Sites of the National Research Council, the principal operating agency of the National Academy of Sciences (NAS), April 10, 1991. The author was invited as a guest to the panel's open sessions.

43 *"the key task for the Academy."* Kevin Doxey, director of the Pentagon's environmental restoration program, addressing the NAS meeting, April 10, 1991.

43 *more than six years in the making.* Interview with Pentagon environmental protection specialist Marcia Read, October, 1991; and U.S. Department of Defense, "Defense Environmental Restoration Program Annual Report to Congress for Fiscal Year 1990," February 1991.

45 *"17,400 contaminated sites at 1,850 installations."* Details about the number of sites included in Doxey's presentation may also be found in U.S. Department of Defense, *Defense Environmental Restoration Program Annual Report to Congress for Fiscal Year 1990,* February 1991, pp. 6–8.

45 *doctrine of "sovereign immunity."* U.S. House of Representatives, Hearing before the Subcommittee on Oversight and Investigations, Committee on Energy and Commerce, *Environmental Compliance by Federal Agencies,* April 28, 1987 (Washington, D.C.: U.S. Government Printing Office, 1987). See also Lieutenant Colonel Richard E. Lotz, U.S. Air Force, "Federal Facility Provisions of Federal Environmental and Statutes: Waivers of Sovereign Immunity for 'Requirements' and Fines and Penalties," *Air Force Law Review,* vol. 31, 1989, pp. 7–29.

46 *drew upon British common law.* Interview with Barry Breen, editor, *Environmental Law Reporter,* Environmental Law Institute, November 1991.

46 *Oliver Wendell Holmes.* As cited by Barry Breen, November 1991 interview.

46 *"unique status of the military."* *Federal Bar News and Journal,* January 1986, p. 38.

46 *Richard E. Sanderson.* Quoted in James Kitfield, "The Military Environmental Quagmire," *Military Forum,* April 1989, p. 37.

47 *Executive Order 12088.* Executive Order 12088, 43 Federal Register 47,707 (1978), concerning federal compliance with pollution control standards. For complete text, see appendix C.

47 *"Hazard Ranking System."* A fact sheet printout, "Hazard Ranking System."

See also U.S. Environmental Protection Agency, "National Priorities List, Supplementary Lists and Supporting Materials," February 1991, "Listing Criteria/Policies."

48 *"can't go out and raise the price."* Michael J. Carricato, quoted in James Kitfield, "The Military Environmental Quagmire," *Military Forum*, April 1989, p. 38.

49 *chemical weapons stockpiles.* See Chapter 14.

50 *major environmental legislation of the 1970s and 1980s.* U.S. Environmental Protection Agency, *Federal Facilities Compliance Strategy*, November 1988, chap. 2, "Summary of Relevant Environmental Statutes and Executive Orders." For more on these laws see appendix C.

Six. Eastern Europe at Home

52 *the "unitary theory of the executive."* For a fuller explanation, see statement of F. Henry Habicht II, Assistant Attorney General, Land and Natural Resources, in U.S. House of Representatives, Hearing before the Subcommittee on Oversight and Investigations, Committee on Energy and Commerce, *Environmental Compliance by Federal Agencies*, April 28, 1987 (Washington, D.C.: U.S. Government Printing Office, 1987), pp. 178–231.

53 *Representative Dennis E. Eckart.* Ibid., pp. 277–278.

53 *F. Henry Habicht II.* Ibid., p. 277.

53 *Hubert H. Humphrey III.* Ibid., pp. 112–127.

54 *Beale Air Force Base.* U.S. General Accounting Office, *Water Pollution: Stronger Enforcement Needed to Improve Compliance at Federal Facilities*, December 1988 (Washington, D.C.: U.S. Government Printing Office, 1988), p. 69.

55 *military installations were twice as likely to violate.* Ibid., p. 3.

55 *"Under federal environmental statutes."* National Governors' Association and National Association of Attorneys General, *From Crisis to Commitment: Environmental Cleanup and Compliance at Federal Facilities*, a report of the NGA/NAAG Task Force on Federal Facilities, January 1990, p. vi.

56 *ruled in favor of the state.* U.S. District Judge James Carrigan, "Memorandum Opinion and Order, State of Colorado vs. U.S. Department of the Army," February 24, 1989, pp. 18–19. Background on case provided by attorney Jim Ellman, Colorado Attorney General's CERCLA Office, July 1991.

57 *Bush pledged.* Reported in David C. Morrison, "Managing Military Waste," *Government Executive*, November 1989, p. 31.

57 *the environmental situation in Eastern Europe.* See Joan DeBardeleben, ed., *To Breathe Free: Eastern Europe's Environmental Crisis* (Washington, D.C.: Woodrow Wilson Center Press, 1991); Lois R. Ember, "Pollution Chokes

East-bloc Nations," *Chemical and Engineering News*, April 16, 1990, pp. 7–16; "Stalin's Legacy of Filth," editorial, *New York Times*, February 7, 1990.

58 *Dennis L. Meadows.* Quoted in Lois R. Ember, "Pollution Chokes East-bloc Nations," *Chemical and Engineering News*, April 16, 1990, p. 7.

59 *The U.S. military has been in violation.* President Carter issued Executive Order 12088 in 1978, stipulating federal facility compliance with all environmental laws (see appendix C). See also Lieutenant Colonel Richard E. Lotz, U.S. Air Force, "Federal Facility Provisions of Federal Environmental Statutes: Waivers of Sovereign Immunity for 'Requirements' and Fines and Penalties," *Air Force Law Review*, vol. 31, 1989, pp. 7–29.

Seven. Lakehurst, New Jersey

63 *The Cohansey aquifer.* For general characteristics of the aquifer and the environment surrounding the Lakehurst Naval Air Engineering Center, see Lakehurst Naval Air Engineering Center, *Nomination for the Secretary of the Navy Environmental Protection Annual Award*, 1984, introduction.

64 *Lucy Bottomley.* Interviews with Lucy Bottomley, environmental engineering supervisor, Lakehurst Naval Air Engineering Center, April 1991. Additional background derives from interviews with Michael Figura, environmental engineer, and Frank Montarelli, press officer, during a tour of the base in April 1991.

65 *A memo that winter.* Memo from the Department of the Navy, Office of the Chief of Naval Operations to all ships and stations regarding the Navy's hazardous materials management program, OPNAV Notice 6240, February 20, 1980.

66 3 million gallons *of contaminated aviation fuel.* Estimate compiled from Naval Energy and Environmental Support Activity (NEESA), *Navy Assessment and Control of Installation Pollutants: Initial Assessment Study of Naval Air Engineering Center Lakehurst, New Jersey*, October 1983.

66 *the story was leaked.* A *New York Times* article in November of 1980 disclosed the discovery of the abandoned fuel dump and allegations of a former employee that hazardous materials were routinely dumped onto the ground at Lakehurst. See also Lakehurst Naval Air Engineering Center, *Nomination for the Secretary of the Navy Environmental Protection Annual Award*, 1981, pp. 3, 12, 13.

66 *Hangar One.* Lakehurst Naval Air Engineering Center fact sheet, Lakehurst press office.

67 2 million gallons *of aviation fuel.* Naval Energy and Environmental Support Activity (NEESA), *Navy Assessment and Control of Installation Pollutants (NACIP): Initial Assessment Study of Naval Air Engineering Center Lakehurst, New Jersey*, October 1983, p. 197.

67 *Several employees, when questioned later.* Ibid.

68 *"Fuel wasn't worth much."* Comment of Robert Kline, director of engineering, Public Works Department, Lakehurst Naval Air Engineering Center, after a hearing before the U.S. House of Representatives, Subcommittee on Transportation and Commerce of the Committee on Interstate and Foreign Commerce, November 20, 1980, documented in press accounts included in Lakehurst Naval Air Engineering Center, *Nomination for the Secretary of the Navy Environmental Protection Annual Award*, 1981, appendix G.

68 *some twenty-nine potentially toxic sites.* Naval Energy and Environmental Support Activity (NEESA), *Navy Assessment and Control of Installation Pollutants (NACIP): Initial Assessment Study of Naval Air Engineering Center Lakehurst, New Jersey*, October 1983, p. 181. "The environmental staff at NAEC Lakehurst had identified 29 potential contamination sites during a survey in 1980. The NACIP team identified 15 additional sites during the on-site survey conducted 21 September through 20 October 1981."

68 *Several of the articles.* Press accounts from this period may be found in Lakehurst Naval Air Engineering Center, *Nomination for the Secretary of the Navy Environmental Protection Annual Award*, 1981, appendix G.

69 *George Marienthal.* Testimony at U.S. House of Representatives, Hearing before the Subcommittee on Transportation and Commerce of the Committee on Interstate and Foreign Commerce, *Hazardous Waste Disposal Problems at Lakehurst Naval Engineering Center*, November 20, 1980, draft copy.

69 *"One day you come up with nothing."* James Gardner, quoted in a *New York Times* article included in the Lakehurst Naval Air Engineering Center, *Nomination for the Secretary of the Navy Environmental Protection Annual Award*, 1981, appendix G.

69 *eight cancer-causing chemicals.* "Analysis of Drinking Water for Chemical Pollutants," Lakehurst Naval Air Engineering Center, July 1981, pp. 4–5.

70 *In a memo about the matter.* Letter from James A. Gardner, supervisory environmental engineer, Lakehurst Naval Air Engineering Center, to Naval Air Command (NAVAIR), July 23, 1981.

70 *forty-four potentially contaminated sites.* Naval Energy and Environmental Support Activity (NEESA), "Navy Assessment and Control of Installation Pollutants (NACIP): Initial Assessment Study of Naval Air Engineering Center, Lakehurst, New Jersey," October 1983, p. 181.

70 *"Drink up!"* Article by Frank Montarelli, Lakehurst NAEC press officer, *Air Scoop*, April 22, 1983.

70 *EPA officials complained.* EPA comments contained in appendix A of Naval Energy and Environmental Support Activity (NEESA), *Navy Assessment and Control of Installation Pollutants (NACIP): Initial Assessment Study of Naval Air Engineering Center Lakehurst, New Jersey*, October 1983.

71 *all of the buried ordnance.* Information on the historical use of Lakehurst for ordnance testing from Lakehurst Naval Air Engineering Center, *Nomination for the Secretary of the Navy Environmental Protection Annual Award*, 1983, p. 17.

71 *before any construction can begin.* Letter from commanding officer, Lakehurst NAEC for general distribution, 1983, reference number OOF:ATP:NAS 8027. "No construction work shall be started in any area suspected to contain buried ordnance until an ordnance sweep has been made by a Navy Explosive Ordnance Disposal Unit and the area certified to be clear of all buried ordnance." A map which accompanied the letter designated nearly half of the installation as "potentially contaminated."

71 *"most advanced in the free world."* Interview with Frank Montarelli, press officer, April 1991.

72 *a leaky valve.* Ibid.

72 *the spill recovery process.* Lucy Bottomley, *Navy Civil Engineer,* Fall 1982, pp. 2–7.

72 *400,000 gallons of contaminated water.* Naval Energy and Environmental Support Activity (NEESA), *Navy Assessment and Control of Installation Pollutants (NACIP): Initial Assessment Study of Naval Air Engineering Center Lakehurst, New Jersey,* October 1983, 6.6.17, "Fuel Farm No. 196, Site No. 17."

72 *12,000 foil packets of phenol.* Lakehurst Naval Air Engineering Center, *Nomination for the Secretary of the Navy Environmental Protection Annual Award,* 1981, p. 14.

73 *"We bring it to the people's attention."* Carol Uhrich, quoted in Naval Air Engineering Center Environmental Management Team, *Chief of Naval Operations, Special Recognition Award Submission,* 1990.

Eight. Grand Island, Nebraska

74 *"I think we had heard."* Interviews with Chuck Carpenter in February 1989 and July 1991. Chronology of events and significant facts verified through document research and requests to Lori Simmers, U.S. Army Toxic and Hazardous Materials Agency public affairs officer.

75 *contributed firepower to every major conflict.* U.S. Army Toxic and Hazardous Materials Agency (USATHAMA), *Installation Assessment of Cornhusker Army Ammunition Plant: Report No: 155,* March 1980, p. 3.

75 *Cornhusker installation.* Early history from installation assessment cited above, pp. 3–4; magazine and load line descriptions from the same source, pp. 18, 23.

76 *Charles Fisher.* Quotes and related material from Tom Harris, "Ammo Plant Packs a Toxic Punch," *Sacramento Bee,* October 3, 1984, p. 37.

76 *thousands of gallons generated.* Installation assessment cited above, pp. 26–27.

76 *"a potential exists for contamination."* Ibid., p. 16.

76 *473 cubic meters.* Ibid., p. 26.

76 *"meandered to the north section."* Ibid.

NOTES

77   *the Army contractor at Cornhusker.* Army confirmation from Colonel Ralph
Wooten, commander of the U.S. Army Toxic and Hazardous Materials
Agency, September 1991.

77   *a Cornhusker official was quoted.* Harold Reutter, "Contaminants Found in
Ordnance Plant Water," *Grand Island Daily Independent*, November 6, 1982,
p. 1.

77   *it could take more than a century.* Ibid.; and interview with Chuck Carpenter.

77   *"significant levels of TNT and RDX."* U.S. Army Toxic and Hazardous Materials Agency (USATHAMA), *Interim Report: Production Records Review*,
1980, introduction.

77   *coulf reach town in just four years.* The speed of the groundwater (and contamination) flow towards Grand Island continues to be a subject of debate.
Grand Island is approximately three and a half miles from the boundaries
of the Cornhusker plant. Andrew Anderson, chief of assessments for
USATHAMA, stated in 1982 that the plume was moving at a rate of anywhere between three inches to one foot per day. USATHAMA's 1980 installation assessment, however, states that "the underground water could
move at any rate up to 4.0 meters per day." Either way, in its tests conducted between 1981 and 1986, USATHAMA badly underestimated the
distance the toxic plume had travelled off base.

77   *the Army had confirmed explosive compounds.* Envirodyne Engineers, Inc.,
Cornhusker Army Ammunition Plant Contamination Analysis Report, Interim
Report Number 3, May 18, 1982, table 4–3 and "Report Documentation,"
p. 2. By August the Army had confirmation that the contamination had
spread off site in Envirodyne Engineers, Inc., *Cornhusker Army Ammunition
Plant Final Report*, August 10, 1982, p. 50.

77   *The Army released a summary.* "Ordnance Pollution Discovered," *Grand Island Independent*, April 4, 1984. See also Harold Ruetter, "Army says 84
Wells West of G.I. Contaminated," *Grand Island Independent*, April 5, 1984.

78   *extremely elevated levels of RDX.* RDX was found in 246 of the 467 wells
tested. 84 of the wells had RDX contamination above the then safety limit
of 35 parts per billion; however, the old detection limit of 2.1 ppb is above
the currently proposed safety standard of 2.0 ppb. Ibid.

78   *RDX below 35 parts per billion.* U.S. Army Toxic and Hazardous Materials
Agency, *Fact Sheet Cornhusker Army Ammunition Plant: Environmental Study
Update March 1991;* John W. Fulton and Roy F. Spalding, "RDX and TNT
Residues in Groundwater of Hall County, Nebraska," an open file report
prepared in fulfillment of a cooperative agreement between the Central
Platte NRD and the Conservation and Survey Division, Institute of Agri-
culture and Natural Resources, University of Nebraska.

78   *Andrew Anderson.* Quoted in Tom Harris, "Ammo Plant Packs a Toxic
Punch," *Sacramento Bee*, October 3, 1984, p. 37.

79   *100-fold "safety factor."* Dr. David Rosenblatt of the U.S. Army Medical and
Bio-Engineering Research and Development Laboratory stated, "When

scientists deal with certain substances, they often put in a safety factor of 100 or 1,000 beyond (the) no observable effects level." Quoted in Harold Ruetter, "Army Plans Meeting to Discuss Contamination," *Grand Island Independent*, February 5, 1984.

80   *a variety of odd health problems.* Interviews with Chuck Carpenter. See also "In Nebraska, His Health and His Finances Suffer," *Newsday*, February 4, 1990, p. 29.

80   *the Army agreed to pay to hook up.* Cornhusker Army Ammunition Plant press release of January 15, 1991, regarding the release of two maps depicting the two plumes of explosives contamination originated at CAAP. A narrative explaining the maps and a bar graph depicting the changes in the level of RDX contamination from 1981 to the present were attached. See also Tom Harris, "Ammo Plant Packs a Toxic Punch," *Sacramento Bee*, October 3, 1984, p. 37.

80   *"de-watering."* For levels of RDX expected to be released, see Peter Wirth, U.S. Army Toxic and Hazardous Materials Agency, *Installation Restoration Program Cornhusker Army Ammunition Plant: Northwest Grand Island, Nebraska Construction Dewatering Well System Evaluation*, July 25, 1985, section 4.0 summary.

81   *the Cornhusker case.* Interview with Chuck Carpenter and Dan Waters, one of the attorneys who represented GNATS.

81   *violated the law after 1965.* President Johnson signed Executive Order 11258 "in furtherance of the purpose and policy of the Federal Water Pollution Control Act." This order states, "Federal installations shall provide secondary treatment, or its equivalent, for all wastes except cooling water and fish hatchery effluents." For more on Cornhusker case, see U.S. District Judge Warren Urbom, "Memorandum on Defendant's Motion for Partial Summary Judgement," September 12, 1989.

82   *an advisory safety standard for RDX.* U.S. Army Toxic and Hazardous Materials Agency, *Fact Sheet Cornhusker Army Ammunition Plant: Environmental Study Update March 1991.*

82   *roughly 40,000 tons of soil.* EPA, Nebraska Department of Environmental Control (NDEC), and Cornhusker Army Ammunition Plant (CAAP), *Federal Facility Agreement(FFA)/Interagency Agreement(IAG)*, Docket No. VII-90-F-004, January 25, 1990. section 6, "Findings of Fact," section K.

Nine. Sacramento, California

83   *only the state government employs more.* Paul G. Brunner, "Environmental Compliance in Operation," McClellan Air Force Base (presentation text provided by the environmental management team, McClellan Air Force Base, during August 1990 visit), p. 1.

83   *Over more than half a century.* For historical information regarding the founding of McClellan, see Air Force Logistics Command, *McClellan Air Force*

Base, installation guide (MARCOA Publishing Incorporated, Inc., under contract with McClellan, 1989), p. 42.

84 *170 separate potentially polluted sites.* See U.S. Department of Defense, *Defense Environmental Restoration Program Annual Report to Congress for Fiscal Year 1990,* February 1991, p. B57.

84 *forced the closure of a municipal well.* For a capsule summary of McClellan's environmental problems, see U.S. House of Representatives, Hearings before the Subcommittee on Transportation, Tourism, and Hazardous Materials of the Committee on Energy and Commerce, *Cleanup at Federal Facilities,* March 3, 10, 1988, (Washington, D.C.: U.S. Government Printing Office 1989), p. 707.

84 *completed its cleanup effort at only one.* U.S. Department of Defense, *Defense Environmental Restoration Program Annual Report to Congress for Fiscal Year 1990,* p. C18.

84 *Mario Ierardi.* Biographical fact sheet on Mario E. Ierardi, United States Air Force Office of Public Affairs, Sacramento Air Logistics Center, McClellan Air Force Base.

85 *delineation into separate "sites" is of little use.* Interview with Mario Ierardi, director of Installation Restoration Program (IRP) Division, Directorate of Environmental Management, and Linda Trogdon, community affairs coordinator, during tour of McClellan, August 1990.

85 *eight sizable polluted areas. The Facts: Information about Environmental Cleanup at McClellan AFB,* newsletter produced by environmental management team, McClellan Air Force Base, no. 2.

85 *A recent internal advisory document.* Paul G. Brunner, "Environmental Compliance in Operation," McClellan Air Force Base (presentation text provided by environmental management team, McClellan Air Force Base, during August 1990 visit).

85 *"The good news is."* Statement of Colonel Keith Findley as reported by Vickie M. Graham, "Cleaning Up Our Act," *Airman,* special issue, "Making a Better Earth," April 1991, p. 30.

86 *this formative period.* McLaren Environmental Engineering, *Final Basewide Report on Contamination McClellan Air Force Base,* Sacramento, Calif., December 1986. Page 10 states, "The monitoring program carried out during November 1979 indicated that groundwater contamination (TCE) occurred both on and off Base."

86 *officials at McClellan routinely withheld.* Interview with Chuck Yarbrough, representitive for the residents of Sacramento on the McClellan Groundwater Task Force, a group which includes members of the surrounding communities, the Air Force, regulatory agencies, and local elected officials and which advises the Air Force about aspects of the cleanup.

86 *legal action was threatened.* Dan Seligman, "State Wants Waste Pit Cleaned Up," *Sacramento Bee,* June 3, 1983; Lee Thelen, "McClellan Warned in Water Pollution Case," *Sacramento Union,* June 7, 1985; and Ricardo Pi-

mentel, "AF Blamed for McClellan Cleanup Delays," *Sacramento Bee*, January 16, 1986.

86 *TCE was detected at 22,600 parts per billion.* Hearings before the Subcommittee on Transportation, Tourism, and Hazardous Materials of the Committee on Energy and Commerce, *Cleanup at Federal Facilities*, March 3, 10, 1988 (Washington, D.C.: U.S. Government Printing Office, 1989), p. 707.

86 *550 homes.* Vickie M. Graham, "Cleaning Up Our Act," in *Airman*, "Making a Better Earth," April 1991, p. 30.

86 *TCE.* U.S. Agency for Toxic Substances and Disease Registry, U.S. Public Health Service, *Toxicological Profile for Trichloroethylene* (Springfield, Va.: U.S. Department of Commerce, 1989).

87 *stripped away a chlorine atom.* Radian Corp., "McClellan Air Force Base, Calif., Off-Base Well Sampling and Analysis Program, Third Quarter, 1986, Informal Technical Report," August 1986, vol. 1, pp. 4–16.

87 *63,000 parts per billion.* CH2M Hill, *Draft Source Control Feasibility Study for Area D: McClellan Air Force Base*, May 1984, table 1–2.

87 average *level in monitoring wells.* Ibid.

87 *exceeding state action levels.* Dan Seligman, "State Wants Waste Pit Cleaned Up, *Sacramento Bee*, June 3, 1983; and "State Plans to Test Private Wells for Toxic Waste from McClellan," *Sacramento Union*, June 4, 1983.

87 *upheld McClellan's sovereign immunity.* For more on *McClellan Ecological Seepage Situation v. Weinberger*, Eastern District of California, see Lieutenant Colonel Richard E. Lotz, U.S. Air Force, "Federal Facility Provisions of Federal Environmental Statutes: Waivers of Sovereign Immunity for 'Requirements' and Fines and Penalties," *Air Force Law Review*, vol. 31, 1989, pp. 7–29.

87 *"I've stayed in the fight."* Interview with Chuck Yarbrough, September 1991.

88 *oust him from the review committee.* Jim Sanders, "McClellan Draws Council's Wrath," *Sacramento Bee*, September 10, 1986; and Ted Bell, "McClellan General Takes Flak for Pollution Panel Ouster Try," *Sacramento Bee*, September 11, 1986.

88 *"Crisis forced change."* Paul G. Brunner, "Environmental Compliance in Operation," McClellan Air Force Base (presentation text provided by environmental management team, McClellan Air Force Base, during August 1990 visit).

88 *cans of spray paint.* Vickie M. Graham, "Cleaning Up Our Act," *Airman*, "Making a Better Earth," April 1991, p. 33.

89 *likely top $10 billion.* Findley quoted in Chris Bowman, "An Enemy Lurks Below McClellan," *The Sacramento Bee*, November 7, 1990.

89 *monitoring wells can actually exacerbate.* Eric P. Jorgensen, ed., Sierra Club Legal Defense Fund, *The Poisoned Well: New Strategies for Groundwater Protection* (Washington, D.C.: Island Press, 1989), p. 54.

90 *a former electroplating facility.* Interview with environmental engineer Doug-

las MacKenzie, during tour in August 1990. Facts verified by McClellan's public affairs office, September 1991.

90   *McClellan's water treatment facility.* Interview with Douglas MacKenzie, during tour in August 1990, and color brochure, "$8 Million Project Cleans Up Contamination," provided by environmental management team, McClellan Air Force Base.

91   *the hazardous gases break down.* See above. Additional information provided by McClellan's public affairs office, September 1991.

91   *a yearly price tag of close to $1 million.* Ibid.

91   *the treated water is tested weekly.* Ibid.

91   *"the Air Force has learned."* Color brochure:, "$8 Million Project Cleans Up Contamination," McClellan Air Force Base.

92   *The cover letter.* Letter from Gary Vest, Deputy Assistant Secretary of the Air Force (Environment, Safety, and Occupational Health), July 10, 1991.

92   *"We are a part of the Earth."* *Airman,* "Making a Better Earth," April 1991, inside cover.

Ten. Hanford, Washington

93   *an unusual two-day symposium.* Institute for Environmental Studies, University of Washington, "Hanford Cleanup—What exactly is it All About? (A Look at Military/Defense Nuclear and Hazardous Waste): A Symposium for Northwest Citizens," April 14–15, 1989, attended by the author.

93   *John Burnham.* Biographical information from symposium program, "Hanford Cleanup."

94   *Burnham said.* Statements at symposium cited above.

94   *unstable radioactive isotope iodine-129:* U.S. General Accounting Office, *Nuclear Waste: DOE's Handling of Hanford Reservation Iodine Information,* May 1988 (Washington, D.C.: U.S. Government Printing Office, 1988), p. 8.

94   *The Hanford Nuclear Reservation.* See Richland, Washington, Silver Anniversary Steering Committee, *Alive! Yesterday and Today: A History of Richland and the Hanford Project.* See also Paul Loeb, *Nuclear Culture* (New York: Coward, McCann & Geohegan, Inc., 1982).

95   *all of the government's nuclear facilities.* U.S. Congress, Office of Technology Assessment, *Complex Cleanup: The Environmental Legacy of Nuclear Weapons Production,* February 1991 (Washington, D.C.: U.S. Government Printing Office, 1991).

95   *at least 750,000 gallons.* U.S. Congress, Office of Technology Assessment, *Long-Lived Legacy: Managing High-Level and Transuranic Waste at the DOE Nuclear Weapons Complex,* May 1991 (Washington, D.C.: U.S. Government Printing Office, 1991), p. 16.

NOTES

95 *nearly half a million curies.* Pacific Northwest Laboratory, *Draft Summary Report: Phase I of the Hanford Environmental Dose Reconstruction (HEDR) Project,* July 1990, p. 4.4.

95 *1979 accident at the Three Mile Island.* GPU Nuclear Corporation communications division newsletter, *Backgrounder,* "Three Mile Island Unit 2: Radiation and Health Effects: A Report on the TMI-2 Accident and Related Health Studies."

96 *an entire reactor core.* For more, see Seth Shulman, "When a Nuclear Reactor Dies, $98 Million is a Cheap Funeral," *Smithsonian,* October 1989.

96 *Marilyn Druby.* Interview with Marilyn Druby, April 1989.

97 *a group of students at Richland High School.* Timothy Egan, "Little Sentiment Here to Ban the Bomb," *New York Times,* January 14, 1988.

97 *documents released in 1986.* The documents initially released are collectively known as the "Hanford Forty-Year Environmental Data" and consist of approximately 19,000 pages of previously unavailable material. The release was a result of Freedom of Information Act requests and legal action taken by two groups, the Hanford Education Action League (HEAL) of Spokane, and the Environmental Policy Institute (EPI) of Washington, D.C. See also the testimony of HEAL spokesperson Jim Thomas, submitted to U.S. House of Representatives, Hearing before the Subcommittee on Transportation and Hazardous Waste of the Energy and Commerce Committee, *Cleanup at Federal Facilities,* February 23, 1989 (Washington, D.C.: U.S. Government Printing Office, 1989), pp. 284–292; and Michele Stenehjem, "Pathways of Radioactive Contamination: Examining the History of the Hanford Nuclear Reservation," *Environmental Review,* Fall/Winter 1989, pp. 95–112.

97 *a special independent panel.* Pacific Northwest Laboratory, *Draft Summary Report: Phase I of the Hanford Environmental Dose Reconstruction (HEDR) Project,* July 1990, p. 1.1. The study is being conducted by Battelle Corp. staff at the Pacific Northwest Laboratory, funded by the Department of Energy and directed by an independent Technical Steering Panel (TSP). See also Seth Shulman, "Hanford Nuclear Radiation Doses Assessed," *Nature,* July 19, 1990, vol. 346, p. 205.

97 *some 400,000 curies of radioactive iodine-131.* Pacific Northwest Laboratory, *Draft Summary Report: Phase I of the Hanford Environmental Dose Reconstruction (HEDR) Project,* July 1990, p. 4.4.

97 *in milk from cows.* Ibid., p. 4.2.

98 *accumulated doses of radiation.* In addition to the dose reconstruction report cited above, see Michele Stenehjem, "Indecent Exposure," *Natural History,* September 1990, p. 10.

98 *radiation considered safe.* See, for instance, League of Women Voters Education Fund, *The Nuclear Waste Primer: A Handbook for Citizens* (New York: Nick Lyons Books, 1985).

98   *Jack Geiger.* H. Jack Geiger, "Generations of Poisons and Lies," *New York Times*, August 5, 1990, Op-ed., p. E19.

99   *Bill Klink.* Interviewed by author during tour of Hanford, April 1989.

99   *The cost of the thirty-year cleanup.* Seth Shulman, "Daunting Costs for Cleanup at Hanford," *Nature*, May 25, 1989, vol. 339, p. 241. A subsequent Department of Energy press release, "U.S. Corps of Engineers to Participate in Hanford Cleanup," July 27, 1990, states that cleanup of Hanford could cost between $1 billion and $2 billion per year for the next thirty years. Michele Stenehjem, a historian who has studied environmental problems at Hanford extensively, estimates costs at closer to $60 billion in "Indecent Exposure," *Natural History*, September 1990, p. 22.

99   *200 billion gallons of radioactive wastewater.* Radioactive Waste Campaign, *Deadly Defense: Military Radioactive Landfills* (New York: Radioactive Waste Campaign, 1988), p. 45.

100   *The price tag to clean this one remote location.* Budget comparison based on an estimate from the Department of Energy's press office that DOE's annual budget is $14 billion; the Bush administration's 25 percent cut in funding is cited in James Franklin, "Nuclear Arms Plant Cleanup is Cut $4.5b," *Boston Globe*, February 22, 1991; education figures as cited in "Education Budget Faces Possible Cuts," *Higher Education and National Affairs*, September 23, 1991.

100   *Hanford's underground tank farm.* U.S. Department of Energy, Richland Operations Office, "Facts About Hanford: Types of Nuclear Waste," and U.S. Congress, Office of Technology Assessment, *Long-Lived Legacy: Managing High-Level and Transuranic Waste at the DOE Nuclear Weapons Complex*, May 1991 (Washington, D.C.: U.S. Government Printing Office, 1991).

101   *the Savannah River Plant.* Radioactive Waste Campaign, *Deadly Defense: Military Radioactive Landfills* (New York: Radioactive Waste Campaign, 1988), p. 99.

101   *Cincinnati's water supply.* U.S. General Accounting Office, *Nuclear Energy: Environmental Issues at DOE's Nuclear Defense Facilities*, September 1986 (Washington, D.C.: U.S. Government Printing Office), p. 20. See also Radioactive Waste Campaign, *Deadly Defense: Military Radioactive Landfills* (New York: Radioactive Waste Campaign, 1988), pp. 116–20.

101   *the Rocky Flats Plant.* U.S. General Accounting Office, *Nuclear Energy: Environmental Issues at DOE's Nuclear Defense Facilities*, September 1986 (Washington, D.C.: U.S. Government Printing Office), pp. 23–24. See also Radioactive Waste Campaign, *Deadly Defense: Military Radioactive Landfills* (New York: Radioactive Waste Campaign, 1988), p. 90.

101   *Idaho National Engineering Laboratory.* Radioactive Waste Campaign, *Deadly Defense: Military Radioactive Landfills* (New York: Radioactive Waste Campaign, 1988), p. 51.

101   *Energy Department contractors knew.* Interview with Robert Alvarez, staffer, Senate Governmental Affairs Committee. See also Seth Shulman, "New

Fears at Hanford," *Nature*, vol. 346, August 9, 1990, p. 501; and Matthew Wald, "Secrecy Tied to Hanford Tanks' Trouble," *New York Times*, August 1, 1990.

102 *"a serious situation."* Letter from John F. Ahearne, chairman, Advisory Committee on Nuclear Facility Safety to James D. Watkins, Secretary of Energy, U.S. Department of Energy, July 23, 1990, pp. 4–6 (as cited in U.S. Congress, Office of Technology Assessment, *Long-Lived Legacy: Managing High-Level and Transuranic Waste at the DOE Nuclear Weapons Complex*, May 1991 (Washington, D.C.: U.S. Government Printing Office, 1991).

102 *"major steam explosions."* Interview with Robert Alvarez, Senate staff; see also Department of Energy press release, "Safety Measures Taken to Reduce Risk from Hanford Tanks," May 24, 1990; and Thomas Lippman, "Danger of Explosion at Nuclear Plant Covered Up, Energy Dept. Probe Says," *Washington Post*, August 1, 1990.

Eleven. Between the Cracks

105 *The Department of Energy has its own program.* The Department of Energy's Formerly Utilized Sites Remedial Action Program (FUSRAP) is a program directed by the assistant secretary for nuclear energy which addresses the cleanup of sites and adjacent properties contaminated by the activities of the Manhattan Project.

105 *some 7,000 locations.* U.S. Department of Defense, *Defense Environmental Restoration Program Annual Report to Congress for Fiscal Year 1990*, February 1991, p. 9.

105 *In Novato, California.* For more on Hamilton Air Force Base, see U.S. General Accounting Office, *Hazardous Waste: Status of Cleanup at the Former Hamilton Air Force Base*, December 1985 (Washington, D.C.: U.S. Government Printing Office, 1985); and U.S. House of Representatives, Hearings before the Environmental Restoration Panel of the Committee on Armed Services, *Overview of DOD Environmental Activities*, March 15, April 5, 11, 25, 26, May 2, 17, 1989 (Washington, D.C.: U.S. Government Printing Office, 1990), pp. 402–3.

105 *in Watertown, Massachusetts.* Watertown Arsenal information derives from interviews with arsenal personnel and a visit to facility. For more, see the Epilogue and Dan Grossman and Seth Shulman, "Toxic Secrets: Closing Watertown's Army Arsenal," *Boston Magazine*, November 1989.

105 *Weldon Spring Ordnance Plant.* U.S. Department of Defense, *Defense Environmental Restoration Program Annual Report to Congress for Fiscal Year 1990*, February 1991, p. E15.

105 *mine shaft in Nevada.* U.S. Department of Defense, *Defense Environmental Restoration Program Annual Report to Congress for Fiscal Year 1990*, February 1991, p. 10.

105   *eroding dunes on Martha's Vineyard.* U.S. Department of Defense, *Defense Environmental Restoration Program Annual Report to Congress for Fiscal Year 1989,* February 1990, p. 9.

105   *"We've got bombing ranges."* Interview with Thomas Wash, director of the Formerly Used Defense Sites (FUDS) Program, August 1991. Wash's estimates confirmed by Philip Loftis, manager of the FUDS database, October 1991.

106   *$247 million we have received.* Interview with Thomas Wash and outline of an internal FUDS presentation prepared by Wash, entitled "DERP-FUDS: Program Review and Analysis," March 1991.

106   *report from the Congressional Budget Office.* Congressional Budget Office, "Federal Liabilities Under Hazardous Waste Laws," May 1990.

106   *preliminary inspections have been completed.* U.S. Department of Defense, *Defense Environmental Restoration Program Annual Report to Congress for Fiscal Year 1990,* February 1991, p. 9.

106   *108 such "remedial actions" to date.* Interview with Thomas Wash, director of the Formerly Used Defense Sites (FUDS) Program, August 1991.

106   *recent internal presentation.* Thomas Wash, "DERP-FUDS: Program Review and Analysis," March 1991.

107   *responsibility for all the formerly used lands.* Interview with longtime Army Corps of Engineers employee Noel Urban, August, 1991; Maureen Ann McCabe, "An Introduction to the Defense Environmental Restoration Program," unpublished masters thesis, George Washington University National Law Center, September 1990.

107   *395 overseas bases.* U.S. Department of Defense, *Defense 90: November/December Defense Almanac,* 1990.

107   *one quarter of all active-duty personnel.* Ibid.

108   *a worldwide investigation.* U.S. Department of Defense, Office of the Inspector General, *Final Report: Review of Hazardous Material/Hazardous Waste Management Within the Department of Defense,* October 15, 1985–February 21, 1986 (Washington, D.C.: U.S. Department of Defense, Office of the Inspector General, 1986).

108   *"The Department of Defense overall management."* Ibid., p. 13.

108   *the directive "was simple and straight."* Statement of Barbara Blum, as reported by Travis Brown, "Program Ignores Bases Abroad," *Sacramento Bee,* September 30, 1984.

108   *foreign bases must obey.* According to U.S. General Accounting Office, *Hazardous Waste: Management Problems Continue at Overseas Military Bases,* August 1991 (Washington, D.C.: U.S. Government Printing Office, 1991), p. 3, the Department of Defense's policy about which laws overseas installations must comply with remains unclear.

109   *the first detailed nonmilitary investigation.* U.S. General Accounting Office,

NOTES

Hazardous Waste: Management Problems at DOD's Overseas Installations, September 1986.

109 *At the congressional hearing in 1987.* See U.S. House of Representatives, Hearing before the Subcommittee on Environment, Energy, and Natural Resources of the Committee on Government Operations, *Hazardous Waste Problems at Department of Defense Facilities*, November 5, 1987 (Washington, D.C.: U.S. Government Printing Office, 1988), p. 81.

109 *the U.S. Air Force admits.* Author interview with Gary Vest, September 1991. See also John M. Broder, "U.S. Military Leaves Toxic Trail Overseas," *Los Angeles Times*, June 18, 1990.

109 *Gary Vest.* Quoted in Dan Charles, "Counting the Cost of the Cold War Cleanup," *New Scientist*, October 13, 1990.

110 *more than 350 contaminated sites in Germany alone.* U.S. Army Europe Public Affairs Office, "USAREUR Responses to Questions About Contaminated Sites." summary provided in response to a Freedom of Information Act request, October 1991. See also Gerd Nowakowski, "The Extent of Contamination at U.S. Military Bases in Germany—The Poisonous Price of Friendship," [Berlin] *Tageszeittung*, November 26, 1990, pp.1–3 (English translation of original German text in FBIS-WEU-90-244, December 19, 1990).

110 *more than 200 in all.* Travis Brown, "Program Ignores Bases Abroad," *Sacramento Bee*, September 30, 1984.

110 *twenty-six known Army sites alone.* U.S. Army Europe Public Affairs Office, "USAREUR Responses to Questions About Contaminated Sites." See also Nowakowski, "The Extent of Contamination at U.S. Military Bases in Germany—The Poisonous Price of Friendship," [Berlin] *Tageszeittung*, 26 November 1990, pp.1–3.

110 *Rhein-Main.* Ibid.

110 *environmental violations on Guam's bases.* For more, see U.S. General Accounting Office, *DOD Installations in Guam Having Difficulty Complying with Regulations*, April 1987 (Washington, D.C.: U.S. Government Printing Office, 1987); and U.S. General Accounting Office, *Hazardous Waste: Abandoned Disposal Sites May Be Affecting Guam's Water Supply*, May 1987 (Washington, D.C.: U.S. Government Printing Office, 1987).

110 *Clark Air Force Base.* Jorge Emmanuel, Alliance for Philippine Concerns, Philippine Resource Center, Berkeley Arms Control Research Center, San Francisco, "Environmental Destruction Caused by U.S. Military Bases and the Serious Implications for the Philippines," paper presented at "Crossroads 1991: Toward a Nuclear Free, Bases Free Philippines, An International Conference," Manila, May 14–16, 1990.

111 *Tinker Air Force Base.* U.S. General Accounting Office, *Hazardous Waste: Tinker Air Force Base's Improvement Efforts*, October 1987, pp. 8, 29.

111 *The Pentagon has recently announced.* Office of the Assistant Secretary of

Defense, public affairs office listing, "Overseas Sites-Return/Reduce/ Standby by Country as of 7/31/91 (1/29/90–7/30/91)." See also Fred Kaplan, "US to Scale Down 79 Bases in Europe," *Boston Globe*, July 31, 1991.

111 *An internal memo.* Jeremiah McCarthy, "Trip Report to the Hague and EUCOM," memorandum for the record, Office of the Assistant Secretary of Defense, Production and Logistics, November 3, 1988, quoted in National Toxics Campaign Fund, *The U.S. Military's Toxic Legacy*, 1991 report, p. 72.

112 *over a billion dollars.* EPA custom printout "Number of Active Foreign Pollution Projects for all Federal Agencies with Non-Zero Budget Amounts for Fiscal Year '92 and Prior," September 27, 1991.

112 *Congress called upon the Department of Defense.* National Toxics Campaign Fund, *The U.S. Military's Toxic Legacy*, 1991 report, p. 76.

112 *"it will be the Germans who pay for it."* Comment of Herman Weyel, mayor of Mannheim, during an interview with the author, September 1991.

112 *"We identified actual or potential pollution."* U.S. General Accounting Office, *Hazardous Waste: Management Problems at DOD's Overseas Installations*, September 1986, p. 16.

112 *Four pages at the heart of the report.* Ibid., pp. 29–32.

Twelve. The Pentagon Gets Religion

This chapter is based on the proceedings of the first Defense and the Environment Initiative Forum, held September 6–7, 1990, in Washington, D.C., attended by author. Quotations in this chapter derive from the author's notes from this meeting unless otherwise attributed below.

115 *"difficult to imagine a gathering like this."* Secretary of Defense Dick Cheney's remarks and a description of the proceedings were also published in the industry trade newsletter *Defense Cleanup*, September 14, 1990. See also Dianne Dumanoski, "Pentagon Takes First Steps Toward Tackling Pollution," *Boston Globe*, September 9, 1990.

116 *The report's summary offers a litany.* U.S. Department of Defense, Office of the Inspector General, *Defense Environmental Restoration Program: Inspection Report*, July 1990 (Washington, D.C.: U.S. Department of Defense, Office of the Inspector General, 1990), pp. i–ii.

116 *a landmark memorandum.* Secretary of Defense Dick Cheney, "Memorandum for Secretaries of the Military Departments; Subject: Environmental Management Policy," October 10, 1989.

116 *Cheney, a former Republican representative.* Biographical information from U.S. Department of Defense, Defense and the Environment Initiative Forum guest speaker and panel member profiles.

117 *"top-priority threat."* Environmental poll by the Roosevelt Center for Amer-

ican Policy Studies, as reported in *U.S. News and World Report*, June 12, 1989, p. 69.

117 *"The Department of Defense's overall management."* U.S. Department of Defense, Office of the Inspector General, *Final Report: Review of Hazardous Material/Hazardous Waste Management within the Department of Defense*, October 15, 1985–February 21, 1986 (Washington, D.C.: U.S. Department of Defense, Office of the Inspector General, 1986), p. 13.

117 *"never be able to achieve a proactive position."* Ibid., p. 6.

117 *"provide the foundation."* U.S. Department of Defense, Defense and the Environment project office, "Defense and the Environment Initiative Fact Sheet," received by author, August 1990.

118 *Admiral David E. Jeremiah.* Biographical information from U.S. Department of Defense, Defense and the Environment Initiative Forum guest speaker and panel member profiles.

120 *only two of Langley's thirty-six toxic sites.* U.S. Department of Defense, *Defense Environmental Restoration Program Annual Report to Congress for Fiscal Year 1990*, February 1991, p. C93.

120 *Trichloroethylene.* Geraghty and Miller, Inc., verification study, *Assessment of Potential Ground-Water Pollution at Naval Air Station/Jacksonville, Florida*, December 1985, p. C5.2 (trichloroethene [alternate spelling for TCE] found at 155,300 ppb in 1983).

121 *almost 5 million people.* U.S. Department of Defense, *Defense 90: November/December Defense Almanac*, 1990.

121 *27 million acres in the United States.* U.S. House of Representatives, Hearings before the Environmental Restoration Panel of the Committee on Armed Services, *Overview of DOD Environmental Activities*, March 15, April 5, 11, 25, 26, May 2, 17, 1989 (Washington, D.C.: U.S. Government Printing Office, 1990), p. 14.

122 *only some 400 toxic sites.* U.S. Department of Defense, *Defense Environmental Restoration Program Annual Report to Congress for Fiscal Year 1990*, February 1991, p. 7; 296 sites at current facilities have been cleaned up, and Thomas Wash, director of the program for formerly used sites, estimates 108 FUDS sites have been cleaned up.

122 *a private industry trade journal.* Defense Cleanup, September 14, 1990.

123 *Air Force Plant No. 44.* Background derives from the Military Toxics Network, *Touching Bases*, June 1991, p. 8, and author interview with Dan Opalski, remedial project manager for EPA, Region 9, October 1991.

123 *Adrienne Anderson.* Quoted in Dianne Dumanoski, "Pentagon Takes First Steps Toward Tackling Pollution," *Boston Globe*, September 9, 1990.

124 *"The tide is finally turning."* Military Toxics Network, *Touching Bases*, vol. 1, November 1990.

124 *"mission essential."* As reported in *Defense Cleanup*, September 14, 1990.

125   *in the midst of a "culture change."* Interview with Gary Vest, conducted with Daniel Grossman at the Pentagon, September 1991.

125   *Senator John Glenn.* For a fuller account, see Senator John Glenn, *New York Times*, January 24, 1989, Op-Ed., p. A21.

Thirteen. Dead Guppies Make Waves

126   *"one of the worst cases."* Judge's statement recounted by Jane Barrett, U.S. Department of Justice, Assistant United States Attorney in the District of Maryland, November 1991.

126   *employees of the U.S. military were found guilty.* Major John J. Bartus, U.S. Air Force, "Federal Employee Personal Liability Under Environmental Law: New Ways for the Federal Employee to Get in Trouble," *Air Force Law Review*, vol. 31, 1989, p. 45.

126   *"I would be lying if I said."* Admiral Bitoff's comment made at the Department of Defense's Defense and the Environment Initiative Forum, Washington, D.C., September 6–7, 1990. For more on the forum, see Chapter 12.

127   *Records show.* See Robert Benjamin, "Army Memo Cites Hazard at Aberdeen Testing Plant," *Baltimore Sun*, February 2, 1986, and Michael Weisskopf, "The Aberdeen Mess," *Washington Post Magazine*, January 15, 1989, p. 55.

127   *"a Pandora's box."* Ibid.

127   *Jim Allingham.* Quotes from author interview with Allingham, press officer at Aberdeen Proving Ground, September 1991.

128   *inspector Parks, presumably chagrined.* Interview with Jim Allingham, September 1991. See also Robert Benjamin, "Army Memo Cites Hazard at Aberdeen Testing Plant," *Baltimore Sun*, February 2, 1986.

128   *more than 100 different toxic compounds.* Interview with former U.S. Attorney for Maryland Breckinridge Willcox, September 1991.

128   *"It was a run-down, seedy facility."* Interview with former U.S. Attorney for Maryland Breckinridge Willcox, September 1991.

129   *"can ignite* SPONTANEOUSLY." U.S. National Institute for Occupational Safety and Health, *1990 Pocket Guide to Chemical Hazards* (Washington, D.C.: U.S. Government Printing Office, 1990), p. 124.

129   *The men who ran the Pilot Plant.* Biographical background of Dee, Lentz, and Gepp from Michael Weisskopf, "The Aberdeen Mess," *Washington Post Magazine*, January 15, 1989, p. 54.

130   *"A number of Aberdeen safety inspections."* Ibid., p. 55.

130   *five criminal counts.* Legal brief for *U.S. v. Dee et al.*, courtesy of Jane Barrett, Assistant United States Attorney in the District of Maryland. For more, see Major John J. Bartus, U.S. Air Force, "Federal Employee Personal Liabil-

ity Under Environmental Law: New Ways for the Federal Employee to Get in Trouble," *Air Force Law Review*, vol. 31, 1989, pp. 45–46 n. 3.

130   *A base safety officer said.* Legal brief and trial proceedings as recounted by Breckinridge Willcox, September 1991.

130   *An aerial nerve gas test.* See Charles Piller and Keith Yamamoto, *Gene Wars*, (New York: Beech Tree Books, 1988), pp. 51–52.

132   *General James Klugh.* As recounted by Breckinridge Willcox, September 1991, and verified by Jane Barrett, November 1991.

133   *"The general rule is straightforward."* Major John J. Bartus, U.S. Air Force, "Federal Employee Personal Liability Under Environmental Law: New Ways for the Federal Employee to Get in Trouble," *Air Force Law Review*, vol. 31, 1989, p. 52. See also Jane F. Barrett and Veronia M. Clarke, "Perspectives on the Knowledge Requirement of Section 6928(d) of RCRA after United States v. Dee," *George Washington Law Review*, vol. 59, no. 4, April 1991, pp. 862–88.

134   *"represents the interests of the United States."* Major John J. Bartus, U.S. Air Force, "Federal Employee Personal Liability Under Environmental Law: New Ways for the Federal Employee to Get in Trouble," *Air Force Law Review*, vol. 31, 1989, p. 52.

134   *"we worry about provisions."* "Environmental Issues of Concern for the U.S. Defense Industry," circulated at the Defense and the Environment Initiative Forum, Washington, D.C., September 6–7, 1990. For more on the forum, see Chapter 12.

Fourteen. Nerve-Wracking Prototype

136   *sirens blare at 8:04.* For more on the incident see John L. Menke et al., *Evaluation of the GB Rocket Campaign: Johnston Atoll Chemical Agent Disposal System Operational Verification Testing*, June, 1991 (McLean, Va.: MITRE Corporation, 1991), p. 3, 156.

136   *4 million pounds of chemical weapons.* Author estimate based on John L. Menke et al., cited above, pp. 1.4, 2.23 and Vicki Kemper, "Deadly Debris," *Common Cause Magazine*, July/August 1990.

137   *Army chemists say.* Interview with Marilyn Tischbin, Army spokesperson for JACADS program, September 1990. See also Seth Shulman, "Bomb Burning in the Pacific," *Technology Review*, October 1990; and Seth Shulman, "First Test of Incineration," *Nature*, vol. 346, July 5, 1990.

137   *the tiny island is "extremely crowded."* Ibid.

137   *Full-scale operation.* This operation was carried out between July 1990 and February 1991 as the "GB Rocket Campaign," the first of four phases of the testing program being carried out at Johnston Island. For more on this phase of the program, see John L. Menke et al., *Evaluation of the GB Rocket*

Campaign: Johnston Atoll Chemical Agent Disposal System Operational Verification Testing, June 1991 (McLean, Va.: MITRE Corporation, 1991).

137 *nerve agent GB.* "GB" is the Department of Defense's designation for isopropyl methylphosphonoflouridate, or sarin. For more on GB, see J. B. Neilands et al., *Harvest of Death: Chemical Warfare in Vietnam and Cambodia* (New York: Free Press, 1972), pp. 85, 289.

138 *forced the facility to shut down.* Menke, et al., *Evaluation of the GB Rocket Campaign: Johnston Atoll Chemical Agent Disposal System Operational Verification Testing,* table 2-2 and pp. 2.3 to 2.10.

138 *the JACADS plant was plagued.* Project manager's log included in Alfred Picardi et al., *Alternative Technologies for the Detoxification of Chemical Weapons: An Information Document,* May 1991 (Washington, D.C.: Greenpeace International, 1991), appendix G. See also John L. Menke et al., *Evaluation of the GB Rocket Campaign: Johnston Atoll Chemical Agent Disposal System Operational Verification Testing,* June 1991 (McLean, Va.: MITRE Corporation, 1991), pp. 2.73 to 2.76; and U.S. General Accounting Office, *Chemical Weapons: Stockpile Destruction Delayed at the Army's Prototype Facility,* July 1990 (Washington, D.C.: U.S. Government Printing Office, 1990), pp. 15–16.

138 *took exactly twice as long as planned.* John L. Menke et al., *Evaluation of the GB Rocket Campaign: Johnston Atoll Chemical Agent Disposal System Operational Verification Testing,* June 1991 (McLean, Va.: MITRE Corporation, 1991), p. xxvi.

138 *VX—the Army's most potent nerve agent.* "VX" is the Department of Defense designation for a nerve agent the precise structure of which is secret. For more see J. B. Neilands et al., *Harvest of Death: Chemical Warfare in Vietnam and Cambodia* (New York: Free Press, 1972), pp. 85, 293.

139 *Environmental Protection Agency agreed.* Interview with Julia McHaig, EPA official, October 1991.

139 *"exudes liquid that solidifies."* Charles G. Pritchard, "The Greening of U.S. Military Bases," *International Defense Review,* January 1991, p. 32.

140 *the other 93 percent.* Distribution percentages provided by Marilyn Tischbin, June 1990. The eight facilities are Anniston, Alabama; Pine Bluff, Arkansas; Pueblo, Colorado; Newport, Indiana; Lexington, Kentucky; Aberdeen, Maryland; Umatilla, Oregon; and Tooele, Utah.

140 *Tooele Army Depot.* Based on the estimate that the U.S. stockpile contains 30,000 tons of chemical weapons (see Vicki Kemper, "Deadly Debris," *Common Cause Magazine,* July/August 1990, pp. 20–25 and Seth Shulman, "First Test of Incineration," *Nature,* vol. 346, July 5, 1990) and distribution percentages provided by Marilyn Tischbin, June 1990.

140 *"environmental consequences of major proportions."* See U.S. Department of the Army, *Chemical Stockpile Disposal Program: Final Programmatic Environmental Impact Statement,* 1988, as quoted in Vicki Kemper, "Deadly Debris," *Common Cause Magazine,* July/August 1990, pp. 20–25.

140 *a worst-case scenario.* The army's environmental impact statement gives estimated number of deaths caused within a certain radius by a variety of accidents at each site. The figures stated in the text are estimates of the number of people living within the radius of danger at each site. See U.S. Department of the Army, *Chemical Stockpile Disposal Program: Final Programmatic Environmental Impact Statement.*

141 *sophisticated computer modeling technique.* U.S. Department of Defense, *Defense Environmental Restoration Program Annual Report to Congress for Fiscal Year 1990,* February 1991, p. 24.

141 *"Of course landfills will leak."* Statement of William Ruckelshaus before a hearing of the California Water Resources Control Board, Division of Water Quality, Sacramento, October 3, 1989, included in Lenny Siegel et al., *The U.S. Military's Toxic Legacy: America's Worst Environmental Enemy* (Boston: National Toxic Campaign Fund, 1991), p. 41.

141 *Most of the other options.* For more background on cleanup technology, see U.S. Environmental Protection Agency, *Innovative Treatment Technologies: Semi-Annual Report, First Issue,* January 1991 (Washington, D.C.: U.S. Environmental Protection Agency, 1991); U.S. Congress, Office of Technology Assessment, *Coming Clean: Superfund Problems Can Be Solved . . . ,* October 1989 (Washington, D.C.: U.S. Government Printing Office, 1989); and U.S. Congress, Office of Technology Assessment, *Are We Cleaning Up?: 10 Superfund Case Studies,* June 1988 (Washington, D.C.: U.S. Government Printing Office, 1988).

141 *bioremediation.* U.S. Department of Defense, *Defense Environmental Restoration Program Annual Report to Congress for Fiscal Year 1989,* February 1990, p. 22.

142 *vacuum extraction.* Ibid., p. 21.

142 *Public Works Center in Guam.* Ibid., p. 12.

142 *halogenated organic compounds.* For more on these toxins, see Mary Jane Schneider, *Persistent Poisons: Chemical Pollutants in the Environment* (New York: New York Academy of Sciences, 1979).

142 *a test of vitrification technology.* U.S. Department of Defense, *Defense Environmental Restoration Program Annual Report to Congress for Fiscal Year 1989,* February 1990, p. 24.

143 *so-called vacuum extraction.* Twin Cities Army Amunition Plant, "Fact Sheet No. 87-11: In-Situ-Volatization," May 15, 1987, Office of Public Affairs.

143 *organic compounds like TCE.* U.S. Army Toxic and Hazardous Materials Agency, *Installation Restoration Program: Preliminary Assessment of the Twin Cities Army Ammunition Plant,* February 1988, prepared by U.S. Department of Energy, Argonne National Laboratory, Argonne, Ill., p. 8.43.

143 *Tucson, Arizona, at Air Force Plant No. 44.* This site is not listed as a federal facility Superfund site but rather as a part of the larger Tucson Airport Superfund site. Background and cost estimates derive from author interview

NOTES

with Gary Vest, September 1991; the Military Toxics Network, *Touching Bases*, June 1991, p. 8; and author interview with Dan Opalski, remedial project manager for EPA, Region 9, October 1991.

143 *$560 million price tag.* U.S. General Accounting Office, *Chemical Weapons: Stockpile Destruction Delayed at the Army's Prototype Facility*, July 1990 (Washington, D.C.: U.S. Government Printing Office, 1990), p. 3.

144 *an overall cost of roughly $6.5 billion.* Alfred Picardi et al., *Alternative Technologies for the Detoxification of Chemical Weapons: An Information Document*, May 1991 (Washington, D.C.: Greenpeace International, 1991), p. 14.

144 *expected to rise a full third.* U.S. House of Representatives, Hearings before the Committee on Armed Services, *National Defense Authorization Act for Fiscal Year 1991*, February 27–May 15, 1990 (Washington, D.C.: U.S. Government Printing Office, 1991), p. 746.

144 *the program is jointly managed.* U.S. General Accounting Office, *Chemical Weapons: Stockpile Destruction Delayed at the Army's Prototype Facility*, July 1990 (Washington, D.C.: U.S. Government Printing Office, 1990), pp. 11–12.

144 *handle their environmental contracts differently.* Statements quoted were made at U.S. House of Representatives, Hearings before the Committee on Armed Services, *National Defense Authorization Act for Fiscal Year 1991*, February 27–May 15, 1990 (Washington, D.C.: U.S. Government Printing Office, 1991), p. 745–46. See also U.S. Department of Defense, *Defense Environmental Restoration Program Annual Report to Congress for Fiscal Year 1989*, February 1990, pp. 12–17.

145 *staff turnover was 29 percent.* U.S. General Accounting Office, *Chemical Weapons: Stockpile Destruction Delayed at the Army's Prototype Facility*, July 1990 (Washington, D.C.: U.S. Government Printing Office, 1990), p. 71.

145 *A 1991 Army report.* John L. Menke et al., *Evaluation of the GB Rocket Campaign: Johnston Atoll Chemical Agent Disposal System Operational Verification Testing*, June 1991 (McLean, Va.: MITRE Corporation, 1991), p. xxxv.

Fifteen. A Military Toxic Network

147 *unexploded grenade.* Interviews with Joel Feigenbaum, April 1987, November 1988. Similar problems have surfaced at many locations. See, for instance, "Another Live Grenade Found," *Brookhaven News*, the newsletter of the Brookhaven National Laboratory (and former Camp Upton Army base) in Long Island, New York, September 1, 1989, p. 1. According to the Brookhaven article, five separate grenade incidents occurred at the base during 1989 alone.

147 *Massachusetts Military Reservation.* Background from U.S. Department of Energy, HAZWRAP support contractor office, Oak Ridge National Laboratory, *Installation Restoration Program: Engineering Evaluation/Cost Analysis CS-4, FS-25, and FTA-1 Study Areas Removal Action, Massachusetts Military Reser-*

vation, Cape Cod, Massachusetts, June 1991. See also U.S. Environmental Protection Agency, Region I, U.S. Department of Defense, National Guard Bureau, and the United States Coast Guard, Federal *Facility Agreement Under CERCLA,* July 1991. See also Jeff McLaughlin, "Cleanup of Toxics—Long in Coming—Under Way on Cape," *Boston Globe,* November 11, 1990, p. 87.

148   *"it feels like a war zone."* See Stephanie Pollack and Seth Shulman, "Pollution and the Pentagon," *Science for the People,* May/June 1987.

148   *highest cancer rates.* See "Cancer Cases Up Again on Cape," *Boston Globe,* March 10, 1991, p. 35; Jeff McLaughlin, "Cancer Incidence Up on Part of Cape," *Boston Globe,* February 4, 1990, p. 63; "Higher Rates of Disease Trouble West Cape Cod," *New York Times,* April 20, 1986; "Officials Expand List in Cape Cancer Study," *Boston Globe,* December 18, 1986, p. 17.

148   *A path-breaking epidemiological study.* Prospectus courtesy of Ann Aschengrau, Boston University School of Medicine, Department of Environmental Epidemiology. Interview with Aschengrau (conducted by Shawna Moos), July 22, 1991.

148   *6 million gallons of aviation fuel.* See *Conservation Law Foundation v. Lt. Gen. Emmet Walker, Jr., Chief of National Guard Bureau, et al.,* U.S. District Court, Massachusetts, Civil Action 86-1044-S, April 1986. See also U.S. Department of Energy, Oak Ridge National Laboratory, *U.S. Air Force Installation Restoration Program Phase I: Records Search, Air National Guard, Camp Edwards . . . Facilities at Massachusetts Military Reservation,* Final Report: Task 6, December 11, 1986.

149   *"lifestyle factors."* See Jeff McLaughlin, "Cleanup of Toxics—Long in Coming—Under Way on Cape," *Boston Globe,* November 11, 1990, p. 87; Ellen Cantarow, "U.S. Military Attacks Environment," *In These Times,* February 25–March 10, 1987, p. 3.

149   *"cancer rates are horrendous."* Interviews with Joel Feigenbaum, April 1987, November 1988.

149   *making an example of Feigenbaum.* Teresa M. Hanfin, "Activist Found Guilty in Otis Air Base Protest," *Boston Globe,* January 17, 1987, p. 15.

149   *Air Force Plant No. 44.* "Poisons in the Pentagon," *Frontline,* Public Broadcasting Service, originally broadcast April 5, 1988; and author interview with Dan Opalski, remedial project manager, EPA Region 9, October 1991.

150   *a class-action lawsuit.* Details of Tucson's Southside case from local interviews. Affected Tucson citizens are bound by their legal settlement to silence. See also Military Toxics Network, *Touching Bases,* November 1990; Bill Turque and John McCormick, "The Military's Toxic Legacy," *Newsweek,* August 6, 1990, p. 20.

150   *"ready to march on our bases."* Major General George E. Ellis, Air Force director of engineering and services for logistics and engineering, as quoted in James Kitfield, "The Military Environmental Quagmire," *Military Forum,* April 1989, pp. 37–38.

151 *The Military Toxics Network.* Comments of Dyan Oldenburg and Lenny Siegel from interviews, September 1991.

151 *the Network flew several activists to Washington.* See the account compiled by Lenny Siegel, Military Toxics Network, *Touching Bases,* November 1990.

151 *The Military Toxics Network's overall agenda.* See National Toxics Campaign Fund, Military Toxics Network, "Citizen's Agenda for Pentagon Environmental Responsibility," distributed at the Defense and the Environment Initiative Forum, Washington, D.C., September 6–7, 1990. For more on the forum, see Chapter 12. See also National Toxics Campaign Fund, *The U.S. Military's Toxic Legacy,* 1991 report, preface.

153 *Representative Richard Ray.* Comments from U.S. House of Representatives, Hearings before the Committee on Armed Services, *National Defense Authorization Act for Fiscal Year 1991,* February 27–May 15, 1990 (Washington, D.C.: U.S. Government Printing Office, 1991), p. 753.

153 *The armed forces have promised.* Since the mid-1980s the military has publicly declared this goal. It is formally incorporated in the Department of Defense directive, "Hazardous Materials Pollution Prevention," DOD Directive No. 4210.15, July 27, 1989.

154 *which ones to address first.* See Chapter 5 for more on the Defense Priority Model.

154 *a billion dollars per year.* U.S. House of Representatives, Hearings before the Committee on Armed Services, *National Defense Authorization Act for Fiscal Year 1991,* February 27–May 15, 1990 (Washington, D.C.: U.S. Government Printing Office, 1991), p. 733.

155 *a striking example.* For Air Force/Hughes Aircraft cleanup deal and Mike Synar comments, see U.S. House of Representatives, Hearing before the Subcommittee on Environment, Energy and Natural Resources of the Committee on Government Operations, *Hazardous Waste Problems at Department of Defense Facilities,* November 5, 1987 (Washington D.C.: U.S. Government Printing Office, 1988), pp. 91–92.

155 *a "Strategic Environmental Initiative."* See *Congressional Record,* Senate, June 28, 1990, pp. 8930–43. See also Patrick E. Tyler, "Senators Propose Shift of Defense Funds to Study Environment," *Washington Post,* June 29, 1990, p. A7; Philip Shabecoff, "Senator Urges Military Resources Be Turned to Environmental Battle," *New York Times,* June 29, 1990, p. A1. For concern expressed, see, for example, Jessica Tuchman Mathews, "How Green the Pentagon," *Washington Post,* June 19, 1990, p. A23.

155 *"a planet far more crowded."* For this and other Lester Brown comments, see Lester Brown, "Beyond Earth Day," *WorldWatch,* Spring 1990, draft copy.

156 *"paint the Pentagon green."* Lead editorial, *New York Times,* July 7, 1990.

156 *"it should clean up its own backyard."* National Toxics Campaign Fund, Military Toxics Network, "Citizen's Agenda for Pentagon Environmental Responsibility," distributed at the Defense and the Environment Initiative Forum, Washington, D.C., September 6–7, 1990. For more on the forum

see Chapter 12. See also National Toxics Campaign Fund, *The U.S. Military's Toxic Legacy*, 1991, p. xiv.

Epilogue

157 *"Why travel all the way out there?"* Interview with Mary Allingham, then a public affairs officer, U.S. Army Toxic and Hazardous Materials Agency, spring 1989.

157 *my local facility.* For facts about contamination at the Watertown Arsenal, see Dan Grossman and Seth Shulman, "Toxic Secrets: Closing Watertown's Army Arsenal," *Boston Magazine*, November 1989. The article was based on an intensive three-month investigation of the facility.

157 *ordered shut by Congress in 1989.* For more on closure plans, see U.S. Army Corps of Engineers, New England division, *Army Materials Technology Laboratory Closure Final Environmental Impact Statement*, August 1991, prepared for U.S. Army Materiel Command.

157 *the Watertown Arsenal has an illustrious history.* U.S. Army Laboratory Command, Materials Technology Laboratory, *U.S. Army Materials Technology Laboratory*, installation guide.

158 *"may have been used as backfill."* See U.S. Army Toxic and Hazardous Materials Agency, *Preliminary Assessment of the Army Materials Technology Laboratory, Watertown, Massachusetts*, March 1988, pp. 127–29.

158 *"brick by brick—wrapped."* The statement appeared first in a local press account, but was confirmed by Wright and press officials at U.S. Toxic and Hazardous Materials Agency in written correspondence of September 6, 1989.

158 *1969 spill of radioactive wastewater.* U.S. Atomic Energy Commission, Region I Division of Compliance, "Report of Inspection" dated May 8 and 9, 1969. Page 11 states, "An unplanned release of 4900 gallons of radioactive liquid waste occurred during the period of February 20 and 27, 1969."

158 *a plume of fuel oil.* U.S. Army Toxic and Hazardous Materials Agency, *Preliminary Assessment of the Army Materials Technology Laboratory, Watertown, Massachusetts*, March 1988, p. 127.

158 *continues periodically to burn.* Tommy Peterson, "Arsenal Article Debated," *Watertown Sun*, November 15, 1989, p. 1.

158 *as much as $100 million.* Thomas Content, "Removal of Toxic Waste Could Cost Arsenal $133 Million," *Watertown Sun*, March 27, 1987.

159 *The GSA acquired the property.* Details about the GSA site from interviews with Frank Camacho, director, Boston Facilities Support Center for the General Services Administration, autumn 1989 and 1991. See also U.S. Department of Energy, Argonne National Laboratory, *Formerly Utilized MED/AEC Sites Remedial Action Program, Radiological Survey of the Former Watertown Arsenal Property GSA Site, Watertown, Massachusetts*, Argonne, Ill., October 1983.

NOTES

159 *contractors began decontamination.* Ibid.

159 *"The Army's record."* Interview with Frank Hinxman, summer 1989, with Dan Grossman.

160 *an independent technical expert.* Federal aid was requested—and denied—for the town to hire an environmental consultant in December 1989 through the Pentagon's Office of Economic Adjustment. The decision to hire the consultant with town funds was made soon thereafter. See, for instance, Bob Rawson, "Federal Aid Asked on Army Lab Re-Use, Initial Answer 'No,'" *Watertown Press,* December 14, 1989, p. 1.

160 *Army agreed to throw out.* See Bob Rawson, "Army Lab Testing Is Going to Be Re-Done," *Watertown Press,* November 16, 1989, p. 1.

161 *they held a press conference.* See Bob Rawson, "AMTL Spokesman Defends Lab's Safety, Rebuts Magazine," *Watertown Press,* November 16, 1989, p. 1.

161 *sent a delegation.* For accounts of the December 6, 1989, town council meeting, see Bob Rawson, "Federal Aid Asked on Army Lab Re-Use, Initial Answer 'No,'" *Watertown Press,* December 14, 1989, p.1.

161 *to suppress publication.* Correspondence from Stephen J. Plumeri, New England Development, October 20, 1989.

161 *mall's parking lot.* U.S. Department of Energy, Argonne National Laboratory, *Formerly Utilized MED/AEC Sites Remedial Action Program, Radiological Survey of the Former Watertown Arsenal Property GSA Site, Watertown, Massachusetts,* Argonne, Ill., October 1983.

161 *give the town a bad name.* See Tommy Peterson, "Arsenal Article Debated," *Watertown Sun,* November 15, 1989, p. 1.

162 *1983 "Perimeter Survey."* Comments included in EPA document "Potential Hazardous Waste Site Identification and Preliminary Assessment, NUS/FIT Trip Report," dated August 23, 1983.

162 *Rose Toscano.* Comments from interview, autumn 1989.

162 *a set of principles.* Watertown Citizens for Environmental Safety, "Principles for Responsible Closure," March 1990.

Index

Aberdeen Proving Ground (MD), 32–34, 126, 140, 144; bureaucratic hierarchy of, 131; contamination at, 34–40, 41–42; legal case against, 126–35

"Aberdeen Three," 126, 129–35

Accountability, importance of public, 154

Achille Lauro, 119

Acrylonitrile, 69, 71

Ahearne, John F., 102

Air Force, U.S., 13, 22, 46, 104, 105, 107; atmospheric nuclear tests of, 137; bioremediation project of, 142; changes in compliance in, 125; cleanup efforts of, 145; computer to predict migration of contaminants of, 141; contamination of overseas airfields of, 109–10; and DS2, 29; Logistics Command of, 25, 84; and TCE, 15–16; use of solvents by, 15–16, 24–26. *See also* McClellan Air Force Base

Air Force Law Review, 133–34

Air Force Plant No. 44 (AZ), 123, 143, 149–50, 155

Alameda Naval Station (CA), 126

All-American Family Institute, 11

Allen, Mark, 25

Allingham, Jim, 127, 128, 129, 131, 133

Allingham, Mary, 161

American Federation of Government Employees, 159

Andersen Air Force Base (Guam), 15, 110

Anderson, Adrienne, 123

Anderson, Andrew, 78

Aquifer, 110, 148; Cohansey, 12, 63–65, 68; Snake River, 101

Arizona, University of, 150

Armor, Richard, 21, 28–29

Army, U.S., 13, 24, 104, 105, 110; cleanup efforts of, 144–45; contaminated water supplies of, 27; and DS2, 28, 30; JACADS of, 136–46 *passim;* Toxic Assessment Program of, 78; use of solvents by, 26. *See also* Aberdeen Proving Ground; Cornhusker Ammunition Plant; Jefferson Proving Ground

Army Corps of Engineers, 105–7, 124, 144, 145

Army Material Technology Laboratory, *see* Watertown Arsenal

Army Ordnance Museum, U.S., 32–33, 34

Army Signal Corps, 23

Army Toxic and Hazardous Materials Agency, U.S. (USATHAMA), 144–45, 157

Arnold Air Force Base (TN), 142–43

Arsenal Task Force, 162–63

Arthur, Stanley, 31
Atomic bomb, 94
Atomic Energy Commission, 95
Atwater, William, 32–33
Augustine, Rose Marie, 123

Baca, Thomas, 120–21, 123
Baltimore Sun, 127
Beale Air Force Base (CA), 54–55
Benzene, 34, 71
Berteau, David J., 144
Bhopal disaster, 21
Binary chemical weapons, 129, 131
Bioremediation, 141, 142
Bitoff, John, 124, 126
Blum, Barbara, 108
Boston magazine, 162
Bottomley, Lucy, 64–66, 68, 69, 72, 73
Breen, Barry, 8
Brown, Lester, 155–56
Brunner, Paul, 88
Bryan, Hayden, 6
Bukowski, Grace, 151
Burnham, John, 93–94, 95, 96
Bush, George, 56–57, 100, 131, 158

Camacho, Frank, 159
Cancer rates, elevated, 148, 149
Cape Cod, MA, 147–49, 150
Carbon tetrachloride, 69
Carcinogens, 69, 71, 78, 86–87, 101
Carpenter, Chuck, 74–75, 77, 78–79, 80–82
Carricato, Michael J., 8, 48
Carter, Jimmy, 47, 50–51, 52, 66, 108
Center for Defense Information, 23
CERCLA, *see* Superfund
Cesium-137, 100, 102
Charles River, 158, 159
Chemical treatment solutions, 141–42
Chemical weapons: binary, 129, 131; halt in production of, 130; and JACADS, 136–46 *passim. See also* Aberdeen Proving Ground
Cheney, Dick, his Defense and the

Environment Initiative, 115–25, 153
Chernobyl plant, radioactive accident at, 98
Chloro-fluorocarbons (CFCs), 24
Chloroform, 71
Citizen Alert, 151
Citizens groups, 148–52
Civil War, 158
Clark Air Force Base (Philippines), 110–11
Clean Air Act, 66
Cleanup technologies, 141–43
Clean Water Act, 55, 66, 135
Coats, Dan, 4
Cohansey aquifer (NJ), 12, 63–65, 68
Cold War, 57, 59, 125
Collinsville, CA, toxic and explosive chemicals found in, 20–31 *passim,* 72, 152
Columbia River, 96, 99
Conahan, Frank, 11–12, 13
Congressional Budget Office, 23, 106
Conservation Law Foundation (CLF), 149
Cornhusker Ammunition Plant (NE), 12, 104, 143; pollution from, 74–82
Couch, Cindy, 34
Curies, 95, 98

DANC (Decontaminating Agent Noncorrosive), 38
DCE, *see* Dichloroethylene
Decontaminant Solution #2, *see* DS2
Dee, Bill, and Aberdeen case, 129–35
Defense, Department of (DOD), 7, 8, 10, 12, 17, 18; auctions of surplus and waste material held by, 21–22, 28; and Defense Priority Model, 43–45, 47–50, 56; and doctrine of sovereign immunity, 46, 47, 50; and DS2, 29, 30; fuel oil purchased by, 23; and Lakehurst Naval Air Engineering Center, 69; and McClellan Air Force Base, 87; Office of the Inspector General of,

108–9, 112, 116, 117; and Toxic
Release Inventory, 56; and
Watertown Arsenal, 162. *See also*
Pentagon
Defense and the Environment
Initiative, 119, 122, 125, 126, 134,
153; inauguration of, 115–18
Defense Authorization Act (1991), 112
Defense Cleanup, 122
Defense Environmental Restoration
Program (DERP), 45, 106–7, 108
Defense Logistics Agency, 13, 121
Defense Priority Model, 43–45, 47–
50, 56
Defense Reutilization and Marketing
Service (DRMS), 28–29, 30, 72,
152
Department of Energy, *see* Energy,
Department of
DERP, *see* Defense Environmental
Restoration Program
Dichlorobenzidine, 71
Dichloroethane, 79
Dichloroethylene (DCE), 87
Dickey, Dean M., his reminiscences
of Aberdeen's contamination, 34–
40, 41–42, 126
Dinitrotoluene (DNT), 27, 28
DNT, *see* Dinitrotoluene
Donnelly, Mike, 124
Doxey, Kevin, 43–45, 47–50
Druby, Marilyn, 96, 103
DS2 (Decontamination Solution #2),
28–30
Dukakis, Michael, 149
Dunn, Nancy, 29

Earth Day, 117, 119, 155
Eastern Europe, environmental
situation in, 57–59
Eckart, Dennis E., 53, 56
Eddystone Chemical Company, 71
Edgewood Arsenal (MD), 33, 34, 35.
See also Aberdeen Proving Ground
Eglin Air Force Base (FL), 142
Electroplating, 24, 26, 90

Energy, Department of (DOE), 47, 58,
100, 105, 117, 155; and Hanford
Nuclear Reservation, 94–102
passim, 104; National laboratories
of, 145; nuclear weapons
production facilities run by, 7–8,
154; and Watertown Arsenal, 159
"Environmental Issues of Concern for
the U.S. Defense Industry," 134
Environmental Law Reporter, 8
Environmental Protection Agency
(EPA), 6, 7, 12, 13, 14, 124; and
Aberdeen Proving Ground, 128,
131; on aging ordnance, 139; and
contamination of overseas bases,
108, 111–12; and Defense Priority
Model, 44; efforts of, to regulate
federal facilities, 18; "Hazard
Ranking System" of, 47; and
Lakehurst Naval Air Engineering
Center, 64, 67, 69, 70–71, 73;
limited jurisdiction of, 51, 52, 53,
55; and Massachusetts Military
Reservation, 149; Office of
Drinking Water of, 82; and PCBs,
142; and RDX, 78, 79, 82; regional
office of, 153; and Rocky Mountain
Arsenal, 56; and TCE, 86; and
Watertown Arsenal, 162; and
Wright-Patterson Air Force Base,
25–26
Executive Order 12088, 47, 50–51,
108
Executive Order 12580, 52, 54
Exxon, 23

FASCAM, 5
Fazio, Vic, 21–22
Federal Bureau of Investigation, 47,
132
Federal Facilities Compliance Act,
proposed, 56, 151–52
Feeds Materials Production Center
(OH), 101
Feigenbaum, Freda, 148
Feigenbaum, Joel, 148, 149

Findley, Keith, 85–86, 89
Fisher, Charles, 76
Florio, James J., 69
F-117A Stealth fighters, 84
Formerly used defense sites (FUDS), 105–7
Freedom of Information Act, 54, 112, 152, 162
FUDS, *see* Formerly used defense sites

Gardner, Booth, 99
Gardner, James, 69, 70
GB, 137–38
Geiger, Jack, 98–99
General Accounting Office (GAO), 11–12, 15, 54, 55, 109, 112; and JACADS, 146
General Services Administration (GSA), 159, 163
Gepp, Carl, and Aberdeen case, 129–35
Germany: environmental problems in, 57–59; reunification of, 57; U.S. military's contaminated sites in, 110, 111, 112
Glenn, John, 102, 125
Goldman, Alan J., 45
Good Neighbors Against Toxic Substances (GNATS), 79, 81, 82
Grand Coulee Dam, 96
Grand Island, NE, *see* Cornhusker Ammunition Plant
Grand Island Daily Independent, 77
Grossman, Dan, 157, 158, 160
Groundwater, 12, 63–64, 76–77, 81, 120

Habicht, F. Henry, III, 53
Halon, 24
Hamilton, Lee, 6
Hanford Nuclear Reservation (WA), 57, 93, 104; contamination at, 93–103
Hansen, Alfred G., 25
Hatch, Henry ("Hank"), 124

Hayton, Robert, 41
Hazard Ranking System, 47
Hindenburg, 66–67
Hinxman, Raymond, 159–60
Holmes, Oliver Wendell, 46
House Committee on Energy and Commerce, 53
Hughes Aircraft, 123, 149, 150, 155
Humphrey, Hubert H., III, 53–54
Hussein, Saddam, 118
Hydrazine, 129

Idaho National Engineering Laboratory, 101
Ierardi, Mario, and contamination at McClellan Air Force Base, 84–91
Incineration, 139–41, 146. *See also* JACADS
Injection wells, 101
Interim actions, 50
International Defense Review, 133, 139
Iodine-129, 94, 100
Iodine-131, 97–98

JACADS (Johnston Atoll Chemical Agent Disposal System), 136–46 *passim*
Jacksonville Naval Air Station (FL), 120
Jasper, Ron, 5
Jefferson Proving Ground (JPG, IN), 157; contamination at, 3–9
Jeremiah, David E., 118, 119, 123
Johns Hopkins University, 45, 129
Johnson, Lyndon B., 81
Johnston Island, *see* JACADS
Joint Chiefs of Staff, 118
JP-8, 88
Justice, Department of, 52, 53, 55, 56, 131–32, 134

Keystone Center, 122
Kirtland Air Force Base (NM), 29
Klink, Bill, 99, 100, 102
Klugh, James, 132
Knouf, Kenneth, 9
Korean War, 81, 84

Lakehurst Naval Air Engineering Center (NJ), 104, 154; Hangar One at, 66–67; toxic waste problems at, 12, 64–73 *passim*
Landfills, 141
Langley Air Force Base (VA), 120
Lawrence Livermore National Laboratory (CA), 95
Leaching pits, 76
Lentz, Bob, and Aberdeen case, 129–35
Lewisite, 40
Los Alamos National Laboratory (NM), 95
Los Angeles Times, 109
Love Canal (NY), 65

McClellan Air Force Base (CA), 83–84, 104, 154; contamination problems at, 84–89; water treatment facility at, 90–92
MacKenzie, Doug, 90–91
Manhattan Project, 94, 95
Marienthal, George, 69
Marine Corps, 145
Martinez, Matthew, 17
Massachusetts Military Reservation (Cape Cod), 147–49, 154
Matney, Bill, 23
Meadows, Dennis L., 58
MESS (McClellan Ecological Seepage Situation), 87, 88
Methyl di-isocyanate, 21
Methylene chloride, 69
Migration, contaminant, 141
Milan Army Ammunition Plant (TN), 27, 31
Military Toxics Network, 124, 151–52, 154, 156
Montarelli, Frank, 71–72
Muniz, Bennie, 151
Mustard gas, 36, 37–39

Nagasaki, atomic bomb dropped on, 94
Napalm, 37, 38, 39

National Academy of Sciences, 43–44, 47
National Governors' Association, 7
National Guard, 147, 148, 149
National Institute for Occupational Safety and Health, U.S., *Pocket Guide to Chemical Hazards* of, 129
National Priorities List, 24–25, 27, 47, 82, 105, 120
National Reserve, 63
"National sacrifice zones," 94, 103
National Seashore, 147–48
National Toxics Campaign, 123, 150–51
Naval Facilities Engineering Command, 145
Navy, U.S., 12, 13, 22, 104, 105, 107; cleanup programs of, 145; contamination sites of, 16; disposal of paints by, 24; and DS2, 29; and PCBs, 142; use of solvents by, 26. *See also* Lakehurst Naval Air Engineering Center
New Hampshire, University of, Institute for Policy and Social Science Research of, 58
New Jersey Pinelands Preservation Area, 63
Newsweek, 31
New York, City University of, Medical School, 98
New York Times, 68, 69, 156
Nixon, Richard, 130
Norfolk Naval Base (VA), 16
Nuclear facilities, *see* Hanford Nuclear Reservation
Nuclear Regulatory Commission, U.S., 102
Nunn, Sam, 155, 156
Nydam, David A., 29, 30

O'Brien, Dennis, 5
Office of Technology Assessment (OTA), 100
Oldenburg, Dyan, 151
Operation Desert Shield, 120

Ordnance, aging, 139
Overseas bases, contamination of, 104, 107–12. *See also* Formerly used defense sites (FUDS)
Oversight, importance of local, 152, 154
Ozone depletion, 24

Parks, David, 127, 128
Parts per billion (ppb), 69, 82, 86, 87
PCBs, *see* Polychlorinated biphenyls
Pearl Harbor, attack on, 83–84
Pentagon, 4, 7, 8, 81, 104; annual report of (1991), 26; and bioremediation, 142; budget of, 121, 144; change in attitude of, 115–25, 133; chemical agents of, 129, 136, 139; and cleanup contracts, 154–55; and Collinsville incident, 30; and contamination of overseas bases, 107–12; disregard of environmental laws by, 50–51; environmental restoration program of, 14, 122, 144; and FUDS, 105, 106; and hearings of environmental subcommittee, 10–11, 13; and Military Toxics Network, 151–52, 154, 156; toxic waste generated annually by, 23. *See also* Defense, Department of
Pentagon Inspector General, 108–9, 112, 116, 117
People Against Arsenal Toxic Hazards, 151
Perchloroethylene, 86
Persian Gulf War, 29, 75, 84, 120, 121–22, 134
Phenol, 72
Phosgene, 128
Physicians for Social Responsibility, 98
Picatinny Army Arsenal (NJ), 41
Picric acid, 128–29
Pine Barrens (NJ), 63, 64
Plume, 77, 78, 81, 82
Plutonium, 94, 95, 97, 99, 100, 101
Pollution Control Agency (MN), 54
Polychlorinated biphenyls (PCBs), 142

Public Health Service, U.S., Agency for Toxic Substances and Disease Registry (ATSDR) of, 27, 87
Public Works Center (Guam), Navy's, 142

Rad (radiation absorbed dose), 98
Radiation, 95, 97–98, 100
Radioactive isotopes, 94, 100, 101
Ray, Richard, 153
Raytheon, 144
RCRA, *see* Resource Conservation and Recovery Act
RDX ("Research and Development Explosive"), 27, 28, 77–78, 79–80, 82
Read, Marcia, 48–49
Reagan, Ronald, 52–53, 54, 56, 57
"Red water," 27, 76
Remedial actions, 50
Resource Conservation and Recovery Act (RCRA), 132, 139
Responsible corporate officer doctrine, 132
Rice, Richard, 16–17
Richland High School (WA), 97
Roche, Jon, 39
Rocky Flats Plant (CO), 101
Rocky Mountain Arsenal (CO), 123, 151, 154, 157; Basin F of, 55–56
Ruckelshaus, William, 141

Sacramento Bee, 78
"Sacrifice zones," 94, 103
Sanderson, Richard E., 46
SARA, *see* Superfund Amendments and Reauthorization Act
Savannah River Plant (SC), 101
Schafer, Carl J., Jr., 13–16, 18–19, 109
Schwarzkopf, H. Norman, 121
Seattle Convention Center, 93
Siegel, Lenny, 151
Sierra Army Depot (CA), 151
Sierra Club, 79, 91
Siler, Harry, 41–42
Silicon Valley Toxics Coalition, 122
Site, 48–49

Smith, Ted, 122–23
Snake River aquifer, 101
Soil venting, *see* Vacuum extraction
Solvents, use of, by military, 15–16,
    24–26. *See also* Trichloroethylene
    (TCE)
Sovereign immunity, doctrine of, 45–
    47, 50, 87
State of the World Report, 155
Strategic Environmental Initiative,
    155, 156
Strontium-90, 99, 100, 101, 102
Subcommittee on Environment,
    Energy, and Natural Resources,
    10–19, 53, 109
Subcommittee on Oversight and
    Investigations, 53
Sulfuric acid spill, at Aberdeen
    Proving Ground, 127–28, 135
Superfund, 34, 35, 53, 56, 65, 73;
    agency managing, 6; and Air Force
    Plant No. 44, 123; National
    Priorities List of, 24–25, 27, 47,
    82, 105, 120
Superfund Amendments and
    Reauthorization Act (SARA, 1986),
    56, 107
Susquehanna National Wildlife
    Refuge, 34
Synar, Mike, 22, 52, 155; and hearings
    of environmental subcommittee,
    10–19 *passim*, 53, 109

Tadewald, Keith, 20–21, 22, 30
TCE, *see* Trichloroethylene
Technical review committees, 153
Tetraethyl lead, 67
Three Mile Island (PA), accident at, 95
Thyroid glands, 98
Tinker Air Force Base (OK), 10, 111
Tischbin, Marilyn, 137
TNT, *see* Trinitrotoluene
Tooele Army Depot (UT), 140
Toscano, Rose, 162
Toxic Release Inventory, 56
Treasure Island Naval Station (CA),
    124

Trichloroethane, 79
Trichloroethylene (TCE), 24–25, 54,
    69, 86–87, 110; at Aberdeen
    Proving Ground, 34; at Air Force
    Plant No. 44, 143, 149–50, 155; at
    Andersen Air Force Base, 15; on
    Cape Cod, 148, 150; cleanup
    technologies for, 143; at
    Jacksonville Naval Air Station, 120;
    at McClellan Air Force Base, 86
Tri-Cities Development and
    Economic Council, 93, 95, 96
Trinitrotoluene (TNT), 75, 76, 77
T-12 "general purpose" bomb, 32
Twin Cities Army Ammunition Plant
    (MN), 54, 143

Uhrich, Carol, 73
Unexploded ordnance (UXO), 5, 6,
    49, 154
Unified commands, 121
Unitary theory of the executive, 52–
    53, 55
Upper Cape Concerned Citizens, 148–
    49
Uranium, 95, 97, 100, 101, 158, 159
Urban, Noel, 107
USATHAMA, *see* Army Toxic and
    Hazardous Materials Agency, U.S.
UXO, *see* Unexploded ordnance

Vacuum extraction, 142, 143
Valdez oil spill (AK), 23
Vest, Gary, 15, 16, 92, 109–10, 125,
    143; on Air Force cleanup efforts,
    145
Vietnam War, 75–78, 81, 84, 124
Vinyl chloride, 34, 87
Vitrification technologies, 142–43
VX, 130, 138

Walker, Lewis, 144
Ward, Thomas F., 30
Warsaw Pact, 57
Wash, Thomas, 104–7
Washington, University of, 93
Washington Post, 130

Watertown Arsenal (MA), 40–41,
    environmental problems at, 157–64
Watertown Citizens for Environmental
    Safety, 160
Watertown Sun, 161–62
Weldon Spring Ordnance Plant (MO),
    105
Westinghouse Corporation, 96
Weyel, Hermann, 112
White, Garland, 41
White phosphorous, 36–40
Willcox, Breckinridge, 128, 131–32,
    133

Wooden, Morris, 3, 4
World War I, 38, 66, 128
World War II, 71, 78, 81, 105, 137
Worldwatch Institute, 155
Wright, Edward, 158
Wright-Patterson Air Force Base
    (OH), 25–26, 31; Air Logistics
    Command at, 25, 84

Yarbrough, Chuck, 87–88

Zeppelin program, 66–67